TUNE IN TOKYO

TIM ANDERSON

ティム アンダーソン

TUNE IN TOKYO
THE GAIJIN DIARIES

チューン イン 東京:

ザ 外人 ダイアリズ

PUBLISHED BY

amazon encore

This book was originally published, in a slightly different form, by Wayward Mammal Publishing in June, 2010.

Printed in the United States of America.

Published by AmazonEncore
P.O. Box 400818
Las Vegas, NV 89140

ISBN-13: 9781612181318
ISBN-10: 1612181317

For Little Man Jimmy.

And for Kelly Guffey (1973–2006),
who sure would have laughed.
(rememberkelly.org)

AUTHOR'S NOTE:

Like everyone, I was deeply saddened by the tragic events that took place in northern Japan in March 2011. In communication with my Japanese friends during the weeks afterward, one sentiment that many of them expressed was the need to have a diversion from the horror and the fear. One friend said, in imperfect but beautiful English, "we shouldn't forget victims, but we need to release our mind apart from this sometime. Otherwise we are stifled with the sadness..." *Tune in Tokyo* is a light-hearted romp through Japan's capital, my love letter to the city and its people. I hope in some small way it can, perhaps, provide a silly diversion for those Japanese folks who happen upon it. And for all those other readers, that it will leave them with a smile on their face when they think of Japan.

CONTENTS

Prologue: Q and A; or, I'm So Bored with the USA............i

Chapter 1: Born Again 1
Chapter 2: Language Barriers 21
Chapter 3: The Next Big Thing 46
Chapter 4: Bad Gaijin...55
Chapter 5: And on Drums...76
Chapter 6: The Vagina Dialogue 100
Chapter 7: The Empress of Ginza 113
Chapter 8: GaijinMan and the Lady-killer 126
Chapter 9: Problem Student...142
Chapter 10: Too Cute 161
Chapter 11: Survivors...171
Chapter 12: Gay Agenda...184
Chapter 13: Jim-zilla Attacks! 194
Chapter 14: Lego My Ego 220
Chapter 15: Karaoke Queens 238
Chapter 16: Look Homeward, Gaijin...............................246

Acknowledgments...265

I got the style but not the grace,
I got the clothes but not the face,
I got the bread but not the butter,
I got the winda but not the shutter,
But I'm big in Japan.

—Tom Waits

PROLOGUE

Q and A; or,
I'm So Bored with the USA

gaijin, 外人 n. 1. foreigner, outsider
2. pest, big fat alien, one who must
be stared at on trains

Why do I to be being here?

This question comes to me one evening when I am in the midst of a two-hour class with two extremely low-level students at the English conversation school where I teach in central Tokyo. Hiromi, Kiyomi, and I are concentrating on question formation: "when," "where," and, of course, "what." They practice asking each other questions in a get-to-know-you kind of exercise, with results like, "What is your sports do you like?" and, "When is month on your birthday?" Then we come to the why.

"Can you think of a 'why' question to ask Kiyomi?" I ask Hiromi slowly, doubtfully. She stares at me with fear and trauma, as if I've just asked her to implicate her mother in the murder of her father.

I've had my share of shit-scared students today, and now I have two more. It's like spending two hours trying to coax a cat out from under the bed: she may take a few steps, but one careless move on your part will have her scurrying out of reach once again, leaving you to pull your hair out.

Staring out the window at the electric Tokyo sky and the Sapporo beer advertisement on a neighboring building—an ad featuring two be-suited Japanese tough guys looking directly at me and asking the pivotal question in English, "Like Beer?"—I come up with a why question of my own:

Why would a college graduate with such impeccable credentials as a BA in English, diabetes, credit card debt, Roman nose, and a fierce and unstoppable homosexuality want to leave the boundless opportunities available to him in the USA (temping, waiting tables, getting shot by high school students) for a tiny, overcrowded island heaving with clever, sensibly proportioned people who make him look fat?

Before I left the U.S., I couldn't figure out what path I wished to tread, like every other lazy, listless Libran of my generation. I was "American by birth, Southern by the grace of God," living in my hometown of Raleigh, North Carolina.

I had three part-time jobs and one boyfriend (the reverse of which being far preferable). *Brightleaf*, a Southern literary journal, was great work experience, Southern fiction being the hot literary genre of the moment, with most of the country only recently realizing that most Southerners can actually read and write without the aid of a spittoon. Here I had the opportunity to read and edit some truly inspired writing. The main problem with this job was the wage: slightly less than that earned by American Heart Association volunteers.

Job #2 was at the Rockford, a downtown restaurant, waiting tables a few nights a week. Here I was nothing if not a jaded waitperson, kind of like Flo on *Alice*, minus the exceptional hairstyle and the long line of trucker boyfriends. (*Sigh.*) Whenever I found myself encouraging my customers to have a nice day, I had to stop and ask myself, "Do they deserve such kindness after giving me just eleven percent?"

Thankfully, the restaurant was as laid-back as they come: no uniform, no split checks, and, praise be to God, no baby chairs. Still, I didn't like the person waiting tables was turning me into. When I bid farewell to my customers as they walked down the stairs to the street below, I didn't see people; I saw walking, talking digestive tracts. I saw beer, veggie burgers, and strawberry cheesecakes sloshing around in stomachs. I saw innards. And I didn't like what I saw.

Which was why I'd sought out job #3. Since I wasn't making enough money at the magazine and couldn't bear the thought of working more than a few shifts a week at the restaurant, I found myself teaching English at the local Berlitz Language Center. A few days a week, I instructed Japanese businessmen on how to communicate effectively (more or less) and confidently (kind of) in a language they feared more than Godzilla.

"We don't just want the best teachers in Raleigh at our school," the head instructor at the school told me during my interview. "We want the best teachers in the *world*." A bold statement, and a bizarre one, since their pay rate was on par with the checkout girls at the local Food Lion, and God knows they weren't the best in the world. If Berlitz expected me to rate with inspirational teachers across the globe, shouldn't they look into paying me more than seven dollars for a forty-five-minute lesson?

Still, it was a job I was happy doing, so I didn't much care about pay. I was getting to know people from all over the place: Mexico, Puerto Rico, Japan, France, Italy, Brazil, Korea. For a few hours a few days a week, I was able to relieve myself of my home-grown ennui and make contact with the outside world.

Because contact with the outside world was what I desperately needed. Somehow, over the years, I had devolved from a social, reasonably charismatic soul who thrived on meeting new people into an introverted, cloistered, and feckless pothead approaching the ripe old age of thirty who rarely explored the world beyond his television screen. Once an attention-whoring child of the stage—with a résumé that included major bit parts in many local Little Theater productions—and an excitable, if music theory–challenged, violin and viola player in school and music camp orchestras, I was now a hopeless recluse with absolutely no confidence, too shy to even pick up my viola and play it for close friends for fear of hitting a wrong note and driving them into the arms of another gay who would better serve their entertainment needs. How had this happened? If the thirteen-year-old me could see me now, he would shake his head, tut-tut, and launch into a wispy rendition of some minuet or other. Then he would look me up and down and slap me in my face.

I looked at my viola, listlessly leaning against its case in my bedroom, aching to be touched, caressed, and gripped forcefully yet lovingly by expert hands. I hadn't picked it up in many months, and the last time I had, I'd gotten the distinct impression that the viola was trying to tell me it would really rather I put it down and find a nice young five-year-old music student to sell it to.

"You really need to get the hell out of this house," my boyfriend Jimmy would tell me as I sucked in my twentieth bong hit of the day and exhaled a plume of smoke out of every orifice in my head. "You're *languishing*."

Now, I take notice when Jimmy uses words with more than two syllables (he generally doesn't care to take the time), and he got me thinking. Maybe he was right: I wasn't just bored, or directionless, or lazy, or confused, or stoned, or scared, or paranoid, or worried about being brutally murdered on the street tomorrow without having accomplished anything in my life. I was *languishing*, like Miss Havisham in *Great Expectations* or Rosanna Arquette in *Desperately Seeking Susan*. (Who will be my Madonna?) When was the last time I'd actively engaged with the world, followed a confused path of my own making, did something remarkable, maybe threatened to stir up some trouble?

Well, let's see. There was that time about a year ago when, in search of a fourth job, I'd visited the temp agency and gotten the highest score they'd seen in months—months!—on the typing test. (I'm a really good typist.) Also, that time last week that I'd woken up, gotten high, and watched a *Today Show* interview with Ann Coulter, marveled aloud at how much her neck looks like the shaft of an erect penis, and then shouted at that squawking blonde dickhead until Jimmy set a plate of cinnamon buns down in front of me to shut me up. But surely there was more to life than that.

Then it came to me: the last time I'd felt totally wide awake and alive was the last time I lived outside the country. After graduating from college, I'd jetted off to London, a city I'd fallen in love with a few years before during a year abroad in Manchester. I'd stayed as long as I was legally able (Americans are only allowed six-month worker visas for the good of the country), living it up in Jack the Ripper's old neighborhood. When I was kicked out by the Home Office, I'd gone home, gotten one job, then another, and then another, and five years later I was neck-deep in the rut from which I was now desperately in need of extrication.

Jimmy was right: I needed to get out of the house, this much was clear. Wake myself up, splash my ashen, sallow face with some cold water, and force myself to at least meet the world halfway. This time, though, I wanted to go where I'd truly be appreciated. Not that England hated me, but it goes without saying that the

English have a love-hate relationship with Americans. To your typical Briton, Americans are loud, hardly ever dressed properly, remain largely oblivious to most events that occur beyond our own borders, and, most importantly, have completely bastardized the English language and simultaneously, through the cultural imperialism of movies and television shows, made "American" the most widely spoken and recognized strain of English in the world. Plus, we use the word "quaint" to describe any house built before 1970. Me, I was ready to go where my status as a U.S. passport holder and card-carrying "American English" speaker was an asset rather than a liability (a list of countries that was shrinking by the second). Besides, I was craving positive vibes, and British people always sound pissed off about something.

Then one day at Berlitz, Hiro, one of my students who loves bluegrass music and playing the banjo, made a suggestion that had been staring me in the face for months: "You should come in Japan!"

And I thought, "You know, I really should." It's on the other side of the world, for one. Also, I wouldn't be able to understand anything anyone said: another plus. Best of all, they don't totally hate Americans there yet, do they?

Here was a race of people who not too long ago had been our enemy, yet now, in the popular American imagination, they seemed to love us—drinking our sodas, watching our movies, building their own copycat of Walt Disney World, sending their children to bed with Snoopy and Woodstock. Who were these people? What were their dreams, hopes, and fears? How the hell did they remember each other's names? Most importantly, what would they think of me?

Japan was much more provocative than, say, Finland or New Guinea. Whenever Westerners speak of Japan and the Japanese, it seems every statement they make—whether it's about their movies, television shows, rock bands, customs, pornography, or fondness for cutting their abdomens—includes the words *crazy* and some variation on *fucking*.

"I saw this crazy fucking Japanese movie about a homicidal videotape this weekend," for example. Or maybe, "I got this crazy fucking Japanese digital camera," or "Jesus Christ, that bukkake live-stream site is fucking *stupid* crazy." I wanted to go behind all these knee-jerk statements and witness the mania myself.

Yes, I would go to Japan and do something insane of my own: I would play my viola on top of Tokyo Tower, write and perform my own haiku on early-morning rush-hour trains, find an unorthodox use for chopsticks, realize my dream of playing keyboards in an all-Japanese New Wave rock band. I would get out there, stomp the pavement, and leave my mark. (Would it be a bloodstain? Time would tell.)

I decided on Tokyo, throbbing heart of the nation, with its sci-fi architecture, kaleidoscopic electric lights, kimono-clad Betties talking on illuminated cell phones, spacepods, decent public transportation, and local celebrities like Yu-Gi-Oh, Mothra, and, yes, Hello Kitty.

Tokyo is a giant city of 5.3 bazillion people. Though it was largely decimated by American bombers during World War II, it has risen from the ashes and now boasts the highest number of giant television screens per square mile of any city in the world. The seat of the world's second-largest economy, this gigantic humongous gargantuan extra-stupendously titanic megalopolis stands bravely in the face of typhoons, earth tremors, and Tom Cruise press junkets. And let's not forget the constant barrage of giant lizards, arachnids, and flying insects that habitually wreak havoc on the public transportation system and, even worse, never ever take their shoes off when they enter a room, even when they're asked nicely.

As a young boy, whenever I'd catch an episode of that old documentary series on the Tokyo Godzilla attacks, I was always struck by the thought that I could fit in there among those howling masses. After all, I'm really good at running away from things screaming, crawling into inaccessible areas, and using passersby as human shields.

And so now, almost a full-grown man, I would finally go there. The future was neon, and I'd bring my light switch.

Surely a utopian futuristic urban monstrosity awaited me: a place where people didn't walk down the street but stood reading inscrutable newspapers on moving sidewalks. Where they talked to their friends on small, portable video screens. Where they didn't sit in traffic, they simply levitated above the masses of pedestrians and bicyclists and blasted off in their CZX Toyota hovercrafts. A place where huge bronze statues of the Buddha sat happily alongside giant Day-Glo plastic Pokémon figurines.

And me, I would find my place there. I would walk the acid-rain-soaked streets by night clad in a beige trench coat, a cigarette dangling from my pouty lips, a hardened, city-delirious look on my face. I would order steamy ramen from a sidewalk noodle bar using the Tokyo slang so pervasive in whatever part of the city I was haunting that night. The neon would reflect off my sleek black sunglasses. I would begin reading up and down and right to left.

I would be Harrison Ford in *Blade Runner*, scouring the city for replicants. (Or cookies, whichever.) I would follow a trail of tiny origami figures left by a man spookily resembling Edward James Olmos. They would lead me to my destiny. Trouble and unrest were in store, and I welcomed them.

My apartment, on the 237th floor of a giant, fully automated apartment block, would be dark and smoky. It would be lit only by the flashing neon advertisements outside my window and accessible only by a cylindrical glass elevator that spoke fifty languages and could recognize who you were and what floor you wanted by the tone of your voice when you said, "Konnichiwa, XR378-B."

I would have all the Japanese mod cons, like a futon bed that collapsed into the size of a credit card; a Ramenator in the kitchen that would offer a variety of ramen selections with complimentary chopsticks; a mechanical ShowerPal in the bathroom, which would disrobe, soap, shampoo and condition, and finally blow me dry as I watched the news on the hologram television suspended in midair like Princess Leia. My alarm clock would know when I wanted to get up and when I *needed* to get up. When someone approached my door, the scanner in the peephole would tell me their name, address, criminal record, how much they'd had to drink, what they do in their free time, and their favorite color.

I would go there, this Tokyo. I would bravely run away from all of my problems at home and strike out for a new and, fingers crossed, utterly ridiculous place. I would amaze the people of Tokyo with my wit and height. I would drink flaming pastel-green cocktails and sing Elvis karaoke songs to rooms full of adoring and utterly charmed Japanese.

Yes, this city would fix everything. Who would be my Madonna? Tokyo would.

I'm here now, obviously, and things haven't panned out exactly as I'd planned. All the vehicles are in close touch with the ground, traffic is treacherous (and that's just the pedestrians), some Japanese folks would just as soon have me step *in front of* the train as *on* it, and my living quarters leave much to be desired (a kitchen and bathroom, to name just two). And where the hell is Edward James Olmos?

But it's a brilliant city. I finally have health insurance. Every day promises a new and exciting humiliation. And most importantly, I've lost twenty pounds.

I guess it's perfectly natural for me to be asking this "why" question. Surely all travelers at one point or another have been compelled: Gulliver, Ulysses, Bilbo Baggins, Indiana Jones. Each had his own answers—and I have a few of my own. Number one on the list? The world's biggest record store is here. And it looks like a spaceship.

I am no longer simply an American. I am a *gaijin*. These are my stories.

Oh, and Brad Pitt will not play me in the movie adaptation. Sandra Bernhard will.

I want to see Pluto,
I want to have fun,
I want to turn blue,
Under an alien sun.

—Siouxsie Sioux

# of Japanese words learned: 2
# of Japanese words successfully used: ?
Bowls of ramen eaten: 14
Replicants terminated: 0

CHAPTER ONE

Born Again

In which our hero (me) gets distracted and lost and many
other things besides, the explanation of which is certain to
amuse and delight all but the most emotionally unavailable of
readers. Read and learn from his story the unfortunate truth
that you can run from God's country, but you cannot hide.

My spacecraft glides over the Shinjuku district of eastern Tokyo
as I swivel giddily in my captain's chair with all the blinking label-
less buttons on the left armrest. Looking out the window, which
circles the entire ship, I see the blinking lights, sleek skyscrapers,
packed commuter trains, and tiny inhabitants hustling and bustling along sidewalks, across bridges, and into and out of the giant
beating heart of Shinjuku Station. My craft touches down slowly
and alights on top of the Takashimaya Times Square building,
which looks like a giant luxury cruise liner. I rise from my seat,
remove my goggles, and prepare myself to be beamed directly
into the thick of the madness spread out below me. I set the trans-
porter to "Tower Records, Shinjuku," and seconds later, here I am.

(Actually, no. I take a plane and then a train and then walk for a bit and then sleep for seventeen hours and then start work and finally get a day off after two goddamn weeks.)

The giant Tower Records television screen just outside the south end of Shinjuku Station plays a pop video featuring a gaggle of preteen girls dressed in shiny, frilly outfits so bright and cutesy they make American child beauty pageant contestants look like Dickensian street urchins. They dance in formation—not particularly well—and stare at the camera, doe-eyed and hollow. I stand at the bottom of a massive escalator looking up at the dangerous display of chiffon and taffeta and excitedly contemplate the pastel-tinted nightmares I will have about all this later.

I'm wandering around the city for the first time, enjoying my first day off. I interviewed with a popular language school called MOBA before coming, and they assured me they could place me in Tokyo. An empty promise, it turns out, since I've ended up with an apartment in a town called Fujisawa an hour south of Tokyo and a job at a school in nearby Yokohama. A disappointment, yes, like a young small-town Russian with stars in his eyes must feel when he has his heart set on living in the Big Apple and instead is forced to rent a studio in New Brunswick, New Jersey. But I'll make it to Tokyo, no problem. All I need is thousands and thousands of dollars so I can afford to put a deposit and key money down on a fashionable closet or cubbyhole in, say, trendy Shibuya or, perhaps, the East Village–like districts of Kichijyoji or Koenji. It'll happen. I'll just need to teach a few hundred more English lessons, sell my used diabetes syringes and Pia Zadora records on eBay, and limber up for those lap dances. I'll be there in no time.

In the meanwhile, I'll continue my job in Yokohama, where I'm honing my communication skills and preparing myself for a career in front of the camera in ways I never anticipated. I have taught so many lessons that I've begun dropping all articles, prepositions, and sometimes the verb "to be" from my speech just to be more easily understood. ("On weekend went to movie and ate nice restaurant. Food so delicious.") I've also started pointing to my ears when I talk about listening to music, behind me when talking about the past, and in front of me and over a little hill when talking about the future. Even when talking to my two Australian roommates, Ewan and Sean.

MOBA is a popular language school with branches all across Japan. I'd had to fly to Boston for the interview, and though I usually choke during interviews, this one ended, amazingly, with an immediate job offer.

Admittedly, it's satisfying to know that simply by virtue of being born in the right place I have a skill very much in demand in another part of the world. I never really considered my English degree very marketable, and neither has anyone else. College papers touting Jane Austen as England's best Harlequin romance novelist or exploring the homoeroticism in *Bleak House* won't get you very far in the real world, let's face it. But when I decided to travel to a faraway land of people who want to know how to speak like me, I automatically had a highly marketable skill: I speak great English. Jim, the interviewer and a former MOBA teacher, was clearly dazzled. In fact, he'd seemed to have only one concern:

"Now, Mr. Anderson, do you think that, as a full-time teacher, you can deal with being asked day in and day out questions like what your hobbies are, why you came to Japan, if you can use chopsticks, if you speak Japanese, if you like sushi, what your favorite movie is, what kind of music you like, what time you usually wake up, how often you eat out, and what your plans are for the weekend?"

It was a legitimate question, one you could spend days trying to answer appropriately. But when you get right down to it, the question he was really asking was, "Tim, can you talk about yourself until you're blue in the face?" And the answer to that, my friend, is, "I feel confident that I can."

He seemed satisfied with this. Then he'd promptly asked me what my hobbies were.

"Well," I began, licking my lips, "I like reading, traveling, playing the viola, and collecting records. And yoga. And swimming. Oh, and watching movies. Did I say swimming?" Of course, I could have gone on and expressed my love of gossip columns, White House scandals, Speedos, and interracial porn, but I figured in this case less was more.

"That's good, you seem to have a lot of interests," Jim said. "Because the teaching will take care of itself. Your free time really will be your own, and it's good that you'll easily be able to fill it."

And that was that. He said they'd be sending me an official offer of employment in the next few weeks, and he let me go. In hindsight, I think if I'd said my hobbies were reading other people's mail, collecting used handkerchiefs, and having sex with my viola, I would have gotten the same response. He just wanted to make sure I wasn't dangerous and could string a sentence together. I fit both criteria and so got the job. My university degree is probably spinning in its frame.

It was the green Yamanote train that carried me to Shinjuku, and against all possible odds in this city of 13 million, I actually scored a seat on it. I got comfortable in my precious foot and a half of Tokyo real estate as people continued to roll into the carriage, a procession that might have lasted days but thankfully ended when the doors closed behind an old, hunched-over woman carrying three heaving shopping bags.

I stood up quickly to offer the tiny obaasan my seat. Cute as a button, she stood about four and a half feet tall, with sleepy eyes, short stringy silver hair sprouting out from under a white visor with a smiley face on it, and a back arched from years of housework, child-rearing, gardening, shopping, and bowing.

She was clearly one of a breed of elderly Japanese women who appear to be approximately 130 years old and, though they still walk around freely, doing their shopping, taking trains, and looking disapprovingly at young people, always look like they could keel over at any moment, uttering their last "sayonara." Some gaijin folk uncharitably refer to them as *Yodas.* Usually it is those who have come up against the nasty side of these women, commonly displayed when the so-called Yodas board a train and proceed to elbow and smack out of their way any person younger than they are (pretty much everyone) so that they can get first dibs on the scarce supply of seats. So, because I'm a suck-up (and because I have a soft spot in my heart for old women wearing visors), I stood and offered her my seat. She bowed, smiled so wide I feared she may tear her face, and said thank you before sweeping me aside, wiping off the seat with a handkerchief to be rid of my white-man funk, and plopping herself down. I wanted to ask her to be my grandmother, but before I had a chance to come up with a decent pitch, the train pulled into the next station, she rose with all her bags, swatted her way through the crowd, and hopped off.

I sat back down, adjusted my gaze straight ahead, and gave a startled jump. There, staring directly into my eyes, into my very soul, was a young boy of about four years. He looked at me with an eerie, inscrutable expression, like the one a child forms when he's about to command the dark forces to descend upon you. He didn't take his eyes off me; he didn't blink. He just stared, cute and creepy. I averted my gaze as the train began to move, hoping that he'd do the same. After a few minutes I turned back to him, and his expression hadn't changed, though he had tilted his head slightly.

To take my mind off the probing toddler eyes, I stared out at the Tokyo scenery rolling past in the fading light. Actually, scenery might be too fancy a word. Explosion of ugly buildings would be more appropriate. As the train sprinted its way through the metropolis, an endless smattering of ashen-hued structures stood together in a desperate display of jigsaw development. No empty space is left unmolested, every extra block of air smashed to bits by the erection of an edifice with an attached arcade, karaoke box, cell phone stand, convenience store, apartment building, police station, flower shop, or Japanese eatery. The buildings aren't in rows, unless your idea of a row is a slipknot. They face each other according to whichever way completes the jigsaw most effectively. The result is a static architectural orgy, the buildings caressing, groping, slamming, and going down on each other in a manner reminiscent of the last scene in *Caligula* (minus the money shots).

Eventually I brought my gaze back inside and briefly made eye contact with the staring toddler before noticing the attractive young girl sitting next to me. She was digging through her purse and pulling out mascara, lipstick, tweezers, blush, and an eyelash curler, obviously intent on giving herself a quick touch-up. Then she pulled out a lighter. And next the largest hand mirror I had ever seen. It was the size of your average windowpane and probably afforded her a good view not only of her own cosmetic shortcomings, but mine and the sleeping gentleman's on the other side of her. She had more tools than a smack-addled surgeon. I watched out of the corner of my eye as she used each one in turn, impatient for her to get to the lighter. Finally she only had two instruments left, the lighter and the eyelash curler. And sure enough, she used them simultaneously, flicking the lighter and holding the tiny flame over the curved metal end of the curler. When she believed it to be hot enough, she put the piping apparatus up to her eye and gave herself a set of shapely, luscious, twenty-four-hour lashes. I feared she'd put her eye out if the train should make a sudden jerk, but even with the rolling and swaying of the carriage, the girl's expert grip on her tools and the precision with which she performed her tasks continued uninterrupted. Amazed, I looked over at the toddler. He was still staring at *me*.

The train pulled into Shinjuku Station, through which two million people pass in a typical day. I wasn't sure which exit I should go for, but I realized it wasn't up to me when I found myself eased down the nearest staircase by the sheer force of the crowds tugging me like an undertow. They decided I would go out the south exit. That would be fine.

So here I am, staring at a giant television screen full of wide-eyed, dancing preteen cherubs and wondering (1) if Japan has its own Britney Spears, and (2) if she's a cheap dime-store floozy like ours. I hope so.

As a large portion of the two million Shinjuku-goers hustle past and slap me with their shopping bags, I wonder where to go. I have no plan, no idea where anything is. I just want to see some local color. I continue walking ahead and through a concrete courtyard directly in front of the exit. Lots of young folks are hanging out, strumming guitars, playing bongos, simply posing, leaning against railings, comparing wacky hats, and so forth. Up ahead, people sit and slurp at a steaming mobile noodle bar right next to a punk rock band thrashing it out on the sidewalk,

7

surrounded by a dedicated horde of twelve-year-old girls offering their support.

The sounds of Shinjuku—spoken advertisements over loudspeakers; pop music from the Tower Records TV screen; the clinking, buzzing, and whirring of the pachinko parlors and game centers; the piercing recorded voices beckoning you into this shop or that one—whoop and holler around me as I walk. I enter this swirl of activity, feeling like one of those wide-eyed, big-headed aliens seen occasionally in Utah or Nebraska.

I pass a horde of young girls with bleached blonde hair, fiercely tanned complexions, panda-like eye makeup, foot-high platform shoes, and miniskirts of a cut that would make Paris Hilton stand back and go, "Oh, honey, cover that shit up a little!" A cute high school couple—wearing matching kilts and carrying the same handbags, made out of what looks like poodle fur— walks by hand in hand. Not to be outdone, a tall guy wearing Buddy Holly glasses and sporting an afro for the ages walks determinedly behind them, his black shirt screaming in white lettering, "So Fucking What?" Local color—check.

As I look around for something else to gawk at, a friendly looking middle-aged woman wearing flats and a skirt that is, thankfully, knee-length, approaches me.

"Excuse me," she smiles. "You speak English?"

Not waiting for me to answer, she continues. "It's nice to meet you. I am Miho Johnson."

You're *who*? I think. Her English is Japanese-inflected, but her last name most definitely is not.

"May I ask, where are you are from?" she continues. She sports a matronly bob, her bangs cut straight across and hanging just above her thin, painted-on eyebrows. Though she has a smile on her face, it's tempered with a constant look of concern.

Also, she never seems to be looking directly at me. When she asks where I'm from, she appears to be reading from a cue card placed above and a little to the right of my big head.

She has made no assumptions about my nationality, so I am tempted to adopt a strange accent and say Greenland or Siberia while gently taking her hand and rubbing my nose on it, the traditional greeting in my country.

"You are from America?"

"Yeah, actually. How did you guess?"

"Oh, just thinking. How long you are being in Japan?"

I tell her I've just arrived, and at this her pensive face brightens.

"Oh, that's nice. I want to tell you about my church..."

Your *what*? Church? They have those here? Hmm. I was actually hoping she'd be able to give me directions to a good ramen shop, a decent record store, and/or a news agent that sells English-language magazines. Perhaps I'm expecting too much.

"Church? Your...church?" I stammer, trying to think of a means of escape.

"It's lovely place, everyone accepted. We have many meetings and enjoy. Jesus there. It's near to here. Please, let me take you to there."

As she places her open hand against my shoulder to lead me towards Christ, I wonder, can this be true? Can I have traveled all the way across the world from the God-fearing American South to an island known more for its electronics, its love of stately rituals like tea ceremony and flower arranging, and its raging Lolita complex than its faith in Jesus Christ, only to be witnessed to in broken English about the Good News?

"We all God *child*ren. Brother and sister with *Christ*. Jesus love *you*."

Yes, I guess I have.

When I envisioned my first jaunt through vast Shinjuku, it went something like this: I would first circle the city on the Yamanote Line, starting at Tokyo Station in the east and making my way westward, through Hamamatsucho, Shinagawa, Gotanda, Ebisu, and the hot-to-trot districts of Shibuya and Harajuku. Along the way I might pick up a pair of Harajuku girls dressed fashionably in fitted burlap sacks, ten-inch heels, and Mouseketeer hats, and we would walk through Yoyogi Park arm in arm as a band of Taiko drummers followed behind us on a dolly and beat out a rhythm for us to swagger to. We would arrive in Shinjuku and immediately go for a few cocktails at a place called Hello Highballs. The cocktails would be neon blue, and they would turn our lips a fetching shade of fuchsia. After drinks we would spill back out onto the street and hitch rides with a clan of bosozoku motorcycle bandits. They would escort us into the next club, which would have a name like Stark Raving Suzuki. There, we'd have more cocktails—these smoking and gasoline-scented— and befriend the DJ, who would be in the midst of a world tour that had taken him to Paris, Berlin, Rome, Moscow, Hong Kong, Bangkok, and Jersey City. After his set, he'd offer us some magic mushrooms, and we'd gladly accept them. Then we'd take turns at the turntable rocking the worlds of the club kids. As the night slowly came to an end and the crowds dispersed, we'd elegantly take our leave, lock arms again, and step out into the crisp morning air hand in hand, escorting each other to the station, secure in the knowledge that we'd done a little bit of Shinjuku.

Nowhere in my wild imaginings did I consider that the first Japanese person I spoke to socially would be a forceful born-again Christian with nothing but time on her hands and a quota to meet. Because I must say that, all due respect to my parents, who tried their hardest to raise me right, realizing a closer relationship with Jesus is not what I've come to Tokyo for.

"Thank you so much, but I'm really not...able." Not unless your church sells *Details* or *Vanity Fair*. Hell, I'll even take a damn *New York Dog*. "I'm...waiting for a friend."

Either she sees through my lie or she doesn't care.

"We have meeting right now, please, you can come and we food and drink and talk and enjoy with other of Jesus people. We sing about Good News and praise God and Jesus Messiah. You bring your friend. You call from there."

It hits me right then how important correct intonation and word choice are to evangelism. You absolutely must put the right stress on the right words or you'll sound unemotional and disembodied, like Ira, the chatty computer screen consultant on *Wonder Woman*. Because of her flat Japanese intonation, she sounds only vaguely interested in what she's saying. But she *is* pushy.

"You come? You come? It just this way."

"I'm sorry, thank you, but I'm not interested."

She appears confused, disbelieving. I decide to break it down into the simplest possible terms.

"Thank you, I no interest. No can do. Can't. Must with friend and eat." I figure the less sense I make to myself the more I make to her. Wrong again.

"No, please, you must not go tempting! God watching you!"

I see. And what does that mean, exactly?

"It safe in my church. Safe from tempting."

"Thank you soooo much," I say, backing away. "But I meet friend now. I see Jesus later." Then she rushes me.

"Please, take this, you can visit anytime you like." And with this she drops into my hand a flyer and her church's business card with address and directions in English. "You no go tempting," she says with a worried smile.

"Thank you," I say again before turning around and getting the hell out of there. I walk briskly, lest Ms. Johnson should decide to approach again, this time with a bigger, beefier member of her church less inclined to take no for an answer. A rotund black belt named Akira O'Donnell, say. I cross the street and, since I have no idea where I am or what I'm doing, walk towards whatever is ahead of me. I stop under another giant television screen and take a look at the flyer Miho had given me.

On one side is a collection of illustrations seemingly drawn by the good folks at Marvel Comics. In the center is Planet Earth, above which stands—I'm assuming here—God, wrapped in angelic white robes, His arms outstretched, His smile twinkling, His long white hair and beard nicely highlighted by the halo suspended above His head. He stands in the center of what appears to be a meteor shower, but He's unaffected because He's God, and He *made* the friggin' meteors, bitch. In another scene, the Statue of Liberty faces an attack by a thick red, yellow, and evil cloud. And in another, a tall, square-jawed, ruggedly handsome man, dressed in a dark blue shirt and matching cape, walks in front of a dome-shaped building, a religious gathering place, perhaps. Oh, and he's got a sign on his shirt that says "666." Oh, and also there are people bowing down in front of him. (I don't blame them. Look at those cheekbones. The man is *handsome*. Like, *Superman* handsome.)

On the back of the flyer is a lengthy piece of hysteria titled "The Final Signs of the End." I read through it quickly, stumbling through the arbitrary and relentless use of underlined passages and all-caps text. ("ONE MAJOR <u>FINAL</u> SIGN OF THE <u>VERY</u> END that is yet to be fulfilled and that many prophets predicted is the rise of a powerful <u>One World Government</u> led by a bestial

dictator who will actually be fully possessed by Satan himself!—
<u>The Antichrist</u>!") I don't read too much, not wanting to slip into
hopelessness and despair on my first tromp through Shinjuku.
And besides, I don't see anything about the Apocalypse happening anywhere near the greater Tokyo metropolitan area. I put
the flyer in my back pocket so I can look at it later and laugh all
uppity-like.

Let's see, what's next? A-ha! Straight ahead is a narrow shopping street peppered with groups of sharply dressed, incredibly
oily looking young men wearing collared white shirts open nearly to their navels, smoking cigarettes, and looking like they're in
training for the International Sleaze Olympics. Let's go this way!

I notice that every so often, one of these men will see an attractive girl in the throngs of passersby, run up to her, and, walking alongside her, offer her some sort of proposition. He bends
down and speaks directly into her ear as she passes, and more
often than not, she tries to lose him. Eventually, she'll hold up
her hand politely, shielding her face from the guy, and decline
his offer, speeding up her step to outrun him. He doesn't give up
easily, but, as if he's being kept on an invisible leash by his greasy
compadres, he eventually halts, takes a drag of his cigarette, and
swaggers back to his post.

Being naturally curious and, yes, even nosy, I walk the length
of the street up to the next block, turn around, and walk back
from where I've come, just to watch this ritual a few more times
from different angles.

As I expect, every time a particularly attractive or otherwise
qualified young lady passes by, one of the greasers jumps up and
chases her down like a little puppy, speaking softly into her ear,
getting the same polite but unequivocal "no" from the woman
each time. Eventually he backs off and rejoins his boys.

What's going on here? Was he asking her out for an ice cream soda? Complimenting her on her knee-high socks? Challenging her to find his one and only chest hair? Frustratingly, I can't find out. Even if I could speak good Japanese, these guys are obviously young gangsters-in-training. Come on, would *you* approach Christopher from *The Sopranos* and ask him what he wanted from the attractive young women he kept talking to on the streets of New Jersey? Huh? Yeah, that's what I thought.

So I give up and keep walking. While waiting at an intersection with half a million other people, I think about my encounter with Miho Johnson. Did she see in me someone who looked lonely and desperate? A lost, malleable soul? A kid who's treading down the wrong path and needs to be brought back to the Alley of the Almighty? Or did I just look like an easy target? When it comes to the devoutly religious, there's a fine line between those who bow their heads in humble supplication and those who can be convinced to puncture bags of sarin on the Tokyo subway. Which camp is Miho in? The literature she gave me is hysterical, but is she?

They say people are put in your path for a reason. If so, Miho's reason must be to lead me to an entire street of massage parlors and sex clubs, as right in front of me is an entire street seemingly dedicated to getting male Tokyoites' rocks off. It kind of makes sense. Usually when missionaries hang out in huge cities, they tend to place themselves near the dirty and immoral goings-on in order to steer misguided souls away from sin, the possibilities for which typically loom very close by. They loiter in hopes of steering those who are about to enter a sexual healing zone towards a purer destination where the healing is focused elsewhere. I once stayed at a Christian youth hostel in Amsterdam that was right across the street from an S & M store. Yes, Miho had succeeded in pointing me in the direction of Shinjuku's smut district. It's all so dirty and depraved. I can't wait to have a look.

On the other side of the intersection there's a much wider side street exploding with revelers, club bouncers, flyer hander-outers, and drunken businessmen. I set off down this street, and before I know it, smartly dressed men—some Japanese, some African, some Middle Eastern—are approaching me, one after the other, asking me if I'm interested in any number of titillating activities available at their particular den of sin. Massages, lap dances, private scrubdowns, penetrating conversation with a gorgeous hostess: all is offered.

It's new and exciting to be taken for a straight man. I can saunter down the dirty boulevard completely immune, not tempted in the least to take any of these generous gentlemen up on their offers. Now, were these guys offering supple young college kendo masters named Nobu, I might have been more engaged. But as it stands I can breezily decline while enjoying a pleasant tinge of moral superiority.

I walk the length of this very long strip of hilarious heterosexual filth and feel sated, if a little nauseous. You can't behold a Hello Kitty sex toy collection in a shop window—including a vibrator, love oil, and what appeared to be French ticklers—and come away the same person, no matter how prepared you think you are for it. At the end of the day, however, I feel better knowing that if I ever do find myself in dire need of a deep tissue massage administered by a woman dressed up as a schoolgirl of fourteen (or by a girl who is actually fourteen), I know where I can find it.

At this point I've given up on meeting the Harajuku girl of my dreams/nightmares and decide that I will count this evening a success if I can get a good Japanese meal, grab some reading material, and find my way back to the station. I've pretty much gone in one direction, so I figure I'll just go around the block and return the way I came. I do this; I end up lost. And the more I try to set myself on the righteous path back towards the station, the more tangled up in Shinjuku's web of winding shopping streets I become.

I sit down to consult my dog-eared guidebook again, but its detailed maps and extensive explanations tell me nothing. I stand up and look down the street, hoping against hope to catch a glimpse of a gigantic neon sign showing a steaming bowl of ramen accompanied by a flashing message in English exclaiming, "WE ALSO HAVE ENGLISH MAGAZINES!!! AND OREOS!!!" I walk around the corner and start thinking about just giving up when I turn my head towards a news agent and my eyes land squarely on naked male flesh.

Even better than a steaming bowl of ramen or a copy of *Soap Opera Hair*! I've successfully stumbled upon a gay "bookstore." Well, since it's right here and, you know, I don't have Internet yet, I'll just, you know, have a, you know, take just a little, uh…

It's small and incredibly cramped, but boy is it well stocked. I excitedly squeeze through the other gawkers to have a look. There's shelf upon shelf upon shelf of magazines, books, videos, and toys. A porn-a-palooza. Many interests are catered to. Got a surfer fetish? Go straight back and have a look at the top shelf on the left. Into straight guys who are "gay for pay"? Look beneath the surfers. Got a thing for aging, fat Japanese businessmen being stripped naked, hung in a tiny net suspended from the ceiling, and probed with a lit candle? You are sick and should be ashamed of yourself. Look over to the right above the lube.

All the magazines are shrink-wrapped, so I have only the covers to go on, but I haven't seen the stuff in a while, and since these days I'm becoming aroused at the sight of subway advertisements for energy drinks, everything looks good (up to but definitely not including the fat old businessmen). I do the waltz of shame around the shop, trying to wring myself through any tight squeezes and not send a collection of Japanese surfer videos crashing to the floor. After a few minutes of browsing and fending off the advances of an old Japanese man with whom I'm sure I have nothing in common, I make my choice, sheepishly pay my money, receive some free condoms and lotion, and get the hell out.

I feel flushed as one usually does when walking from a porn shop out into public view, and then it hits me. Not only did I "go to tempting," as Miho had so poetically put it, but I'd completely given myself over to tempting—swallowed it whole—and come away with the brown paper bag with the free "love oil" inside that I am now clutching tightly to my side. I think of the flyer Miho had given me with its friendly, approachable God wrapped in white. Then I think of Mr. 666 and wonder if he's a top or a bottom. Is this wrong?

By way of divine punishment, on my way back to the station, I find myself back in the Straight Greaseball District, where the pack of young, sharp-dressed hoods are still gathered. One of them is quickly walking alongside an office lady on her way home with groceries, who wants none of his foolishness and wastes no time in outpacing him. Realizing he's been outrun by a woman in heels, he stops, swishes his hair back into place, and, attempting to save face by opening his phone and pretending to take a call, swaggers back to his fellow navel-baring delinquents. Bada-bing.

As I skirt through the street towards what I can now see is the east entrance of the train station, one excitable Japanese guy chases me down and, his English obviously failing him, simply points to a flyer he's holding in front of my face and says, "SEX!" Can't really disagree, but I politely decline and move on, after which I am chased down by an African guy saying, "Come, man, come on! Hot ladies for you! You come to my bar!" I tell him no thanks, but he continues with his sales pitch. "HOT WOMEN, MAN!! HOT WOMEN!! ALL FOR YOU, MAN!! COME ON!" I speed up and wave him away, at which point he stops, stomps his feet, and yells in mortal frustration, "WHY NOT, MAN??!!" I want to turn around, stomp my foot, and bellow self-righteously, "Because I have too much respect for women!!" But this isn't why.

I take the Yamanote train to Shinagawa Station, where I will transfer to the Tokaido Line and ride all the way to back down to Fujisawa. At Shinagawa the platform is a sea of people. The train soon comes, and as people pile in, two uniformed attendants standing by each pair of doors push, nay cram, the people in, forcing everyone on board to assume positions normally reserved for doctor visits. The carriage is a piece of modern art, each arm, newspaper, briefcase, set of headphones, chin, book, and elbow squeezing into each other like blood cells in a particularly narrow capillary. And just when you think no other living soul can possibly fit into the carriage, a stiff looking businessman leaps in and, as the doors shut, slowly morphs into whatever position the carriage allows (broken cigarette, leather slingback, praying mantis).

The train is so packed that every part of my body is being touched (not an altogether horrible sensation). When the train stops at Yokohama Station the people start flooding out, and I'm nearly strangled to death by my own bag (carrying my precious porn—an irony Miss Miho would have appreciated) because, though the strap is still over my shoulder, the bag and I are apparently separated by a few dozen people; those people, unfortunately for me, live in Yokohama. Thankfully, I'm able to pull it back to me without slicing anyone in half, and the rest of the ride isn't nearly as intimate.

Arriving back at my apartment, I go immediately to my tiny room, flop onto the futon, open my bag, take out the magazine (an imported American one), tear off the shrink-wrap, open it, and gasp.

I gasp not with lust, amazement, or even amusement. It is with disillusionment and disgust that I turn the pages of this very expensive magazine and move my eyes over the glossy, full-color content. Every crotch shot, every hint of man-meat, every flash or flicker of cock and/or balls is scratched out. It is unthinkable. Yes, yes, a very lucky man at some porn importer has the dream job of thumbing through all the magazines coming into the country and taking a big, thick black marker, or sometimes a pencil eraser, to each and every hard, throbbing penis contained within. Such blatant disregard for art and those who buy it I have never witnessed. All those gorgeous photographs laid to waste because of some weird Japanese law against showing the crotch area to those who wish to pay good money to see it.

You can still make out some of the goods, but really, the whole point of porn is that it makes absolutely no demands on your imagination. It puts everything you want to see right in front of you so you can enjoy it briefly before getting on with your life.

I set the magazine down and, lying on my bed staring at the cracks in the ceiling, let out a frustrated laugh. I lean over and pull the flyer that Miss Miho had given me out of my back pocket and look at the illustrations on the front. There's God again, smiling widely in his pristine white robe. When I'd looked at it before, he seemed like a benevolent, soft-featured God with a voice like Morgan Freeman's. Now, it seems, he is smiling knowingly, like he's just told a great joke about a Jew, a priest, and a homosexual and is waiting for me to get it. Did he just wink at me?

A little ashamed of myself, I look over at my porn, its pages open to a photo spread of a farmhand asking his boss for a raise up against a wheelbarrow, a big, thick black blotch running through the best parts. I look back at God, his eyes twinkling, his mouth grinning with a self-satisfied "gotcha!"

Miho Johnson was right. God is always watching. Even when you're hopelessly lost in Shinjuku.

I'll be damned.

# of beers bought from vending machines: 22
# of times train has been late: 0
# of bows taken (big): 13
# of bows taken (small): 1,157

CHAPTER TWO

Language Barriers

In which your new favorite protagonist takes a big, fat, meaty bite out of a new language and, in the process, realizes that the topic of oral sex is so unavoidable in this day and age that it sometimes just brings itself up in the classroom.

My tiny new Japanese cell phone may cause cancer, but it cures it, too. I bought it last night and have been playing with it for the better part of the morning. It's sleek and silver, about the thickness of ten playing cards wrapped in tissue paper. None of the two thousand possible ringtones really appeal to me, so I'm happy to discover I can program in my own songs. The instruction manual includes a picture of a keyboard, each note corresponding to a certain button combination on the keypad, so naturally I've spent an hour programming in the theme song to *Dallas*. The dramatic crescendo could use some work, but I decide to do something else and save my emotional energy.

I've already read the two books I'd brought with me, so I start nosing around the place for any discarded literature. My roommate Sean, the heartbreaker of the household, had recently let me borrow some of his *Playboys*, but I'd lost interest after reading the interviews. Plus, a few too many of the pages were sticking together.

I thumb through the day's *Daily Yomiuri* newspaper before remembering that my other roommate, Ewan, has a shelf full of books in his room, the only traditional tatami room in our small, Western-style apartment. Ewan is a thirty-nine-year-old Australian introvert, possibly the only introvert Australia has ever produced and exported. He is tall and thin, with an angular, friendly face like that of a marionette or that elf who wants to be a dentist in *Rudolph the Red-Nosed Reindeer*. He's soft-spoken, loves pasta and chopping up vegetables, and has never been married. Yep, that's about all I know.

I slide open his door and tiptoe in, my socked feet enjoying the tickle of the woven tatami underneath. From the bare-bones look of the room, it appears Ewan has really thrown himself into capturing the minimalist Japanese decorating style. There's no furniture except for a folded futon on the floor and a small bookcase in the corner. Since I'm a snoop, I pad over to the closet space and start sliding open doors. Each cabinet holds absolutely nothing interesting. There are folded sweaters. Folded pants. Socks. A crate of underwear. A box of envelopes. Some pens. A disposable camera. I close the doors so I don't collapse on the floor and plummet into a deep sleep, and then I turn and step lightly toward the bookshelf, hoping for the best. Since Ewan's a bookish fellow, I figure he'll have a respectable collection of titles to choose from. Maybe I'll finally read *The Brothers Karamazov, Look Homeward, Angel,* or *Dianetics*.

Unfortunately, it turns out that his are the books I would read only if I had a gun to my head. Titles like *If Lions Could Talk,*

Third World Geology, and *The Psychology of Rabbits* abound. My eyes brighten when I see the word "sex" in one of the titles, but it turns out to be *The Sex Life of Plants.*

I search and search his room looking for something, anything, readable. The most exciting thing I come across is a map of Yokohama, which I promptly swipe and have a read through. (It doesn't hold my interest for long, too bogged down with details, unrealistic plot contrivances, soulless narrative…) Then I see a book about learning Japanese kanji characters, and I nearly run away screaming.

Though I planned to take some emergency Japanese lessons at Berlitz before arriving in Tokyo, I never actually got around to it, what with all the emergency CD shopping, emergency bar hopping, emergency beachgoing, emergency Internet surfing, emergency lying around, and emergency last-minute freaking out. I did buy a language book called *Japanese the Fast and Fun Way* and a Japanese-English dictionary, but the extent of my study has so far been a few perfunctory looks at their back covers (very nice: simple, colorful, practical).

Though I learned the two phonetic alphabets without too much trouble, I'm deathly afraid of the kanji symbols that make up the bulk of the written language. Not just because there are twenty thousand of them, each with two pronunciations. Not even because each symbol must also be written in a certain stroke order. (To a guy who mixes his cursive and printed script, and upper- and lowercase letters when he writes—KinD oF LikE this—this is absolutely out of the question.)

The last straw is the fact that kanji symbols are listed in dictionaries according to the number of strokes, so to find a specific kanji I must know that it has twelve strokes and not ten or fourteen. I'm not prepared for that kind of life.

Lying on Ewan's futon is a workbook filled with his, er, stroke practice. I'm impressed. Sure, it looks like they were done by a three-year-old, but at least he's trying, and that's more than I can say for me. Seeing how Ewan is so hard at work learning his letters, I start thinking maybe it's time I finally make that leap into the linguistic unknown. I came here, after all, to shock my system, to give myself over to new and even scary possibilities. So far it's been very easy to live here knowing only a few phrases and hand signals. Some teachers have actually been here upwards of five years and still struggle to understand train announcements. Sure, it might seem incredibly lazy, but if your job is to speak English, then the need for fluency in Japanese isn't so desperate on a day-to-day basis.

Ignorance may sometimes be bliss, but not when you're wondering whether or not you're on the right train or if what you're about to eat is filled with bean paste and not chocolate. Besides, it's my God-given right as an American to speak my mind and fill others' ears with my thoughts, my opinions, my innermost feelings, and my repressed childhood memories. It seems a shame that I should let a tiny thing like a complete ignorance of the language keep me from doing it. I now know only a few more words than most Americans learned from that Styx song "Mr. Roboto." This absolutely must change.

Yes, my honeymoon period is officially over. I am settled. I am working. It is time to hit the books and prepare myself for my future career in Japanese films, television, infomercials, music videos, car shows, or Internet porn, whatever. I decide I'll ask around at work for a good teacher.

I work in the Kamiooka school of Yokohama, situated on a big shopping street across from the gigantic Kamiooka Station/ Bus Terminal/Shopping Center, and above a Burger King, which means that the smell of french fries pervades the entire school and I must eat at least one large order every day.

The pace here, like that at a Burger King, is manic. Every day I teach about seven forty-five-minute lessons and then spend another forty-five minutes in the free conversation room, where students of all levels discuss whatever topic is suggested or move from topic to topic according to interest level. (Mostly the students just sit and stare at the teacher until the teacher says something.) The classes generally consist of three people, unless a student pays extra to have individual instruction. We have ten minutes between classes, during which we're meant to grade each student on a number of points (listening, grammar, confidence, pronunciation, poise, dress sense, etc.), make recommendations, pass the file on to the next teacher, then get the files for our next class, open them up, and quickly choose a lesson that each hasn't done yet or needs to do again based on comments written by a previous teacher.

It's all very stressful and crowded in the tiny teachers' room as we scramble for the limited number of seats, sometimes ending up writing our files while leaning against the file cabinet that other teachers keep needing to use or sitting on someone's lap. This sense of pandemonium coupled with the smell of burgers, fries, and chicken fingers wafting through the room sometimes makes me feel as if I'm not actually an English teacher at all, but a fry cook.

Needless to say, we teachers have been forced to become intimate with one another, much like actors and actresses filming a love scene. Except our love scenes are every forty-five minutes and generally involve not two people, but ten.

And to make our lives that much more exciting, there's the persistent presence of Jill, our head teacher from Australia, a woman who, in spite of her fondness for brightly colored blazers and hair bleach, possesses all the warmth and approachability of a Salem, Massachusetts, prosecutor circa 1654.

Jill likes to lord it over us minions with a firm hand and a furrowed brow. And, sometimes, a hot pink pantsuit. Her most pronounced personality trait, besides a tendency to dribble ketchup and mayonnaise all over herself while eating BK Flame Broilers, is her staunch Australian patriotism, coupled with a similarly staunch dislike of Americans. She's surely the proudest, most irrationally nationalistic person from Australia I've ever met. Of course, most Australians are proud of their country and generally get a massive kick out of being Australian, it's just that their pronouncements about their homeland don't sound like government-sponsored propaganda the way Jill's do.

I'd recently overheard her chiding a student in one of her classes in her high-pitched Betty Boop squeal: "Why do you want to go to America? America is *dangerous*. Australia is much prettier, and the people are so much nicer." Apparently she also works for the Australian Tourism Board.

In Jill's mind, she's not doing her job as an English teacher in Japan if she's not riffing on the international nightmare that is the USA.

A few days ago I'd heard her say to a class of three stern-looking businessmen, "Americans are soooo lazy!" Which is fine, we are, fair enough, whatever. Sure, statistically we work longer days than anyone else in the world, but we also, statistically, probably ingest more kinds of fried potatoes while sitting on the couch for hours on end than any other country. But the fact that this statement is coming from a woman of about five feet eight inches and surely no less than 180 pounds somehow annoys me. She may hate Americans, but she sure as hell seems to love our Ben and Jerry's New York Fudge Chunk Swirl.

During these chaotic breaks between classes, when we teachers are using one another's backs as makeshift writing surfaces so we can recommend that Hiro work on his pronunciation and sentence production or that Masako give up studying English and perhaps take up a more suitable hobby like hang gliding or miming, Jill likes to barge into the teachers' room and pick a playful fight with any available American in the room—like, for example, me—and ask inane questions like, "Why do you people refer to *fringe* as *bangs*? That's so annoying."

Though her outrage at America's total lack of respect for such a mainstay of the English language as the word *fringe* is certainly understandable, I am at a loss as to how exactly we are meant to answer such a charge to her satisfaction. I have no idea how the word *bangs* came into being. Maybe it has something to do with Americans' love of guns and the noises they make?

All I can think to say to this is, "Why do you say *cunt* instead of *can't*?" but I don't say it, because it would bring the conversation down to a level that no one is likely comfortable stooping to just yet. So I keep my comments to myself, look her in the eye, shrug my shoulders, and speak the only Japanese I have learned so far: "Wakarimasen." ("I don't know.")

MOBA is the most popular language school in a country that has as many language schools as the U.S. has places to buy coffee milkshakes, and the students have many reasons for wanting to study English. Some are businessmen and women who do a lot of traveling abroad and need English so they can move up that ladder a little faster or chat people up in hotel bars more easily. Many are housewives with kids in school (or no kids at all) and money and time to kill. There are also a lot of high school and college-aged kids who want to travel, want to be able to speak to the foreigners they see, think "English is cool," or simply want to know what Kanye West is going on and on and on about.

There are also a few people learning English because they're movie buffs and want to be able to watch American movies without reading the subtitles. By far the best justification I've heard for studying English, though, was given by an extremely low-level fifty-something woman named Keiko, who says she is learning English because she wants to teach her son. This I regard as a triumph of convoluted logic. I don't know how old her son is, but surely he's at least a teenager by now. Why doesn't she send *him* to the school? Really, at the rate she's going, she's going to be on her deathbed and her son is still going to be saying things like "This is a pen" and "I enjoy to surfing."

I ask around about Japanese lessons, and everyone says I should talk to Joy, an excitable Latina from New York who seems to have an insatiable appetite for new hobbies.

"Well, I tried at this one school near Yokohama Station that's got a really convenient schedule and everyone seems really nice and you can get private lessons," she said.

"And how did it go?"

"Oh, I didn't go with them because they were too expensive."

"Oh."

"But I heard the community center across the street has really cheap lessons."

"Oh, cheap would be nice."

"Yeah, but all the classes take place in the same room at the same time. It's really loud and hard to hear the teachers."

"Uh-huh. So…"

"So anyway," she continues, "I'm thinking I just won't take lessons right now because I kind of want to join a gym, and I've got my life drawing classes, and I want to study that flower arranging stuff. And learn how to kabuki."

Thankfully, soon after this spirited but useless exchange, I meet Yoko Ojima, an intermediate-level student who takes private lessons. She's about fifty years old and has wispy gold and purple streaks in her short hair. Her face is always immaculately made up, her lips a dramatic dark crimson, her eye shadow echoing the purple in her hair, her skin painted powder white. An active and busy woman, she runs a medical clinic that she co-owns with a male physician, whom she hates. Understandably, she is always at least five minutes late for her lessons, rushing in breathlessly with a few shopping bags, a leather bag overflowing with folders overflowing with papers, and a sheepish smile overflowing with many apologies.

Teaching Yoko is always a nice break from the shy, low-level pupils who make up the bulk of our student population at Kamiooka MOBA. Since she's not a beginner, she can thankfully talk about her life beyond what her hobbies are, how many people there are in her family, what she ate for breakfast, and what her favorite movie is. And she doesn't mess around. The first day I taught her I'd learned that she'd separated from her husband because he'd had an affair and later shacked up with his secretary. We discuss her marital situation at length during each lesson—how he stops by her business every week to drop off money, how his secretary just wants his money, how Yoko won't divorce because if she does, she'll have no legal right to his money due to Japan's weird divorce laws that service the men and screw the women. I begin to feel more like a therapist, who, in addition to offering emotional support and acting as a beacon among the rocks, corrects his patients' grammar and pronunciation.

I mention to her how clearly backwards these divorce laws are to an American.

"Oh my God, Yoko, if you divorced him in the U.S., you could take him for every sorry yen he has."

She furrows her brow and tilts her head to indicate she doesn't understand.

"I mean, in America, you would be able to get his money," I try again, this time adding some hand motions. "He was screwing around on you, right?"

A nod, then another furrow and tilt.

"He was…uh…having sex with his secretary, right?"

"Yes," she says with a roll of her eyes. She obviously feels the same way I do about this. Really, an affair with a secretary? That is about as imaginative as dipping your french fries in ketchup. I would have given the guy a few points if he'd strayed for the love of a trapeze artist or a bass player, but come on, a secretary is just a slap in the face.

"Well," I continue, "all that you would need to do is get a private investigator to follow him around and take pictures of them necking in the park during lunch."

Furrow. Tilt. Nervous smile.

I repeat what I'd said slowly in more basic terminology and act out the parts about the taking of the pictures and the necking. Her eyes widen.

"Then, you take the pictures, text them to your lawyer, and BAM! Money." Here I rub three fingers across my thumb in the international signal for "mucho dinero."

Her brow unfurrows, her head untilts, and she sighs, wishing desperately she could litigate a divorce in New York City. As it stands, they just live separately from each other and Yoko does what she can to bleed him dry of his and his secretary's funds.

She lives in Kamiooka with her twenty-eight-year-old daughter, Fumiko. Both of them are currently studying to be Japanese language instructors, and they are nearing the completion of their course.

"Oh, *reeeeally*?" I think.

I feel like I've started to develop a special closeness with Yoko, one that transcends the confines of our cramped classroom. We've discussed her marriage, her business, and Fumiko, whom she fears is too awkward to ever marry and will live with her forever. Could I maybe take things to the next level and ask her to be my Japanese teacher?

"You know, I am very interested in studying the language."

She says, "ほんとですか？" reverting back to Japanese. "Really?" She pauses. "We can to teach you."

Yessssss. And, better yet:

"We do for free, because these days we cannot charge for to teaching. Not yet get certificate."

Now, if I were the uncertified teacher, I wouldn't likely be paying much attention to such an inconvenient rule, but this is a good example of the tendency of many Japanese towards being honest and law-abiding. There are, of course, exceptions, like, I don't know, the Japanese mafia, whose hobbies include getting ungainly tattoos, carrying automatic weapons, and using their chopsticks to put a person's eyes out, but generally, the Japanese respect the rules, as opposed to Westerners who would cheat their own mothers if it meant turning a profit.

So on a Wednesday evening a few weeks later, I meet Yoko and Fumiko out on the street in front of the school, and they lead me to their home behind the Keikyu plaza, high up on top of a very, very steep hill. For the first time since my arrival here, I realize how deeply disappointed I am that my fantasy of traveling hither and yon (mainly yon) upon a moving sidewalk conveyor has not been realized.

They live on the fifth floor of a giant condominium complex with a lot of security cameras and electronic checkpoints. The little area outside their door is full of Disney garden figurines: the Seven Dwarves, Bambi, Thumper, Daisy, Cinderella's mice, and, inexplicably, the Tasmanian Devil. We go inside, relieve ourselves of our footwear, and Yoko leads me to the dining room table, where we will be doing our studying.

It's a cozy condo. The hallway leads to a tiny kitchen on the left, opening into a dining area straight ahead with a finished wooden table and flanked by a china cabinet full of tiny Japanese bowls and cutlery and a few muted watercolors decorated with swirls of calligraphy. Beyond this is a small sitting room. And the Disney theme continues. A piano stands on the left wall, and next to it is a large shelf full of Disney sheet music and Seven Dwarves tea tins. A big framed puzzle of Cinderella, the Fairy Godmother, and the newly transmogrified pumpkin coach hangs above the piano.

On the dining table are two books: *500 Basic Kanji* and *Japanese for Busy People*. They are shiny and new, and seemingly purchased just for me. The prices for both are scribbled on a piece of paper and placed bookmark style in the Kanji book, so while Yoko and Fumiko begin furiously to prepare a meal, I get some yens out of my wallet to pay them back.

Since I've already done a little studying on my own in preparation for my lessons, I decide I'll be clever and thank them for buying me the books and explain that I have some money to pay them, all in Japanese. I practice a few times silently before taking the plunge and adding some vocal cords.

"本はありがとうございました！かねをもってきました," I say to Yoko when she walks into the room. "Thank you for the books. I've brought some money."

"O-かね," she corrects me, wincing and giggling.

It's amazing the difference one little omitted syllable can make. She shakes her head and waves her hand like she's sending away a bad smell.

I read in one of Ewan's books that the syllable "o" is an honorific, placed in front of some words to make them softer or more polite. I'd omitted it in front of the word "money," and this omission had drastically altered the sound of the sentence, judging from Yoko's reaction. So instead of saying, "Thank you so much for the books. I've brought some money," I'd actually said something like, "Here's your money, you greedy bitch. Thanks a fucking lot."

It is this kind of tiny but pivotal error that seems so easy to make on a regular basis when trying to communicate in Japanese as a foreigner. When learning a new language, especially one completely unconnected to your mother tongue and filled with such contextual nuance, you're naked, totally unprotected, walking blind in a brambly and treacherous terrain full of colloquialisms, multiple meanings, varying levels of politeness, and double entendres. I am terrified that one day, while trying to tell someone they look nice, I'll instead end up saying I want to lick their daughter's underarms. I'm about to learn what it's like to be the student crying over his textbook and not the teacher laughing up his sleeve.

Here's the thing: if you're going to learn a new language, you've got to be unafraid to make mistakes, relax, and have fun. What I tell my students, in other words. I'd thought I'd been blowing out a bunch of useless hot air, but turns out I was wise beyond my own understanding.

During the lesson, I sit at the dining room table with my notebook and books in front of me while Yoko and Fumiko teamteach me. They stand on each end of a dry-erase board that they've wheeled into the room, and both hold large wooden pointers for easier gesturing. Fumiko, a giggly gal with a frizzy bob, proves herself quite the opposite of her exceptionally put-together mother. She dresses in sweats, doesn't bother with makeup, and laughs loudly with her mouth wide open—a no-no for women in Japan. Once, at Yoko's prompting, she covers her mouth and nearly succeeds in knocking a tooth out with her large wooden pointer.

She drills me on basic pronunciations of the phonetic characters and some simple words and phrases, playfully jabbing me with the pointer whenever I make a mistake. Yoko then takes the reins and corrects my mistake, making me repeat after her until I get it right or I feel like I'm losing my mind, whichever comes first.

> Yoko: KonNIchiwa
> Me: Konichywa
> Yoko: No, no. Konnichiwa
> Me: Konichywa
> Yoko: Kon-NI-chi-wa
> Me: Konichywa
> Fumiko: KON-NI-CHI-WA!! [jab with wooden pointer]
> Me: Konnichiwa!
> Everyone: [applause]

The ladies escort me through the wonderland that is basic, bottom-rung, just-off-the-boat Japanese, from the different greetings for the different times of day, to expressions for politely leaving work before someone else, expressions for politely refusing more food, expressions for politely asking where the toilet is, expressions for politely requesting something in a restaurant, expressions for politely saying no, you would rather not eat pizza for dinner because you had that shit for lunch, and about what seems like hundreds of different ways of apologizing for what seems like a hundred different things I didn't realize I could do wrong. We cap things with a session about useful expressions to use when riding in a taxi: saying where you need to go, where to stop, giving directions to a driver, and such. All in all I do pretty well, with a few minor exceptions hardly worth mentioning.

> Yoko/Taxi Driver: Where would you like to go?
> Me: Can you please take me to the park? First, drive straight. And then take a left at the next stoplight. After that, go straight.
> Y/TD: OK, I understand.
> Me: Now please rent a room on the right at the next stoplight.
> Y/TD: Um, I don't understand.

We stop the lesson after thirty minutes and prepare to have our meal. I stand nervously, wondering what I should do, while Fumiko sets the table with plates, chopsticks, and teacups and Yoko finishes the yaki soba and salad in the kitchen. Fumiko looks at the job she's done setting the table, tilts her head in consideration, and goes back into the kitchen and whispers something to Yoko. This prompts Yoko to come survey the table, tut-tut, and do some rearranging. She asks me to sit, and she and Fumiko bring out the food: a heaping pan of yaki soba and one whopper of a salad.

"いただきます!" Yoko says, prompting me to repeat this standard phrase one says when receiving food.

"Itydikimasoo!" I beam, and we all dig in. The ladies enjoy a few giggles over my use of the chopsticks. Don't get me wrong, I can use them, but since I'm left-handed, I have a special way of holding them, just like we southpaws have a unique way of holding pencils and pens. We don't hold them, per se, we grab them, as if we were trying to strangle the life out of them. I can feed myself with chopsticks, but I prefer to do it alone in a dimly lit room and not in front of a peanut gallery of Japanese critics.

After dinner, I make my way to the toilet, while Yoko and Fumiko clear the table, clean the dishes, and presumably argue about when the hell Fumiko is going to find a goddamn man and move the hell out of the house. I am delighted to discover in the bathroom a Washlet, one of those high-tech toilets you find in the nicer Japanese restrooms. It has a slew of useful functions, like a butt sprinkler, a heated seat, and a dizzying selection of sound effects to muffle the user's unseemly emissions.

Toilets are a national obsession in this country of 100 million people and, if all goes well, 100 million daily turds. But the sheer volume of human waste isn't the main reason these Washlets are so necessary. It's the waste of water resulting from the tendency of Japanese women to flush repeatedly in order to mask their own excretory noises. These toilets solve that problem, allowing you to have a seat, choose a rushing water or an oscillating fan sound (a laugh track might be fun), sit back, and let it loose, giving yourself a sprinkle afterwards. And even though I'd gone in there just for a piss, I'm unable to leave without sitting my bare bottom on the heated seat (*ahhhhh*) and giving myself a little splash. I'm sure I'm blushing on the way out.

I return to the dining room table to see it set again for the dessert course. But this is no ordinary dessert. Yoko and Fumiko stand by their chairs until I come back to the table, then gesture for me to sit down. They join me, and Yoko begins an elaborate and carefully executed procedure of making and serving the tea. This here, I think to myself, is a Japanese tea ceremony. Just like I'd seen in *The Karate Kid Part II*. With any luck, this particular tea ceremony will not end with one of the ladies letting her hair down, reaching across the table, and kissing me full on the lips.

I watch as Yoko performs every action with a studied yet poetic grace. When it comes time for us all to partake, she instructs me on how to turn the cup with three (or is it four?) short, controlled movements and bring it back around to its starting position, at which point she indicates, with nods in my and Fumiko's directions, that we should now raise the cup to our lips and taste its delicious greenness. We do and then place the cups delicately down onto their saucers.

We also enjoy some small cakes Yoko had picked up from the local bakery. She slices each in half before passing them to us on saucers and providing us each with a fork the size of Homemaker Barbie's spatula. I see that the cakes are filled with a mysterious thick brown substance and hope to God it isn't one of those Japanese concoctions that looks to be filled with chocolate when actually it's stuffed with a semisweet bean paste. I bite into it with a smile and, my fears totally confirmed, swallow it as quickly as possible. Lying through my teeth, I proclaim it "おいしい！" or "Delicious!"

No sooner have we finished our tea and cakes than Yoko turns to me and asks, "Do you want hear Japanese harp? Maybe I can play for you now."

Wow. I've had a free Japanese lesson. A delicious free Japanese meal. A front-row seat at a free Japanese tea ceremony. A free Japanese bean paste cake thingy. And now she's offering to play me music? Of course I want to hear the Japanese harp, that goes without saying. But I have a sinking feeling that I'm setting myself up for some bad karma, accepting all this free stuff without giving anything back. I mean, I had offered her an ear to vent about how awful her husband is, but surely she's overcompensated me by this point. Let's see…I could stand and recite the Pledge of Allegiance, follow this with my famous rendition of "Look at Me, I'm Sandra Dee," and finish things off by doing that thing I can do with my left eyeball, but it always takes me so long to uncross my eyes after that.

Plus, I remember something I'd read in the welcome packet that MOBA had sent me before I'd left the U.S.:

If you should lose a personal item, such as your wallet or purse, cheer up. It is highly likely that it was turned into the station master or the nearest kōban (local police box). Simply show up and make a clear identification.

No, not that one. This one:

The Japanese are very preoccupied with maintaining the status quo. It is of utmost importance not to offend anyone, and they are generally uncomfortable saying a direct "no" to a request. So instead of saying "no," often they will utter a noncommittal "maybe." This should be construed as "no."

Yoko had said the word "maybe." So does she really want to play the Japanese harp for me, or is this just her Japanese way of saying,

"OK, Tim, look, I've given you a lesson, I've fed you, introduced you to my daughter, hell, I even did a dang tea ceremony for you, which I've never even learned to do properly. What's next? Need a haircut?"

What to do? I really want to hear that harp. I'd also been hoping that later she would bring out her samurai sword and kendo sticks.

I finally decide that I'll bring my viola and washboard to the next lesson and give Yoko and Fumiko a little show. I'll also get Jimmy to send me some Pepperidge Farm Sausalito cookies and S'mores Pop-Tarts so I can impress the ladies with some sweet, sweet Americana.

"That'd be great," I reply.

Yoko and Fumiko promptly stand and move into the living room, where they start rearranging the furniture. They shove the coffee table against the far wall, open one of the sliding doors and chuck a sitting chair into the bedroom, and move a bunch of potted plants out onto the balcony. The gaping hole left in the middle of the living room is soon filled with the arrival of a humongous Japanese harp—a giant ocean liner coasting into a harbor. Yoko and Fumiko bring out the four-foot-long instrument, place it on two stands, one on each end, and start positioning little white plastic pieces under the strings in order to tune it.

I'd never known the Japanese harp was so massive. I'd seen old drawings of men and women sitting cross-legged on the floor strumming them, but in contemporary Japan, everything seems to get smaller and smaller with time, from cell phones to computers to cameras to paperback books to quantities of breathable air. Seeing the ladies drag in this bulky and unwieldy piece of polished wood with dangling strings and begin to transform it into an instrument, I think how, in Japan, size reduction of modern obsessions is one thing, but respect for tradition is another.

"Shrink everything else," I can hear the old Japanese samurai say as they collapse their swords down to something the size of toothpicks and place them in their back pockets. "But let the harp remain large enough to demand its own room."

Yoko finishes setting the harp to the right pitch, grabs some sheet music off the bookshelf, and then brings a chair over and sits down with the harp before her. She slides the little string picks on her fingers, bends toward the harp, and begins to strum and sing along to an old Japanese ballad. It's a vaguely familiar melody, yet I can't figure out why.

"I've heard this before," I say as Yoko continues singing and Fumiko starts picking her cuticles.

"Sakura...Sakura...Sana denchi to o-mo-u..."

Yoko stops. "You want play?" she asks.

"Oh, no, I can't. I..." I can't think of a decent reason not to. So Yoko stands and allows me to take her place in front of the harp. She instructs me briefly on how to read the notes of the Japanese score she'd been playing. Then she gives me the picks off her fingers so I can put them on. But I can't. They're too small for my fingers, naturally.

"No ploblem," Yoko assures me as she goes into the other room. "More large size I have." She reappears, bringing a few more picks for me to try on. As I attempt one after the other without success, I decide that big Western men were not meant to play this instrument.

"You can play no picks." Freestyle.

I strum the notes of the song, and slowly, pluck by pluck, I get the hang of it. Yoko and Fumiko sit watching me, Fumiko intermittently gnawing on her fingernails and sucking up the blood, Yoko looking at her disapprovingly. There are lots of stops and starts and plenty of foul notes plucked, but I get through it without hurting myself or damaging the instrument, which I consider a victory. Yoko and Fumiko obviously do as well, for their applause at the end of my performance is impassioned and relieved.

It's getting late, so after the women dismantle the harp again and dock it in another room, I gather my books and papers and prepare to leave. As I put the books into my backpack, Yoko tells me my homework is to learn to write the first ten characters in the Kanji book and to study the two phonetic alphabets, Katakana and Hiragana. I come very close to crying and begging for her benevolent mercy, but I can hardly say no after the good time she's shown me.

So I tell her I'll do my best, bow, say goodbye to Fumiko, who's standing with her hands behind her back cracking her knuckles, give Yoko a gentle American handshake, almost fall over trying to put my shoes on while bowing and saying goodbye, and step out into the hall.

Yoko and Fumiko smile at me from the door as I walk to the elevator, their bright faces flanked by those of Bambi, Thumper, and a half dozen dwarves. All the way home I think of the gloating I'm going to do about all the Japanese culture I'd imbibed in one evening.

The next day at work, I walk into the teachers' room and greet everyone warmly, waiting desperately for someone to ask me what I did last night or why I was in such a good mood or how to ask a Japanese taxi driver to drive me to the train station.

I see Joy and light up, because I know she's also taught Yoko, and given her current interest in all things Japan, she'll probably be very interested in hearing about my evening of cultural immersion.

"I had my first lesson with Yoko last night," I begin.

41

"Oh, cool!" she said. "That's great! Did she do the tea ceremony for you?"

"The what?"

"The tea ceremony. When I went a couple nights ago, she and Fumiko did a tea ceremony for me, and then we all sat around and took turns playing the Japanese harp. It was really fun."

Am I just one of many? It can't be. I am chosen.

"Oh, and she made yaki soba, and I learned how to give directions to a cab driver."

"Uh…that's cool. Yeah, we did all that."

"She also showed me a little bit about Japanese flower arranging, which was kind of cool, because, you know, I was wanting to take a class or something, and now I think I'll just pay her, you know, because she'll give me a good rate I think, and she'll, like, teach me Japanese at the same time. But you know what? To tell you the truth, I was most interested in the beautiful kimono collection she has. Did she show them to you?"

"No."

"God, you should see some of the designs! Oh, and her bonsai garden! Absolutely gorgeous. That woman can do anything, I swear. Oh! And she wants me to teach her Spanish! *Que magnifica*, no?"

"Oh, yeah, Spanish, that's great. And the bonsai garden was… you know, just totally amazing. Very artistic." The lies just pour out of me.

I sit down to look at my first students' folders and pick a lesson, wondering if I should ask if Joy knows about Yoko's husband's philandering and her problems getting Fumiko married. I decide not to, figuring I need to hold on to something of the whole Yoko experience that is mine and only mine, even if it's also everyone's.

I pick out a lesson for my class and pull out my new Japanese book, starting in on the first chapter.

The first bell rings, and the other teachers begin flooding in. Joy tells everyone about my night at Yoko's, and the questions start flying:

"Did you have those tiny cakes?"

"Wasn't her apartment beautiful?"

"Did she play you any Disney songs on the harp?"

"Fumiko is always messing with her fingers!"

Hmph.

So my experience at Yoko's wasn't my own. That's OK. The key is that I have begun to break down that language barrier and expose myself to the other side of the world. And I'm eating some great food in the meantime. It will happen brick by brick and stone by stone, but it will happen, and one day, I'll look straight through to where a wall once stood with my Western eyes and not only be able to give a taxi driver directions, I'll be able to ask him his opinion of the flat tax and banter with him good-naturedly about how dumb the U.S. health care system is.

But let's not get ahead of ourselves. There are some basics we must cover before shooting for the stars. Like talking about food in the free conversation room, for example.

I have a free period and decide I'll pop in on Bob, a gigantically tall teacher from Wales who is in what we call the free-con room with about ten students.

I open the door and hear him saying, "Yeah, I really don't like the taste; it just doesn't appeal to me."

I put on a smile as I look around at the students, all of whom have a look of utter horror on their faces.

Bob turns to me. "Tim, do you like manko?"

"Manko…manko…," I think aloud. "Oh, manko! Isn't that that bean paste stuff?"

He nods, looking around and wondering what the students find so horrifying about someone not liking manko.

"Yeah, I don't like that either. The first time I ate manko I was expecting it to taste like chocolate, and it just didn't at all." I screw my face up into a look of distaste. "I was so disappointed. Because, really, what's more delicious than a creamy, chocolate-filled doughnut?"

The students are still in shock about something, and a few of the ladies cover their mouths and giggle, red-faced. Things are clearly getting a little uncomfortable, so I do what I usually do when this happens. I walk out of the room and let the other person deal with it.

A few minutes later the bell rings and Bob comes into the teachers' room looking redder than any Welshman I've ever seen.

"Oh my God, oh my God!!" he bellows in his resonant baritone. "I've just made an awful, terrible, horrible mistake! I can never go back into that room again! I want to die and be buried immediately. Immediately! Shit! Fuck!"

Between his exclamations of "Oooooooooh, I wish I were invisible" and "Aaaaaaaaah, I want to go back to Wales," we get his story.

In class, they'd been discussing Japanese food, and the students had asked Bob what food he really doesn't like. Bob answered that he really doesn't care for bean paste, a perfectly reasonable answer. It's the answer I would have given and, in fact, had given when I'd stuck my head in. Unfortunately, he'd used the wrong word for bean paste. Instead of "anko," which means bean paste, he'd said "manko." Manko means pussy. He'd just told the class he really didn't like eating pussy.

And I had too.

All the teachers squeal and cover their mouths.

Right on cue, in walks Jill with a smirk on her face, oblivious to the atmosphere of confusion and despair engulfing us all and still intent on bringing the American empire down, colloquialism by colloquialism.

"You know my least favorite American word?" she squeaks. We are dying to know, absolutely can't wait for her to tell us.

"*Mom*. Why don't you just say *mum*?"

I wrack my brain trying to think of a good reason why we Americans refer to our mothers in such a venomous and disrespectful way. But I'm too appalled right now to take this bait.

I flop into a chair and look sadly at my Japanese book, wondering if there's a handy way to politely apologize not only for saying the word "pussy" at least four times in a ten-second period, but also for expressing that I don't really like eating it.

I decide maybe I should go down to Burger King and get some fries. I've got a really horrible taste in my mouth.

# of kanji characters studied: 40
# of kanji characters forgotten: 34
# of sexually inappropriate things said to Tokyo's
cashiers when just trying to be nice: ?

CHAPTER THREE

The Next Big Thing

In which a small prayer is offered to the God of Large Things.

I wake up in my neighbor Julia's apartment with the taste of moldy vodka and tonkotsu ramen on my breath. I'm not usually much of a drinker, but I make special exceptions when everyone else is doing it. Last night everyone else was doing it.

I rise up and see Ruth, Julia's roommate, passed out on the floor perpendicular to me. Turning left I see Julia in the kitchen heating the kettle and looking like she would very much prefer to be dead.

Last night we'd made our very first entrance into the kaleidoscope of Tokyo nightlife. We'd felt we deserved it. Collectively we have taught hundreds of lessons at MOBA over the first few weeks. We were tired of being polite and encouraging, tired of speaking broken English. We wanted to speak dirty English. Nasty English. Get-your-booty-on-the-dance-floor-baby-and-shake-that-ass English. It was time to make our way into the city for some booze and boogie.

It was off to Tokyo, to the neon-soaked streets and the sake-soaked locals. While getting dressed and lubing ourselves up with cocktails, we'd made a modest list of things we wanted to accomplish during our evening out:

1. Drinks with some kogyaru ("cool girls") in some DJ bar in Shibuya. They should have bleached hair, fake tans, boots that give a whole new meaning to the word "platform," sparkly, raccoon-style eye makeup, and bright white lipstick making their lips look frozen to their burnt faces.

2. More drinks, maybe some dancing to irritating house music?

3. Street performers! Let's see some street performers!

4. Drugs? Yeah, should try to find drugs.

5. Random dance floor groping.

6. House party on the top floor of the Park Hyatt Hotel in Shinjuku; green tea slammers; handstand contest, which we will win.

7. Our prize: a four-hour access ticket to penthouse suite on the fifty-ninth floor; pillow fight.

8. Trannies, clowns, geishas, geisha trannies, Jaeger shots, Red Rover.

9. Pie.

Yes, we'd figured it would go something like that.

To our complete and utter amazement, it didn't. Julia and Ruth got wasted before we even left Fujisawa and had to be dragged up to Tokyo by Charlie and me, who were a half hour more sober. It was an epic journey that involved falling down train station staircases (and being stepped on and over by impatient commuters), many emergency trips to the nearest bathroom, and much drunken apologizing to people for being in the way, being loud and Western, and being too tall.

We ended up dancing (kind of) at a club in Shibuya that was hosting a hip-hop night where the crowd and the dress code were a good five to ten years our junior.

"Yeeeahhh!" a disembodied MC shouted into a mic, doing his best impression of Chuck D, as we headed to the dance floor. It must be said, it is exceedingly difficult to dance to hip-hop with any credibility when you're a white guy weaned on New Wave and Euro-pop like I am. I lack the swagger, the confidence, the massive low-swinging balls to pull off successful hip-hop moves. Amid all the oversized hoodies, giant sneakers, and sideways baseball caps, we all felt more like chaperones at a dance than young kids out for the night. So we hit the bar and drank more to make ourselves feel younger. Once we were walking and stumbling into walls like three-year-olds, we figured we were young enough and, after a few more attempts at dancing, left.

We finished our evening at a ramen shop, Julia and Ruth passed out with their heads on the counters, Charlie trying to eat with one chopstick, and me sitting and waxing on and on about how cute the shop employees were behind the counter.

"Look at them, oh my God, kawaii city! Look!! With their little hats and their giant ladles. See? He's holding that giant ladle in his tiny, adorable little hand! Charlie! Ruth! I want one of those hats! Julia! Don't you want a hat?! Oh my God, I just wanna eat them up!!"

I can still taste the ramen in my nasty mouth as I hear a muffled attempt at speaking.

"Large night, eh?" I hear Charlie mumble from the corner, where he's been sleeping rolled up like a cat. He is right. It was a large, large night. Rubbing my eyes, I see Julia has the scars on her legs to prove it.

I peel myself off the floor and walk over to the kitchen table, damning the daylight, damning vodka, damning ramen, and, most passionately, damning hip-hop to hell. I try not to open my eyes too wide for fear that the birds fluttering their wings inside my head might get antsy and flap harder.

Magazines, yesterday's newspaper, and photos are strewn about on the kitchen table. I pick up the pictures to have a look. There's Ruth in front of a beautiful Japanese garden. There's Ruth ladling water over her hands, presumably at a shrine of some sort. There's a blurry Ruth in close-up squinting to cover up her nasty case of red-eye and holding a hand out toward the camera. There's Ruth standing and smiling in front of a giant Buddha statue. Upon seeing this last one, my heart skips a beat: I do so love humongous statues.

"Wow, what is *this*?"

"It's the Big Buddha in Kamakura," Julia strains to say as she sits down and lowers her head onto the table. "Close to here," she mumbles.

"Really?! Where?" I demand.

"That way." She points out the window.

Wow. The Big Buddha. A giant, glorious statue offering the promise of enlightenment and inner peace, sitting among the beauty and languor of a lush and reassuringly symmetrical Japanese temple ground. The perfect antidote to last night's asymmetrical booze opera.

Mankind has had a long and storied obsession with creating giant structures of humans, gods, and mythical beasts to pass the time. You have your Sphinx, you've got your Statue of Liberty, your Christ the Redeemer, and your Michelangelo's David, all of which are testament to man's endless desire to painstakingly construct and then sit back and gaze upon giant representations of the mythic, the massive, the messianic, and the supple and drop-dead gorgeous.

It's this obsession I share with generations of humans before me that makes me feel most connected to my ancient antecedents. Or something. In any case, plunk down a giant statue, building, stone pillar, lighthouse, or fire-breathing monster, and I will buy a ticket, stand in front of it, gawk, and maybe even tear up; if it's big and famous, I want to see it.

I used to have dreams in which I was standing on the crown of the Statue of Liberty looking out over the city. In the dreams, Lady Liberty did not have her own island. No, she lived in Midtown. Her spiky crown afforded me a convenient little bridge to the roof of any number of the other city skyscrapers. The wind would rip through my tousled blond hair and push me ever closer to the edge of that tiara as Juice Newton's "The Sweetest Thing (I've Ever Known)" filled my eardrums. I would lift my head towards the sky and spread my arms out like a member of the Von Trapp family. Then usually the vertigo would get to me and I'd lose my balance, plummeting headlong towards the pavement.

As a child, I would visit my aunt and grandmother in Jamestown, New York, every summer, and one of the highlights of the trip was always the frequent drives into the tiny downtown area. To get there, we would have to drive over a bridge connecting the neighborhoods to the city center, and off to the right, on top of a factory building, was a massive, twenty-five-foot statue of a shirtless Indian brave. He stood at attention, one arm by his side, the other lifted high above his head, palm facing the sky. In his palm, also standing at attention, was a big bottle of Stroh's beer.

I was devoted body and soul to that Indian brave, and I looked forward to seeing him every year. My sister Laurie never cared for him, preferring the much more approachable and friendly looking Mr. Donut figure situated downtown. This meant I didn't have to share him with anyone. I should note that I didn't love him only for his massive muscles, his stern and manly expression, and his alluring headdress. It wasn't his rippled stomach, his tight-fitting calfskin trousers, his bulging pectorals, or his erect, brick-red nipples.

It was that he was damn huge. I was afraid of him and drawn to him at the same time. He sent chills down my back. He was dangerous and unattainable, a perfect object of desire.

Yes, for many of my preteen years, I was in love with a twenty-five-foot statue of a beer-swilling Native American.

Of course, the Indian is only famous in the greater Jamestown area, but since him I've seen many big and famous things: Big Ben, the world's most celebrated gilded phallus; Stonehenge; Seattle's Space Needle; the Empire State Building; the Metronome in Prague; my own North Carolina's Cape Hatteras Lighthouse; the seven-foot penis in Amsterdam. Most importantly, I saw Michelangelo's David in Florence, which turned my knees to Jell-O and gave me the sweats for days. He inspired a euphoria I hadn't known since my old red friend. But where the Indian stood defensive and defiant, David stands blithe and somnambulant. Where the Indian seemed to forbid anything more than a casually appreciative glance, David the attention whore coaxes you into looking more closely. Where the Indian wore calfskin trousers, David is stark naked. I'd stared at him for what seemed like hours, from every conceivable angle.

So, needless to say, I'm very excited about seeing the next big thing, this so-called Daibutsu, or Great Buddha, and I'm happy to hear that he sits just down the road from us by train, perched cross-legged among the trees in the innermost area of a temple in nearby Kamakura. And while I know the Big Buddha may not excite me in the same way Big Red and Big Dave did (it would be wrong to become aroused by a statue of the Buddha; it would be wrong to become aroused by a statue of the Buddha), he still has sheer size to offer.

"Oh, let's go! Let's go!" I demand of my friends at Hangover House. After all, there's nothing to help a hangover more than stepping out into the white light of morning, hopping a train that weaves and buckles through several tiny towns, and walking a few winding uphill roads to see a big holy tub of bronze.

"You've got to be kidding me," Julia manages to say without hugging her temples. "I'm not going anywhere."

Charlie has fallen back asleep leaning against the wall, and Ruth had never come to to begin with, so I figure this sojourn will be a solitary one. That's OK, I think. I'll come back the most enlightened one on my floor.

Construction of the Great Buddha was finished in 1252. He's cast in bronze and weighs nearly 850 tons. Most importantly, my guidebook tells me, he is 11.4 meters tall. He sits out in the open surrounded by the beautiful greenery of Kamakura. It was not always so. He was once housed in a great hall, until 1495 when a tsunami washed it away. So after a good five hundred years of sitting outside, he's understandably a bit weathered and blotchy. Who wouldn't be?

The Daibutsu is a stunning sight: a giant figure blissfully hunched in a pose of poetic reflection; a symmetrical, robust giant clad in a loose robe, with lowered eyes and bare feet. He is the picture of serenity. And he is B-I-G. But where David and the Indian had both seemed well aware they were being watched, Buddha, if he knows, doesn't appear to give a damn. He is in his own world, his massive head slightly lowered, his robe falling open in the center, revealing the midsection of his chest and curved belly, his eyelids hanging low over his shadowed eyes, eyes that might be looking down, might be looking straight at you, might not even be there.

The atmosphere of the temple grounds is serene and reverential. Out-of-towner Japanese folks bow and pray, write out prayer wishes and attach them to the prayer board, and do the ritualistic cleansing of the hands and mouth using the bamboo ladle at the entrance. A few Buddhist Westerners sit off to the side in the lotus position. Children chase each other around the statue.

Meanwhile, I take pictures from all sides, circling him from the left and slowly winding my way around, trying to avoid the speeding kids, capturing every angle of his greatness. As I make my way to the right side, I see a little entryway where you can go inside for a mere twenty yen. There's no saying no to an offer like that, so I pay my twenty yen, lower my head, and cross the threshold. As soon as I alight, on the first step there in the darkness, I experience an emotional spasm, like when you realize your boyfriend's birthday was yesterday and you'd completely forgotten. I realize that not only have I *found* the Buddha with the help of the good Lonely Planet people, but I now stand *inside* him. I am in the Buddha's belly. My God, I think, I should be having a real existential experience right now, shouldn't I? If only I were Buddhist. Were I Catholic and standing at the foot of the giant Jesus in Rio de Janeiro, I'd surely be weeping, crossing myself, and feeling really guilty about what I'd gotten up to at the bar the previous evening. Alas, I haven't found my particular religious path yet, so my reaction to stone embodiments of the divine is aesthetic and wholly secular. Contemplating the existence of God while gazing at a religious sculpture never leaves me with questions answered, convictions affirmed, or fears assuaged. I may leave wanting to be a better human, but I'm at a loss as to how I go about it.

I will say this, though. Walking around the Great Buddha so many times, examining every curve and swoop of his robe, staring fixedly at the way his hands perfectly meet each other as they lay in his lap, makes me feel even more asymmetrical than usual. Thanks a lot, Buddha.

Though I don't have a spiritual awakening, we do share a moment, and my hangover feels tons better. Also, I swear, as I exit out around the right side and emerge back around the front, I look up to his mysteriously guarded eyes and they meet mine as he murmurs, "Big enough?"

"Yes," I reply, clasping my hands together in a bid for symmetry. "Big enough."

# of times since arrival I've said
"thank you": 5,423
"I'm so sorry": 5,424
"It's a shame about that baby": 2

CHAPTER FOUR

Bad Gaijin

In which our hero's new roommate becomes an
international metaphor for something god-awful.

People have all sorts of reasons for leaving their home country
to live in a completely foreign land where they stick out like sore
thumbs. Some are good reasons (personal fulfillment, sobering
up, wanderlust, cultural curiosity), and some are questionable
(avoiding the law, drug smuggling, sex tourism). MOBA, one of
the most popular language schools in Japan, doesn't care what
the reason is, as long as you can pretend to know how to speak
English.

I've had my doubts about MOBA's hiring practices from the
very beginning, and not just due to the fact that my roommate
Sean only has a high school education, has never met a double
negative he didn't like, and had no problem getting a job as an
instructor. I've also noticed a tenuous command of the English
language on the part of a few of my coworkers who can barely
string a sentence together correctly without breaking into a cold

sweat. Like Stanley from New Zealand, who brings a briefcase the size of a tuba case to work and says things like, "Yeah, but he didn't play like do that right down the middle without your mum crickety bum licker." Or Pete from Pennsylvania, whom I recently overheard in a class explaining what the word *broke* means like this:

"You know if you have something, like a dish or a glass, and you drop it on the floor? *Broke* is what it becomes. For example, 'My watch is not working. I think it is broke.'"

As an English teacher, and a kind of anal retentive one, when overhearing such egregious misteachings of the language in an adjacent classroom (we can hear everything through the thin walls), I often wish I could leave my class, jump into a phone booth on the street below, squeeze into my spandex, grab my magic Declension Dildo, and quickly emerge as some sort of costumed English language superhero (Conan the Grammarian?) whose mission it is to save people across Japan from the dangerous consequences (i.e., sounding stupid) that can result from mixing up the past and the present perfect forms of verbs.

"Here I come to save the day!" I would sing as I flew into master villain Pete from Pennsylvania's room, slapped the hapless teacher silly with the Declension Dildo, and corrected the students before the mistake could be permanently etched into their brains. "Brok*en*! His watch is brok*en*!"

"How can we ever thank you very much?" the grateful students would say.

"Just use 'broken' in a sentence correctly," I'd reply with a wink before sheathing my weapon, flying out of the room, and quickly returning to my class in normal clothes. My own students, having taken the opportunity of my being out of the room to have a quick conversation in Japanese, would be none the wiser.

But my doubts about MOBA's commitment to excellence in English instruction have been confirmed beyond repair ever since the arrival of my new roommate, who took Sean's place when his MOBA contract had ended. Sean is on his way back to Melbourne and his job as a customs agent at the airport.

"I've done what I set out to do," he told me with a wink and a nudge over a farewell drink at our local bar.

Even without the wink and the nudge, I'd pretty much known he wasn't talking about fulfilling his lifetime goal of scaling Mount Fuji or learning the traditional Japanese process of making washi paper. He was talking about making it with Japanese girls.

Sean is one of those guys who come to Japan for no other reason than the possibility of having sex with Asian hotties. It's common knowledge around these parts that Western guys, especially those with limited sex appeal in their own countries, can experience the ultimate image makeover by just stepping off a plane at Narita Airport. All of a sudden, they're exotic and hot. They're like that tuneless, unwashed, and insufferable local band in your town that nobody goes to see but somehow develop a huge following in Japan thanks to some obscure seven-inch they managed to get released there because of their cute mugs and the voracious appetite of young Japanese girls for white boys playing guitars. In Australia, Sean was a pale, stocky, simian type, perpetually squinting like he is always staring directly into the sun. In Japan, he's a sexual dynamo, in spite of the fact that, when he speaks Japanese to his lady friends, he sounds like Crocodile Dundee ordering a kangaroo burger at a sushi bar.

But what had Sean's plan been in specific terms, I wanted to know.

"Six in six," he says proudly, taking a swig of Asahi Super Dry beer.

I've never been too good with numbers. Was I meant to divide, multiply, add? Surely not subtract. I'm confused by it.

"Six ladies in six months," he clarifies, looking at me.

Oh, I see. A girl a month. A cross-cultural experience of a lifetime easily reduced down to simple mathematics and sex. Cheap and calculating, yes, but I must say it's always encouraging to hear about someone reaching his goals with little to no effort. But such little ambition! Surely he could have shot for nine or ten.

A few weeks after Sean's departure, Ewan and I both receive faxes at work informing us that we're getting a new roommate on Friday. His name is Ron Faust and he's from the U.S., and that's all the information they give us. Though we are both a little nervous at the idea of our home life being altered, it's in the back of our minds that this Ron Faust could be a really cool guy who might breathe new life into the AF Building.

"Maybe he'll be a good cook," Ewan says.

"Maybe he'll be a flutist," I offer.

"Maybe he'll be a necromancer!" says Ruth.

"Maybe he'll be a fugitive," says our neighbor Julia, who used to work at a prison in England. We all giggle in blithe amusement for the last time that week.

By the time Friday rolls around, we've prepared ourselves as much as we can. Ewan cleaned up the kitchen and common area and even bought some wine and crackers that he arranged on the kitchen table as a welcoming gesture. I put new batteries in the TV remote.

I wait around with Ewan for a while watching the Discovery Channel, but I eventually get sick of waiting for Ron to show up and leave to visit Julia two doors down. We get drunk and continue the "maybe he'll be a…" game until things get really stupid.

"Maybe he'll be," Julia stammers, her head bobbing on her hand, "Madonna!!"

"Yes!! Or," I begin, holding my index finger in the air to emphasize the seriousness of my point, "it's also possible that he's Cher."

When I come back at midnight, the mythical Ron Faust still hasn't arrived, and I see that Ewan has opened the wine, downed a few glasses, and even started in on the cheese and crackers.

Ron, it turns out, doesn't arrive on Friday. Nor does he arrive the next day. After a few more days, Ewan calls the Tokyo head office of MOBA to find out what's happened to him. All they know is that, apparently, he hadn't shown up at the airport for his flight.

Three days later he still hasn't arrived, and Ewan and I are happily getting used to the idea of not having a new roommate and maybe turning the unused bedroom into a fitness/meditation room. Then, two weeks after the day that he was meant to arrive, who should ring our bell at ten p.m. on a Friday but Mr. Faust himself. He is drunk and from Philadelphia. And he looks like a pirate. He has a scraggly, unkempt beard, glassy eyes, and when he says, "Hello, I'm Ron," it sounds as if he's just released a small collection of rocks from his lungs.

Stunned, I say hello and welcome him in. He limps inside, dragging his left foot along the floor as he walks, and I help him with his stuff. After we deposit his things—a bookbag, a rucksack with what looks like a rolled-up one-person tent attached at the top, and four plastic grocery bags—on the floor of his room, he stumbles back to the door and spends a good ten minutes making sure he's able to use the key properly, repeatedly sticking it in, turning it round until the lock clicks out, turning it back until the lock clicks in, and pulling it out again until he feels he's mastered the drill.

"Just wanna make sure," he grumbles, sounding not unlike car wheels on a gravel road.

Afterwards, he comes into the kitchen where Ewan and I are sitting and takes a load off. Ewan and I sit looking at him and each other nervously, unsure what to say to break the ice. (I'm thinking, "Wow, you're totally fucking wasted!" would be appropriate.) Ron sits slumped in his chair, breathing heavily like he'd just killed a person with his bare hands. He pulls a tall can of beer out of his jacket pocket and cracks it open, sucking up the rising fizz and foam. I guess he stopped by the 7-Eleven first?

Now, God knows I hate to judge, but this man does not appear to be in any shape to instruct Japanese people in the finer points of English idioms or irregular past verb forms (especially not irregular past verb forms). He looks like he'd been scraped off the streets of Philadelphia and shipped to Japan while still viciously intoxicated—without being told why. My guess: a Philadelphia MOBA headhunter had been desperate to meet his quota, went out onto the street, found Ron drinking from a brown bag and talking to his imaginary friend Crabcake, and thought, "Now there's a MOBA English teacher!"

Visibly freaked out, Ewan soon retires to his room with a book he'd just bought about the history of furniture.

"Good night, guys," he says in his affable way. "Nice to see you, Ron."

"Yeah, ghghsshgrighsfheigls," Ron replies, one eye looking toward Ewan, the other at the floor.

I am now left alone with our new tenant. I sit and try not to stare at him as he finishes the tall beer he'd opened only a few minutes before. He lifts the can above his gaping mouth and shakes the last precious drops in, his lips slurping against the mouth of the can, his tongue reaching out and over to catch any stray dribbles. He smacks his lips, puts the can down on the table, and proceeds to inhale and exhale so loudly he sounds like he's got a mic on him. Satisfied that there is absolutely nothing else in that can, he hightails it to his room, rifles through one of his bags, grumbling to himself all the while, and once again emerges, limping into the kitchen with a bottle of Jack Daniels.

When he sits back down, he does something I totally don't see coming: he takes off his left leg. Or rather, he takes off the prosthetic lower leg part and drops it on the floor. So that's why he was limping. I decide not to ask him about it; he might not be finished taking off body parts yet, and I don't want things to get awkward. Plus, he's busy biting off the cap of the JD bottle.

I kind of want to throw up.

After taking his first swig, he makes a brief and barely understandable reference to being a Vietnam War veteran. It speaks volumes. Then he tries to engage me in a conversation about his girlfriend Debbie, whose husband is a real prick and he really wants to do the right thing by her so he is going to support the baby if it's his and he told this to the husband himself, yeah he did, but he's a prick and he wouldn't listen and he just tried to pick a fight, so what can he do and the husband's the one with the money so it wouldn't be any good for her to leave him because where would they get the money for that cruise they were planning?

"Exactly," I say, wondering if I have enough money to hire a security guard to stand outside my bedroom door while I'm sleeping.

For some reason, I am very hesitant to ask Ron any questions. Maybe it's because I don't see him offering any answer that can be understood by someone who hasn't been drinking highballs for the past two and a half weeks.

My curiosity gets the better of me, though, and almost without realizing it, I ask him, "So why are you here?"

"To get away from Mom," he replies without hesitation.

He's joking, right? This is a joke. I'm being punk'd. OK, guys, I get it, where's the camera? Come on, OK, you got me, ha ha, very funny, didn't see it coming. Ashton, get your ass out here, you nut! You are awful, but I *love* you! Ashton? Guys? Guys??

"And her retarded fucking husband."

I decide then and there that this Ron gentleman is the most fucked-up person I have ever met. Sure, I had some problems before coming here. I was a pothead. I was directionless. I was bored and uninspired. I was a part-time waiter. But this guy? He is like an amalgam of horror movie villains. Does his mother live in his attic? What's wrong with her husband? Where does Debbie fit into this melodrama? A feeling of helpless dread takes me over. It's fight-or-flight time, and since I'm a little fairy at heart, I decide to flee, back over to Julia's, to unload my worries about being beaten to death with a prosthetic leg in my sleep—and to take solace in her well-stocked cabinets of English biscuits.

"It turns out," I tell her as I make myself a cup of tea and arrange some McVities Digestives on a small plate, "that you were not far off with that fugitive comment. And it's also possible, Ruth, that he's a necromancer."

Julia doesn't blink. "Did you happen to see if he has any tattoos, like maybe a series of numbers or a gang symbol?"

I tell her that no, I hadn't seen any tattoos, but that was probably because I'd been preoccupied with the prosthetic leg on the floor, the containers of booze that kept appearing from nowhere, and the fact that he only has one earlobe.

By the time I return a few hours later, Ron is well into his fourth or fifth tall beer and has downed about half of his bottle of Jack. He has somehow managed to pry Ewan away from the cocoon of his bedroom and is talking to him about his girlfriend and his mother and the prick and the baby, and Ewan looks as if he is questioning his very concept of reality. I retire to my room to read and try to get some sleep.

I fall asleep enumerating the various ways one might lose an earlobe. I wake up about an hour later to the sound of Mr. Faust banging around the apartment, cursing, throwing things around, and generally grumbling like Grendel. I get up and peek out my bedroom door. All I can see is his shadow moving along the hallway floor and the shadows of the things he is throwing (the TV remote, a magazine, some Tupperware).

I fall back asleep and awake later to an eerie silence. I get up and clamber out the door and down the hall to the kitchen. It's strewn with beer cans, dirty dishes, cigarette butts, crumpled-up pieces of paper, and small puddles of Jack Daniels.

Among all the crap on the table I find a small letter that he's scribbled to an unfortunate soul by the name of Debbie. It is written in the penmanship of a three-year-old, but I am able to make out its contents. He talks about his new roommates, saying about us that we're "good guys, but I won't be surprised if one of them has to kiss the sidewalk soon." Cue maniacal laughter.

Hmm. Evil's afoot. What is Ron Faust's plan? Is he concocting a plot to get rid of us? Perhaps he's considering making our rooms into fitness/meditation rooms. Ewan's would work better for that, I think.

Since I'm now wide awake, I decide to sit down, have a piece of damn toast, and read the *Entertainment Weekly* a friend has sent me from home. I'm settling nicely into an article about Michael

Jackson, who always makes me feel better about my life, when Ron comes back in and sits down with several more beers and a fifth of vodka. He asks what I'm reading, and I show him. When I stand up to put my dish in the sink, he picks up the magazine, scoffs, and says, "Do you really get off on this stuff?"

"Um...," I mumble, not sure how to answer, "I just read it; I don't touch myself or anything."

He doesn't really appreciate the joke.

"Well, I always read the articles in *Playboy*. They're really good. Course, I look at the pictures, too."

Gross.

Then he starts talking about this woman who'd bought his car a few weeks before he'd made the big move to Japan.

"She had a great stack, though not much of a face, I'll tell you. It wouldn't stop a clock, let's put it that way."

It's very interesting to hear a man who is about as sexually appealing as a toilet seat talk about someone else's lack of physical attractiveness. Kind of like hearing Tony Danza say that he'd broken up with a girl because she sounds stupid.

Ron starts warming up to me once he gets his tenth or eleventh drink in him. He asks if I want to share a Valium with him. He says we're kindred spirits. I beg to differ and decline the offer, though I am *ve-heh-ry* tempted. Instead, I say my good nights and go back to bed.

In bed I wonder what Ron's mother looks like. I wonder if their relationship has ever crossed any moral boundaries, and as I'm drifting off to sleep with the word "Debbie" dancing in my head, I jump awake, having had an epiphany that won't be silenced. His mother and Debbie are the same person! And the husband is his stepfather! And he'd left the country because something terrible had happened that he'd needed to escape from! He got his mom pregnant! I have it! It all makes sense now! *Gross!*

Having had such a monumental breakthrough, I have trouble falling back asleep. I toss and turn for several hours, listening to Ron curse and burp and piss and yell throughout the apartment. The sun rises and I hear him cursing to himself at the front door right outside my room. He opens the door, and I can hear him throwing things out and over the balcony into the garden below.

It is then that the screw turns, and, the sleep deprivation allowing my polite Southern façade to crack, I bolt out of bed, throw open the door, and shriek, "What the fuck are you doing?!!"

I look down at the area where our shoes had once lain just inside the door. They're all gone, except for one of my sneakers that he still has in his hand, poised to toss. Taken off guard, he turns to me and starts fumbling for an explanation, but since in the past five hours he has ingested innumerable beers, a whole bottle of Jack Daniels, a Valium, and an ocean of vodka, an answer isn't forthcoming.

I storm out the door onto the balcony and look over the railing. There, four stories down, is a wonderland of footwear tossed away like so much rubbish.

I turn back and look at Ron, my nostrils flaring, my eyes surely bulging. "Don't you ever touch my fucking stuff, do you understand me? Don't you fucking ever fucking touch my fucking stuff!"

I run down the stairs, stumble into the garden, and start picking up all the shoes and carrying them up to the apartment. It takes me two trips, which gives me a good chunk of time to get even angrier. When I've retrieved all the shoes and brought them back up, I stand at the threshold of the front door and glare at

Ron, leaning against the wall in the hallway looking confused. I am ready to use the "F" word some more.

"You fucking drunk insane fucking idiot, what's your fucking problem?!!"

Meanwhile, Ewan has finally come out of his room and started being my yes-man, punctuating my railings ("You need to fucking dry out! Fucking shit fuck!") with the occasional sober "exactly" or "that's absolutely right."

It turns out that Ron, in his profound delirium, thought Ewan and I were playing a cruel joke on him. He couldn't find his leg on the floor and naturally jumped to the conclusion that we'd thrown it over the balcony.

I ask him why the fuck he fucking thought that fucked-up shit, and he says, "Because of the argument."

"What fucking argument?" I ask with petulant exasperation. "What are you fucking talking fucking about?!"

He must have interpreted our conversation in the kitchen earlier—the one in which he'd offered me a Valium and I'd politely declined—as an epic struggle between opposing forces that had ended in a vengeful prank. I should have just taken the damn pill. (It's not like me to dismiss offers like that out of hand.)

I take advantage of the fact that he's sorry and prostrate, and I send him to his room with no more vodka.

"Go to fucking bed!" I command him. Still confused and very, very drunk, he sheepishly obeys and limps to his room.

I'm awake for good now. Ewan and I have a cup of tea in the kitchen after cleaning up the remnants of the past eight or so hours and try to think of what to do. Meanwhile, Ron is in his room snoring like a hacksaw. Then, of course, he starts talking—screaming, really—in his sleep. At one point I hear him shout, "Hey, fatty!" but since neither Ewan nor I can generally be described as such, I figure he's safely asleep and dreaming of Debbie/his mother.

Ewan and I can't figure out how he had gotten hired by MOBA. Yes, they hire some idiots, but how had Ron stayed sober long enough to get through the interview? Had he not made a bad impression when he'd creamed his coffee with whiskey and then wet his pants?

I spend the whole day at work telling everyone about what happened and worrying about what I will find when I return home. Will he be selling all my CDs for a hundred yen by the side of the road? Will he have turned the refrigerator into a medicine cabinet for his many pharmaceuticals? (Actually, that might be nice.) Will he have killed, crushed into powder, and then snorted poor Ewan?

How could this have happened? Is MOBA so desperate for teachers that they've resorted to raiding American rehab clinics, luring the conscripts out with the promise of limitless Absolut and tonics? It's true, the English conversation school industry in Japan is one of the most fiercely competitive in the country. On trains, magazines, television, newspapers, and billboards everywhere, advertisements for language schools abound. Even celebrities, always up for making a quick buck in the lucrative Japanese market, get in on the fun, allowing their images to be used to convince the Japanese public to say screw it, get a second mortgage, and sign up for some English lessons. Which means you have the baffling phenomenon of Celine Dion's face on an Aeon English School poster beckoning people to come to Aeon and learn to speak English like an overwrought French Canadian.

I understand the need for teachers to meet the demand of an English-starved public. In Japanese grade schools, kids learn English reading and grammar starting in junior high. But since most English teachers don't speak English, they are ill-equipped to prepare their students for any real-world English-speaking scenario. So a handsome student named Tatsuya can graduate from a Japanese high school, walk right up to a native English speaker named Cheryl in a dimly lit bar, say something as basic as "I can buy you any drink?" in order to woo her, and because Tatsuya's pronunciation is so horrendous, Cheryl will promptly hold up her hand and say, "I'm sorry, I don't speak Japanese." Their relationship will end at roughly the same time it started. Very sad.

The tragedy of Cheryl and Tatsuya is why native English speakers are a hot commodity here, and all of the competing language schools understandably need a constant influx of teachers from America, Britain, Canada, Australia, and New Zealand in order to meet the demand. But I'm old-fashioned, I guess. I think prospective teachers should be able to do more than present a valid passport and pass the height requirement. They should at least have to pass a breathalyzer.

I call the accommodations department at the head office and talk to Kevin, the man in charge, who thankfully has already spoken to Ewan, so I don't have to start from the beginning. He apologizes and says that there must have been a mistake.

"We'll try to get him out of the apartment as soon as possible, but since it's the weekend, you know, it's a little difficult to arrange these things."

"Oh, *please*," I say. "Please please *please* get him out of there."

"I'll see what I can do."

He calls me later and says that they won't be able to move him until Monday night—three days hence!—but that they will definitely be moving him then. He offers me a pearl of advice.

"You and Ron should just attempt to stay out of each other's way until then, if at all possible."

Well, that sure ruins my dinner plans. Thankfully, Kevin has spoken to Ron and assures me that he is very sorry and has agreed not to come near us.

When work is over, I prepare myself to return home, with anxiety in my heart and, thanks to my friend and colleague Donna who has a boyfriend at Yokosuka base, a mild sedative in my belly.

Mamta, a teacher from Australia who lives directly below me, says she'll go home with me.

"I know you don't want to be alone with the one-legged man," she says.

When we arrive, Ewan is there, alive and well, but Ron isn't. We all sit down and have some tea and watch a Discovery Channel program called *Travelers* that sends young, wide-eyed Americans to exotic places so they can say things like, "I just love shopping in another culture!" We all agree that Ron is a better roommate than any of the retards on the show would be.

To prove our point, a skinny white girl from Ohio named Kim tries on an African head wrap at a street market and says, "Oh, this is *totally* me!" I start desperately wishing Ron would come back and put us all out of our misery. Right on cue, Mamta looks down the hall at the door and says, "Um, Tim? Yeah, the police are here."

I stand up and walk to the edge of the hallway leading to the door. Just outside it stand two policemen, leaning in and saying to me, "Your friend? Your friend?" while pointing to—you guessed it—Ron. Not surprisingly, he is drunk as a wombat. I speak to the policemen in my rough Japanese, and they explain, with the help of hand signals and mimicry, that they'd found him on the bridge down the road stumbling and generally looking like a scary foreigner. I thank the officers and apologize, going against my gut instinct to fall to my knees and offer them money if they will just stay the night. They leave Ron propped up against the wall just inside the door, and I go back to the kitchen.

Ron stands in the hallway for some time, leaning against the wall so as to remain more or less vertical. I slump down into a chair at the table and exchange unsure looks with Mamta and Ewan.

"I suppose it's good he didn't accidentally fall into the river," Mamta offers, and we all nod in agreement before changing our minds and sheepishly shaking our heads in embarrassed disappointment.

A growling sound comes from the hallway, followed by the words "Can't we talk about this?"

I hear him take a few steps toward the kitchen and say, in a more menacing tone, "Where's that guy who thinks he's better than everyone else?"

"Who's *that*?" I wonder aloud before realizing he's talking about me. I think this evaluation of my character is completely unfair. Sure, I am most definitely better than certain people, like most of the people I went to middle school with, all the gorgeous guys who have ever ignored me, and anyone who has ever told me I look like Bert from *Sesame Street*. But I don't argue. Nor do I raise my hand and say, "Over here!"

I stand and walk over to the kitchen drawers. "There you are," he says. Meanwhile, I start pulling all the cutlery out of the drawers to hide in my room.

Finally he makes it to the kitchen, launching into a litany of good deeds that he's performed today.

"I did all the dishes." I look at the drying rack. He's washed two soupspoons and a rice bowl.

"See how I washed all the dishtowels and hung 'em up?" he adds, pointing to the balcony. I go out to the balcony and find hanging two formerly white towels covered with big brown blotches and smelling like Ron's breath had the night before. He must have wiped up the Jack Daniels puddles with them, I figure.

"And I took out that big trash bag."

"Where did you take it?" I ask him.

He looks uncomfortable and says nothing.

On a hunch I look down to the street and see the bag slumped against some shrubbery, a milk carton sticking out and leaking droplets onto the greenery.

"Great," I say, coming back inside and taking a seat at the table. "Thanks."

He twitches and tilts his head, detecting a lack of authentic appreciation. Then he looks at me the way a person looks when he's about to snap another person's neck, gets in my face, and says, doing a spot-on imitation of Jack Nicholson in *The Shining*, "You wanna live here? I just bought this building. And I ain't leaving."

He steps back and lifts his arms and shoulders into a shrug.

"Guess *you'll* have to."

"You, um, bought the AF Building, Ron?" I ask.

"Yes sir," he spits. "It's just gonna take a few days for the money transfer to go through." Then he turns and plods off to the bathroom.

I look at Mamta and Ewan, utterly speechless.

"Look!" Mamta says, pointing to the television in the corner of the room. "He didn't break the TV!" Bless her, she's grasping.

I don't know whether to laugh or cry. It's beginning to look like I've traveled all the way around the world to the safest country on earth only to be drawn and quartered by an unhinged Philadelphian. Monday night seems so very far away.

"Listen," Mamta whispers, "why don't you and Ewan just bring some of your important stuff down to my place. You know, just to be safe."

We agree this is probably a good idea, since there's no telling when the Beast will decide to start throwing things over the balcony railing again. So I pick up my laptop and a stack of CDs. Ewan collects all his books.

We go downstairs and drop off our stuff. Ewan stays with Mamta, and I go up to Julia's to see if I can stay the night if things become life-threatening. As I'm filling her in on the recent developments in the saga, the doorbell rings. Julia answers and it's Mike, who lives in the apartment between Julia's and mine.

"Hey, do you know what's going on in Tim's flat?" I hear him ask.

I run out of the apartment and look towards mine. The door is wide open, the police alarm from the kitchen is sounding, and Ron is inside screaming. I go down to Mamta's and get Ewan. We decide to go up and get everything of importance out of the place, in case Ron has started a fire or something. I grab the rest of my CDs, and some work clothes and shoes. Ewan gets more books. Mamta offers to help, and Ewan quickly makes use of her, handing over his encyclopedia of arthropods and his giant collection of historical maps of the world.

But our mass exodus is halted when we can't get the front door open. The handle won't turn. Ron is on the other side, blocking us in. We can hear him outside shouting at Mamta's roommates, who had come to make sure we were alright.

"Oh my God, we're trapped!" I say, clearly kind of starting to enjoy the drama. I look at Mamta and Ewan with their arms full of useless books, and we all laugh. Then we look worriedly toward the door, because we really are trapped.

I could force the door open, but I am really afraid to do anything that will result in Ron being thrown off balance, for there's a second balcony and he's standing directly between it and the door. So we put everything down, go into my room, open the window, and watch as Ron wields a fire extinguisher to keep at bay the group of MOBA teachers from nearby apartments who have gathered around him, some people looking scared, others covering their laughing mouths.

We wait at the window until he finally moves away from the door. We quickly gather up everything and make a run for it. As we bust through the door, Ron is busy threatening the others congregated outside—the entire floor of tenants at this point, including a few mystified Japanese people who have never seen a real American crazy before.

"What's your name?" he demands of Mike.

"I'm not telling you," Mike says.

"What's your name?" He points to Julia.

"Thaddeus," she says.

"What's your name?" Holly, Mamta's roommate, this time.

"I don't have a name."

"Well," Ron growls, "I'm going to remember your names and I'm going to find you and you're going to be sorry!" Then he burps and kind of sneezes.

We sneak behind him and spirit our stuff down to Mamta's. From above someone yells down that two police officers have arrived, yay!

I run up the stairs ready to tongue-kiss both of them at the same time and, with a wink and a lick of my lips, invite them over to Julia's later. Turns out the two officers are the same ones who had brought Ron home earlier, after the bridge incident.

The party has moved back inside my apartment, so I open the door and see the two cops standing over Ron, who's sitting in a chair in the middle of the darkened hallway, his arms folded, his expression defiant, his face beet-red and shiny.

Erica, one of Mamta's friends who's half Japanese, serves as interpreter.

"I own this place! This whole place!"

Erica translates directly with a wink wink, nudge nudge.

The officers look at each other, confused. After a long, winding conversation that takes in all of Ron's hijinks as well as Erica's attempt at explaining that not all English teachers behave like this, the officers tell us they can't do anything because it isn't illegal to be publicly drunk in Japan, and anyway, he hasn't hurt anyone. (But what about what he's done to my *feelings*?!) They take down our details as a formality, and after accepting my heartfelt apologies on behalf of my entire country, they leave.

The door closes behind them, and we all silently turn our heads to look at our tormenter.

The good thing about a drunk like Ron is that, though he can ingest award-winning amounts of booze, he will reach his stopping point, and suddenly. Leaning back further in his chair and struggling to keep his eyelids raised, he reaches that stopping point. Down, down, down he goes, backwards toward the floor, the chair giving way under his greasy girth. He roars and spits all the way down to the floor, a trip that happens in slow motion. Then thud. Binge over. Yay, gravity.

Folks gathered outside begin to scatter now that the show's main performer appears to have passed out in epic fashion. "Goodbye, y'all," I say. "Thanks for coming. Yeah, I'll see you tomorrow. G'night. Be safe."

I step over Ron and walk to the kitchen, where Ewan sits looking tired, confused, and desperate to take up smoking. "It's over, Ewan," I say, patting him on the shoulder. "Let's go to bed."

The next day, I receive a call from the MOBA head office at work. He is out. They've moved him somewhere else; I don't ask where. I get home that evening and find that all of his stuff is gone. I walk back to the kitchen and see a final parting gift from Ron on the tile floor: a big brown turd. I turn around and walk to his room. It is completely empty, except for one item on the floor: a small paperback book that had presumably fallen from his bag on the way out. The title: *Networking in Japan: Making Those Important Contacts.*

Also, my *Entertainment Weekly* is missing.

A few days later, gossip swirls that Ron has gone missing from his new digs and still hasn't shown up for work. All of us gasp at the idea that Ron is freely walking the streets of Fujisawa carrying all of his belongings and throwing empty beer cans at old grandmas on the street. What if he decides to pay us tenants at the AF Building a visit? He is our landlord, after all.

Finally, after two weeks have passed, Ron calls the MOBA head office and says, no doubt slurring every syllable, "I'm ready for work!" But at this point MOBA has written him off and decided to do something unprecedented in their history: pay for a teacher's flight back home before he's even started work. It's the right decision—for the security of the nation.

That night, Mamta sees a particularly interesting item on CNN. A flight from Japan's Narita Airport bound for New York's JFK had to make an emergency landing in the Midwest because an unruly American guy had attacked a stewardess.

I'd bet my very soul that this guy had been drinking Jack Daniels. And reading my *Entertainment Weekly.*

*# of times I've visited Takashimaya department
store just to use their fancy, high-tech "Washlet" toilet: 3
# of train suicides that have made me late for work: 2*

CHAPTER FIVE

And on Drums...

*In which we learn that our hero's rock
star wet dreams can indeed come true—
if he just stays asleep long enough.*

Since the Ron fiasco, I've been seriously questioning my future
not only in my apartment but also with MOBA. Sometimes it
seems like getting a job teaching at this school is about as difficult
as finding work as a homeless person on the streets of New York.
It takes no credentials whatsoever and anyone can do it, which
means that in day-to-day life you run the risk of clashing with
drug-addled assholes who don't know when to shut up and go to
sleep.

Or just normal everyday idiots, like Paul from Canada who
recently dedicated an entire class to teaching his students the
nicknames English speakers have for Japanese people, most of
them extremely unflattering ("slanty-eyed midgets," for one).
When I asked him why he felt compelled to do such a thing, he
said simply, "I just thought they should know."

Then there's Australian Mark, who recently had the brilliant idea to teach a lesson in impenetrable, slangy Crocodile Dundee–inflected speech, because "they're gonna have to deal with it if they ever come to Australia." I watched from my classroom as his three mid-level students had three separate mid-level nervous breakdowns.

Not that I'm any kind of Einstein. I've made my share of idiotic remarks in class. Sometimes it's unavoidable when your job is to talk all day and try to maintain enthusiasm. Recently I was teaching two men, both engineers and advanced-level students, and we were talking about Japanese electronics, architecture, and design. At one point I proclaimed in a commanding tone, as if I were saying something really quite unprecedented and insightful, "Japanese engineering is just, like, totally amazing, and, you know, the architecture and, like, electronics, I mean, you know, *my God…*" I wanted to die even as I rambled on, and from the look on my students' faces, they wanted the same thing.

I decide to use the whole Ron thing as an excuse to finally make the big move to Tokyo. It's time to move on, to head north, onwards to the city to take a large, sloppy bite out of the Big Rice Ball.

I find a room in Minato Ward, South Tokyo, in what is called a guesthouse. There are two showers, two toilets, two sinks, and one tiny hot plate in one tiny kitchen.

I've made the unlikely and not altogether fabulous transition from living with two gaijin to living with five. There's Talvin from England, a MOBA teacher in Tokyo; Amelia from Australia, who hates her job at a gimmicky "English Through Drama" language school for kids; Hans, a banker from Germany; Chain-Smoking Jerry, a freelance English teacher (yes, I said a freelance English teacher) from Canada who, though he's got to be nearly sixty, hasn't let it keep him from snagging a beautiful young Japanese woman (in this case, the lovely Keiko) and getting her to cook for him. They're all pretty nice.

But my new best friend is Rachel from California. She's the girl next door. Not in that bobby sox–wearing, let's-go-to-the-hop kind of way; she lives in the room next to me. I loved her immediately because, since she's from California, she has a disposition at least as sunny as mine. She is an ex-MOBA teacher who now works at Lane, a school with four branches in Tokyo.

When I move in, I have to pay a deposit and a month's rent in advance, but thankfully no "key money," which is a customary monetary gift of at least three months' rent that new tenants in Japan offer their new landlord just for being such a great guy. I avoid this odious practice by going through an agency that specializes in finding housing for poor, helpless gaijin. Unfortunately, I am also paying for my Fujisawa apartment, so right now, I'm paying two rents. And eating lots of Cup Noodle.

Because of my lack of cash flow, I had to move all of my stuff myself using only my hands and the train. A sane and more financially solvent person would have loaded all of their stuff into a cab and put any of the overflow into boxes and had them sent through his local convenience store delivery service (because there is absolutely nothing you can't do at a freaking convenience store here). But all of this costs money, and I have zero disposable income. I'm borrowing money from teachers at the school just to eat, and if I could have gotten away with it, I would have walked around Fujisawa Station with a cane, a pair of Speedos, some dark glasses, and a coffee cup made of tin begging people for spare yen for a few hours a day. Unfortunately, if you're a white man in Japan—even one with a limp and a vision impairment—you are (correctly) assumed to be making the big bucks, because more likely than not you are an English teacher. So that shit wouldn't fly here. I simply had to bite the bullet and move everything myself. And though I could've done without having to wheel my TV/DVD player behind me on a little trolley down a five-lane city street from Shinagawa Station to my new place, I got through everything all right, and the TV only fell over twice.

Soon after I move in, I'm hanging out with Rachel on the couch in the tiny sitting room/kitchen while Chain-Smoking Jerry gives Keiko a lecture about the first Thanksgiving and what it means to Americans and Canadians alike. As he exhales a huge plume of smoke in our direction while relating the history of maize cultivation in North America, Rachel tells me that her language school is looking to hire a few new teachers.

"I'm such a dork, I totally forgot to tell you about it," she apologizes.

"Oh my God, get me a job! Get me a job *immediately!*" I demand.

"Totally, yeah, I'll put in a good word for you."

And with that brief exchange I am on my way to a new teaching position at two of Lane's schools in Shinjuku and Ginza. I send in my résumé, and a few days later they call me in for an interview.

This interview is a little different. While Drew, the head teacher, does ask me about my interests and hobbies, the Lane folks seem a little more preoccupied than MOBA with their teachers having a decent command of the English language. To that end, there is an hour-long, ten-page exercise that tests my knowledge of English grammar, from comma splices to misplaced modifiers to restrictive and nonrestrictive relative clauses. Although it's a bit of a harrowing experience struggling to recall how *affected* and *effected* are different, and although I seriously doubt the need for the general Japanese population to know what distinguishes a simile from a metaphor, it is comforting to know that the school is interested in hiring me for my thorough knowledge of the language and not just my American passport, valid working visa, and jazz hands. Still, I'm more than a little worried about how I'd performed on the test.

I get a call the next day from Craig, the other head teacher, offering me a job with the school.

"Really?! Did you not look at the grammar test?" I say.

He says no, they did, and that I made a pretty good showing, actually. In fact, I received the highest score they've ever seen. Those Latin classes served a purpose after all.

I am ecstatic. Not only because I will be working in central Tokyo, but because I will be making more money, have more vacation time, have all national holidays off (at MOBA, national holidays have been our busiest days), and, most importantly, I will never ever have to see or hear Jill again, ever, as long as I live, ever.

"You bitch! You're leaving me alone with that cow?!" Donna says after I sing her the good news to the tune of "America" from *West Side Story* during one of our after-hours drinking binges. We've grown very close in our time at MOBA together. We'd initially bonded out of our mutual loathing of Jill, only later discovering we also had a mutual love for text messaging, sukiyaki, and men in uniform.

But she wishes me well, and we promise each other that our life together is not over. Sitting at our favorite Kamiooka izakaya bar getting sloppy on foamy mugs of beer, we make a solemn vow that we will, as Donna put it, "go somewhere fucking fabulous on holiday together and be complete pigs." We toast to it, clinking our glasses together and spilling beer onto our tiny plates of complimentary pickled relish.

All settled in Tokyo now, I decide it's high time I hatch the next part of my big "I'm Waking Up to Myself" party: yes, it's time to go out in public with my viola. I place an ad in the English-language *Metropolis* magazine looking for people to play music with. It would be nice, I figure, to have a regular quartet, marching band, or heavy metal orchestra to meet with, and it's been a while since I last played music with other people, considering I typically play by myself in my apartment when nobody else is home with the shades drawn and a rolled-up towel pushed up against the bottom of the door. But even though I've played for years, I'm still a little lacking in confidence, and this insecurity may have seeped into the wording of my ad:

AMATEUR VIOLA PLAYER, AMERICAN
SEEKS OTHER AMATEUR MUSICIANS TO PLAY MUSIC
JUST FOR FUN.
MUST BE AMATEUR. FOR FUN.

I think my ad also suffered from bad placement, since it was positioned right under an ad reading:

HI! FEMALE SINGER/DRUMMER HERE!
AUSTRALIAN, BLOND, EARLY 20'S
SEEKS PATIENT, UNDERSTANDING GUITAR TEACHER
FOR PRIVATE INSTRUCTION.
I CAN TEACH YOU ENGLISH!!

I'd guess 99 percent of the people looking for musicians to work with that week answered her ad. But I do get a few responses:

Hello,
I'm writing to your ad. I like viola player. I sing, but not so well. Let's make a music!
    Hide Saito

Dear Mr. Viola,
I play the bass and like a rock music. You like a rock? I'm not sure viola okay for this kind of style music. Maybe we try. You e-mail me.
    Kenji
P.S. You like the Genesis?

Hmm. Not too promising. I'd sooner peel off my own face than play Genesis songs on the viola. Then I get an e-mail from a piano player named Toru in Yokohama.

Dear Tim:
My name is Toru and I play the piano. I saw your ad and I would be very interested in playing music with you. If you are interested, please write. Thank you.

Wow. He writes English better than I do. I write him back, and we strike up an e-mail friendship. A few weeks later we meet in Shibuya for coffee to get to know each other and discuss what music we should play. I learn that he's been teaching himself English for about twelve years, starting when he was thirteen, and he'd improved by practicing on his foreign friends. He suggests we try the Brahms sonatas for viola and piano. Blissful in my ignorance, I quickly agree, and we are off to the Yamaha store to buy some sheet music. Toru already has the piano music, so we just need the sheets for viola, which he quickly finds among the thousands and thousands of papers on the shelf and hands to me with a smile.

I hesitate to look at the music as an old demon creeps into my consciousness: Though I'd started playing violin when I was seven, switching to viola in my twenties, I don't sight-read music very well. When I took up the violin, I learned via the Suzuki method, which emphasizes ear training at the expense of music reading. Though I later learned to sight-read, it was always a struggle for me, and my natural tendency was always to ignore whatever sheet music my teacher had assigned for the week and just pick things out that I wanted to play ("Edelweiss," "You're the One that I Want," the themes from *E.T.: The Extra Terrestrial*, *The Golden Girls*, or *L.A. Law*). Once I knew what a piece was supposed to sound like—either by listening to my teacher play it or by obtaining a recording of it—I could rattle it off with relative ease. But given the same piece of music and no assistance whatsoever, I'm doomed. Doomed.

Long story short, I am a string player deathly afraid of sheet music.

This phobia would've been my undoing had I been playing in the era of Mozart, when rehearsal time was extremely limited and most people sat down and just sight-read their way to riches, glory, and designer pantaloons. Had I had the gall to ask Wolfgang before a performance to just hum a few bars of what I was meant to play, I would've been laughed off the stage, my fluffy white wig a web of tomatoes, eggs, and spittle, my legs beneath my secondhand pantaloons lashed repeatedly by violin bows, my fluffy blouse ripped to shreds and set on fire, my head nearly split open with an almond cheese log.

Thankfully, I'm living in more liberated and patient times. I have a look at the first movement, and it seems pretty manageable. Then I turn to the second movement and nearly faint. The notes are crowded together on the page like, well, like Tokyoites of all shapes and sizes standing, sitting, swaying, knocking about, picking fights with each other, and looking up each other's skirts on a rush-hour train. I stare at the two pages comprising the movement and panic, feeling like a complete phony, desperate for Toru to just agree to play sitcom theme songs and familiar show tunes and let me off the hook.

But then I think, "Hey, I never shy away from a challenge." But then I think, "Actually, Tim, you ALWAYS shy away from a challenge. I've never seen you NOT shy away from a challenge."

"This looks fun," I say to Toru, trying to wipe the fear off my face, and we make a date for me to come to his house in Yokohama's Higashi Totsuka area and give Brahms a whirl.

Meanwhile, I get this intriguing reply to my ad:

Hi, My name is Nabe, I saw your ad in Metropolis. I am interested in your viola to join the project that I and my freinds are doing. The project is a kind of a musical community. We have not given name for. But, the main idea or theme of this project is making music with others who have totally different background each other, but nobody force nobody. In the other words, it could be expressed as "Encounter with others through music or sound." Well, all you need is enthusiasm and free mind about sound. So, if you are interested in our project, give me a e-mail. Of course, you can ask me any question about the project, I also got a lot of things to tell you about it. Maybe, to begin with, we should meet for each other and share the idea. In addition, I play the guitar (both electric and accoustic), didgereedoo, harmonica, termin, etc. I am looking forward your response!?

This sounds great. It is exactly the kind of laid-back, creativity-friendly atmosphere I am seeking. Just people playing music for fun. Although the project sounds like a glorified jam session, and I can't really picture myself "jamming" on the viola, I figure what the hell, at least I won't have to read music. I e-mail him back, saying I'd love to join his group.

The next Sunday I show up at the practice studio Nabe has reserved for us in Koenji, an East Village-ish neighborhood full of college students and aspiring musicians and artists in West Tokyo. Assembled at the studio are two guitarists (Nabe and Ryunosuke), a drummer (Kiyoshi), a tuba player (Masako), a bassist (Yu), and a viola player (me). The studio, like every other place in Tokyo, is small and cramped, and since I'm the last to arrive, the only space left is that next to Masako and her tuba, so I squeeze past Nabe, Ryunosuke, and Yu and all their amps, stepping over the tangle of black cords on the floor, and pivot into an empty chair next to Masako after dropping my viola on her foot.

"ごめんなさい!" I say to her. "Sorry!"

"だいじょうぶですよ!" she replies. "It's OK!"

Nabe, ostensibly the leader of our band of misfits, had spent four years in Tennessee when he was younger, which is why he can speak English. Unfortunately, no one else does, so he acts as interpreter when my Japanese fails me, which is almost every time I speak.

He gives a short greeting to everyone and talks for a few minutes in Japanese, presumably about why we are here, what we are going to do, and who the handsome white stranger is sitting next to Masako and her tuba.

Then he switches to English and says to me, "I just tell them that we going to just plug in and play and jam for little while and see how we can make a music. Is OK?"

"Sure, sure," I nod, wishing I had an amp for my viola.

The guitarists plug everything in and start some soft strumming, and Masako and I play some scales to get warmed up. It's nice to hear the music bouncing around me, and everyone seems to be tuning in to each other and getting in the zone. Things go a little quiet as everyone decides they're warmed up enough. Then the drummer hits his drumsticks together and launches into a mid-tempo beat. From there, everyone just joins in whenever they feel the urge. The result is a sound not unlike a car being eaten by a lawnmower. The drums bicker with the bass, the guitars vie for supremacy, and the tuba trudges along underneath like a tortoise at a NASCAR speedway. And me? My viola is buried far, far beneath all of it, gasping for air, begging for its life and the life of its strings.

Our noise lasts for a good fifteen minutes without pause. After the first few minutes, though, I just give up trying to improvise anything because no one will hear it anyway, and I don't want any accidental genius to be wasted. I start practicing my scales and then launch into the first movement of the Brahms sonatas that Toru and I had picked out, figuring I could use the practice. It is painfully obvious that, as great and romantic as Nabe's idea of having "free mind about sound" is, some type of structure and order will be necessary in order to make music that doesn't make people vomit.

As each of us tire of playing, the noise comes to a gradual finish, the last sputtering sounds that of the rumbling snare drum and a lonely little tuba. We sit in silence for a few moments, not sure what to say. Should we apologize to each other? Shake hands and say "good game"? Sniff some paint thinner and try again?

We try again without any greater success, though Yu does mix things up by putting down her bass and yelping into the nearest microphone. This time I detect more of a reggae vibe, and my viola tries its best to fit in. Things shift gears several times before finishing semi-triumphantly with a standoff between Yu and Masako's tuba bouncing atop Kiyoshi's ominous drumbeat, which, if memory serves, is the same as that in the song "In the Air Tonight" by Phil Collins. (Is there no escaping the Genesis?)

At the end of our session, Nabe asks me to meet again the next week, and I say I will, though I'm not sure anyone else will. Everyone says their polite goodbyes and we leave.

At work the next day, Eric, a teacher at Lane, asks me if I'm interested in renting a room in the house he lives in with a girl named Akiko, as their other roommate is moving out. The house is in Koenji, funnily enough, so I hop on it, move all my things again, and set about weaseling my way into the local scene, going to the Penguin Live House and hanging out occasionally at the Morgan Café, a tiny upstairs diner down the street from our house where the young husband and wife owners can't speak a lick of English but love American indie rock.

The next week, we participants in Nabe's music experiment meet in a different studio in Koenji. This time a guy named Kawano shows up, who is a singer and guitarist. There is also another bassist friend of Nabe's, going simply by the name M. The guys plug in all their stuff and start playing, Kawano improvising some vocals. His singing style can best be described as "interpretive squawking." Nabe tells me before we start that Kawano likes to make up his own language while he's singing, which is fine by me, since it means I won't be the only one who doesn't understand him.

While they warm up and start jamming, I get my viola out to tune it and rosin my bow. But when I reach for my bow in its usual resting position in the case, I realize with horror that it isn't there. I must have forgotten to put it back in the last time I practiced. So I am left with only a viola to pluck while the others fill the air with the screams of their own instruments. I will never be able to compete.

They continue playing while I sit and impotently pluck my viola into my microphone, which, let's face it, won't bring the house down. The guys eventually stop playing, remember I am there, and look at me curiously.

"Yeah, I, uh, kind of forgot my bow," I say. "Yeah, my...my bow...it's not here."

Nabe informs the players in Japanese of my predicament.

"Do you play any other instruments?" he asks.

"Not really," I say, still lamely plucking the strings of my viola, wishing I were invisible.

"How about you wanna to try drums?" he suggests. Hmm. We don't have a drummer today, and I've always wanted to play. And look, there are some drumsticks right over there on the stool!

"Sure, I'll give it a try." Infused with a new energy, I sweep up the sticks, hop behind the kit, and start pounding away. I don't really know what I'm doing, but psychologically it feels right. And as a gay man, I naturally have a solid sense of rhythm, of course. The guys follow my lead, and we tear through a few improvisations like fourteen-year-olds in their parents' garage. When we finish our session, the guys bow slightly to each other.

Kawano says, adjusting his Buddy Holly glasses, which have slipped down his nose, "いいね." "Cool, huh?"

The next week I get an e-mail from Nabe:

Whaaazzaaaap, Tim-san!!!! ? ? How was the last session? Actually, Kawano-san (a crazy singer whom you saw last week) loves your drumming. I and Kawano-san talked abuot the band, and you should play drum for us as well as you play your veola. The sound of your druming is cool, because you are the beginner. It was like a drum from some gararge bands. Well, we don't even know where the direction should be. What we are doing now is like a trial and error, but also making music, is like a problem solving as well (that's why I keep making music.). We are planning to have a session on this Sunday, too. So, let me know whether you are coming or not. ?
Nabe

The next week I bring my bow and a new pair of drumsticks I got from the Yamaha store in Shibuya. This time it's me, Nabe, and Kawano. Nabe had brought some of his recording equipment, so we decide to record our session. I hop behind the drum kit and start pounding. Nabe soon chimes in with some guitar, and then in comes Kawano with some otherworldly yelping, hemming, hawing, and rhythm guitar. There are no verses and no choruses, just one long odyssey of noise, piss, and vinegar. Yes, that's what it is, a thirty-three-minute odyssey through rock and roll's primitive passions. By the twentieth minute I'm drenched with sweat and I start having trouble holding on to the drumsticks, but I'm bound and determined not to let this moment—this exceedingly long moment—end. I hang on to them for dear life. I'm the captain of this Viking ship, after all, and it is my duty to steer the vessel through the treacherous waters of modern rock, to take up the hammer of the gods and smite any pretenders to the throne or John Mayer fans I find in my path. That's my duty, right?

After we finally career to a graceless finish, Nabe suggests that next time I should give them a nod when I'm ready to finish, otherwise they won't know when to stop and Kawano might feel the need to, as Nabe put it, "keep to singing."

We practice for a few more hours and record everything. After finishing our allotted time at the practice studio, we decide to walk back to Nabe's place in Koenji to listen to our session on his sound system. We pack up the guitars, my viola, and Nabe's portable recording equipment, pay our bill for the three hours we used the studio, and, all six of our arms occupied with equipment, start down the stairs to the street.

It is a sweltering August evening, and Koenji is in the middle of its summer matsuri, or festival, so we find ourselves exiting onto a narrow brick shopping street brimming with festival-goers standing on the sidelines of a long and winding parade of men and women dancing in traditional matsuri garb: men crouch and stomp around dressed in short yukata robes and handkerchiefs on their heads with corners tied together between their noses and upper lips, a misguided aesthetic choice if ever there was one; women stand in formation with their hands raised doing a more subtle and mannequin-like dance in unison, dressed in white kimono with pink sleeves, black waist wraps, and what looks like big bamboo placemats folded in half and placed on their heads; then there are the drummers, the flutists, and the blue kimono-clad band of men carrying the giant mikoshi, or shrine, on their shoulders. It is the best parade I've ever been to (except for that one where I saw two guys on a float dressed as hot lumberjacks making out against a giant inflated ball sack—that was a little better).

We squeeze ourselves out into the flow of traffic on the street, Nabe leading, Kawano following, and me bringing up the rear, each of us struggling to keep our grips on our instruments in the press of people around us. The smells of yakitori, grilled octopus, and beer hang deliciously in the air as we push our way through the throngs of people. After a good twenty-minute crusade through the thick of the celebration, we duck down a tiny side street leading to Nabe's "room," as he'd called it. We are soon there, and, well, he wasn't lying. It is a room with a loft bed, the tiniest of bathrooms, and a hotplate.

Kawano and I take a load off as Nabe cues up the minidisk on which he'd recorded our practice. I brace myself for the inevitably disappointing result, but I am pleasantly surprised to hear that it sounds OK. Especially the drums. Can I have been a rock god all this time without even knowing it? God, the wasted teenage years spent playing in orchestras when I could have been just hitting things with sticks and getting laid!

We listen to our thirty-three-minute opus, which in all honesty really starts to drag after the first five minutes. As the music continues, Nabe and Kawano have a discussion in Japanese, their heads nodding and brows furrowed as if they're talking about something very grim, like Japan's strained relationship with China. Then their faces brighten into toothy smiles as if they've just figured out how to fix it.

"Tim-san," Nabe says, "you wanna be a band?"

"Yeah," I say, flushed and feeling as if I've just been asked to the prom. "We should give it a try."

Nabe and Kawano further discuss China and then move on to the demilitarized zone of the Koreas. Then Kawano smiles and nods his head again, clearly having solved the problem of how to deal with Kim Jong-Il. He tries to say something in English to me.

"We…in…band. I…あの…friend…have…girlfriend. She work…あの…live house…"

I nod and smile, having just gotten to the bottom of the West Bank issue, and consider Kawano's words. What do they mean, exactly?

"Kawano-san has a friend," Nabe explains. "He knows guy who has friend who have girlfriend who work at live house. He say maybe she can help us get gig there."

It sounds so complex, but we are all so full of enthusiasm that the odds don't matter.

And after a number of beers, we come up with a name, inspired by our love of the Absurdists, our passion for the free-form ideals of the Beats, and most importantly the bilingual magazine that is sitting on Nabe's floor. Our name: Thighbone Trumpet Ikiru, which translates roughly to, um, Thighbone Trumpet Living. (Better not to translate, I think.) Now, what should our first album be called, and what will I wear on the CD sleeve?

The next week we get together at the same practice studio in Koenji to rock the roof off the fucking place. We try to play the song we recorded the week before, but none of us can really remember it, so we just jam for a while, taking a journey through a rock and roll wonderland, traveling to the ends of the sonic universe, riding the gargantuan waves of human drama and emotion one can only experience when beating things with a wooden stick or screaming an imaginary language into a microphone.

As I sit at the drums, pounding away and imagining my image plastered on teenage girls' rooms across Japan, I start writing our rock bio in my head, from our humble beginnings at a Koenji practice space to headlining at civic centers across the country. I have our band member personalities all figured out. Nabe will be the cerebral one, the real musical backbone of the band. In interviews, he will be soft-spoken, his words carefully chosen. The girls will really go for his smoldering, reserved sexuality. And he will, naturally, really go for the girls. Kawano will be the eccentric lead guy who will be just as likely to play the Burmese flute as strum a guitar and who will lie his way through interviews, saying he was raised by she-wolves on the northern tip of Hokkaido, where he lived until he was eighteen when he went south to Tokyo to study mapmaking. And I will be the big, weird, foreigner guy who in interviews always comes out with controversial sound bites that will fascinate and electrify the Japanese tabloids, statements like, "Any person who has bought an Alanis Morrissette album should be completely stripped of their human rights. Period."

One day after completing our first national tour, during which we will have played in front of sold-out crowds from Fukuoka to Sapporo, we will come back to Tokyo a full-on phenomenon, and when asked about our early days in television interviews, I will explain playfully in a British accent, "It was quite lovely, actually, the way it all came about. I'd done something bloody stupid and left my viola bow at home, so Nabe, silly old tart that he is, suggested I pop behind the drums and, sort of, you know, give it a go…"

The next record will be moodier, with more keyboards and guest appearances by Lou Reed and Chrissie Hynde on backing vocals, Stevie Nicks on timpani, Siouxsie Sioux on eyeliner, and David Lee Roth on spandex. There will also be a massive viola solo that I will perform wearing only a sweater vest and some boxer briefs. We'll branch out into different forms of music, ignoring the record company's preferred pigeonhole for us and following up a platinum-selling ska disc with a brassy show tunes record. Then, when we start laying down tracks for our flamenco-flavored German rock opera...

"Tim-san!" Nabe says, waving his arms at me. He and Kawano are starting to unplug their guitars and pack them up.

"Time is over. We must to leave."

Even though I leave my viola in its case during my jam sessions with the Ikiru boys, I don't forsake it altogether. Under the influence of Thighbone Trumpet Ikiru, my practices with Toru become a little more spirited. My playing is less measured, I've developed a certain swagger (if a viola player can be said to have swagger), and I've begun to play like a man unafraid to make mistakes and let what happens happen. Even if it sounds like a bird being strangled by a piano wire. Toru appreciates my enthusiasm, though he really wishes I could play the damn third movement without getting to the end of the piece before he does. What he doesn't know is that the reason I'm playing so fast is because I'm trying to resist the urge to swing my bow and hit something, like this stack of magazines or that potted plant or the grand piano over there. I've got drum fever in me, and like the Hulk in Bill Bixby or the gay in Tom Cruise, it's desperate to get out.

For the next month, the three of us—Nabe, Kawano, and I—become a kind of posse, going around town together after rehearsals, hanging out at rock shows, drinking a lot, and passing out in Nabe's room. We have nothing in common but a love of music, Beat Takeshi movies, and Kirin Ichiban beer. And yakitori. But it is a bond strong enough to hold us together at least through each weekend. I never ask much about Nabe or Kawano-san's personal lives, and they remain ignorant of my history of manic pole-smoking, but these gaps in our awareness of each other's lives create a healthy tension that feeds our music. Or something. That's how I explain it to myself, at least.

It does start to bother me a little that, though we've been rehearsing for weeks now, we haven't written a proper song yet. And we do have a tendency to practice for three hours, record our sessions, go back to Nabe's place with a bunch of beers, and listen to what we'd recorded without gleaning anything more from it than that we really should start to think about adding a trombone somewhere. Sure, Kawano's psychotic singing style has started to grate, and yeah, maybe Nabe's guitar playing could use a little variation. But the drumming is perfect. And the backbone of any band is its drummer. Just ask Ringo Starr.

One night we go to a used bookstore/clothing boutique in Kichijyoji, west of Koenji, where Yu, the bassist from the very first music session who is a sort of punk rock performance artist who also dabbles in apocalyptic woodblock prints and illustrations, is holding court. In a small, unfurnished room off to the side of the main merchandise area, Yu kicks her drum machine on and begins maniacally strumming her guitar strings, creating a cacophony of blistering noise that she then hollers on top of. This is no verse-chorus-verse arrangement. It is more scream-strum-stomp-kick the wall-scream. While it isn't something I would choose to listen to while, say, house cleaning or curling my hair, her performance is brilliant as pure spectacle. The ten or so people in the audience watch with rapt attention as she takes one of her guitars and starts beating it against the drum machine, shutting it off. She then moves on to the wall and the floor, smashing that naughty guitar until it's a gangly mess, all the while screaming into the microphone, which she is holding like a phone between her head and shoulder. All the while, a tall, lanky guy dressed in black with an art house goatee and librarian glasses sits on a stool off to the side quietly strumming a mandolin with his eyes closed. At one point, as Yu is slamming her guitar against the wall, he answers his cell phone and talks for a few minutes.

When Yu is satisfied that she's proven her point, she picks up another guitar, which is wrapped in a leather jacket and fastened with a black electrical cord, unwraps it, kicks the drum machine back on, barks three times, and starts over.

I take a break and walk around, checking out the merchandise. There's a lot of local art, zines, self-released CDs, and photographs, plus locally made clothing, shoes, hats, scarves, and washi paper. I pick up a few things that look interesting—a yellow sticker with a radiation symbol on it that says "BIG DRUNK PIG" and a homemade manga graphic novel with a picture of a young guy on a subway reading the newspaper dressed only in tight underwear—pay, and make it back to the other room just in time to see Yu commence the destruction of some of her own giant woodblock prints.

"Damn, I would have bought that one," I think as she jumps repeatedly on top of a print depicting two lovers making out in front of a towering inferno and then picks it up and throws it out the window.

So much destruction. A metaphor for something. But what? Is it a symbolic breaking out of the box that Japanese society has put her in as a woman with an asymmetrical haircut? A tirade against the sociocultural stoicism she sees around her? A bold, tragic statement on the ephemeral nature of art? Is she just a good old-fashioned psychotic deconstructionist? What?

The next week I have to cancel a practice at the last minute, and then the week after Kawano is a no-show. I don't hear from

Nabe about when the next practice is. I e-mail and call him several times, but he never gets back in contact with me. He has disappeared.

About a month later I run into Kawano-san at the Tsutaya video shop in Shinjuku where he appears to now be working. He is dressed in the standard blue Tsutaya collared T-shirt and carrying a stack of videos, on the top of which I see *What Ever Happened to Baby Jane?* We have a very difficult discussion, me speaking in my broken Japanese, him in his broken English and, I think, bits of his imaginary language:

"Why do we not meet anymore for play our song?" I ask in Japanese.

"ええейとね 。。。 You no can tell…we don't have never think to be indygooten," is his mysterious multilingual reply.

"Ummmm. Yeah, so Nabe did not to call me very much," I say, again in Japanese, trying to keep the conversation monolingual.

"そうだね 。。。 playing guitar ですから 。。。 あの… cannot to be showing faces to phsnraaaanksu…"

I nod, smile, put a friendly hand on his shoulder, and say softly in my mother tongue, "I have no idea what the hell you just said."

He seems distracted and uncomfortable around me. I wonder if I have at some point committed a social offence I wasn't aware of. Should I not have left in the middle of Yu's performance to shop around? Do I sweat too much during my drum solos? Am I just too tall? Or—oh shit—did they somehow find out about my history of manic pole-smoking?

Kawano smiles and indicates by picking up *Baby Jane* and angling his head towards the American Classics section that he needs to get back to work.

I wave, bow slightly, say goodbye, and exit the store.

A few weeks later I'm sitting in Morgan Café chatting with a friend of a friend of one of the owners, telling her that the bassist in one of her favorite bands, Superchunk, is a friend of a friend of mine.

"ほんと??" she says. "Really??"

"ほんとだよ!" I answer. "Yes, really!"

"すごい." "Cool."

While I'm basking in the afterglow of convincing someone that I know someone I don't, I look over and see Yu walking in carrying a stack of orange papers.

"こんにちはゆうさん！ おひさしぶり!" "Hey Yu! Long time no see!"

"あっ 。。。ティムさん、こんにちは! げんき?" she says, surprised. "Oh, Tim-san, hey! Doing OK?"

Yu has brought flyers for her next show. This will be a more low-key affair. Just some of her drawings and watercolors. The flyer shows an impeccable drawing of a kitchen fire. I tell her I'll definitely be there. Then I ask if she's seen Nabe, and she shakes her head.

So, my rock and roll dreams have come to a frustratingly abrupt end, for now at least. Yes, there were problems, among them no communication within the band, no coherent plan of operation, no songs. Sure, we were unable to understand each other without an interpreter present, but we could have made it work. The language barrier disappears if you're grooving to the right beat, man. We were going to take over the island of Honshu!

But I guess it's time for me to take a break from the drums for a while and pick up that viola again. Brahms is calling, and there's sheet music to be deciphered. I'm not saying my pelvis-thrusting, bass-drum-thumping, slave-to-the-rhythm days are over. Thighbone Trumpet Ikiru may yet rise again, phoenix-like, to play on a street corner or a surprise party somewhere in the Tokyo suburbs. I just need to mellow out for a while, you know? There's more to life than being a pinup.

Perhaps David Lee Roth would agree.

# of times I've told my students
I'm diabetic and been laughed at: 11
# of times I've had to explain to students that just because
I'm diabetic that doesn't mean I used to be a big fatty: 11

CHAPTER SIX

The Vagina Dialogue

Our hero is not afraid of vaginas.
They don't scare him or make him the least bit uncomfortable.
What? They don't, for real.
(Shut up.)

"It's a mate of mine who's throwing the party, so we can get in cheap," my friend and fellow teacher Grant says by way of convincing me that we should spend our Saturday evening in ooky Roppongi at a club party.

Roppongi, even more so than the sin-city of Shinjuku, is the district of Tokyo historically known for being a popular hangout for the Japanese mafia. It is also the hangout of choice for foreigners and the Japanese people who love them. It abounds with hostess bars; hostess bars that are actually sex clubs; dance clubs; dance clubs that are actually a cover for underground gambling rings and money laundering operations; and Western-themed places that in the U.S. would be called sports bars, the advertisements for which show busty non-Asian girlies all hugging on each other and probably saying something like, "Who wants a titty shot?" while drunk Western jarheads look on admiringly. Roppongi boasts more Westerners per block than any city in America. It's dirty, loud, sleazy (in a bad way), and it makes me want to wash my hands every five minutes when I'm there. It's like the world's biggest frat party, minus the free beer. If a person (me, for instance) ever wants a quick reminder of why he is glad to be away from his home country (America, say), this is the place to visit.

Amazingly, Roppongi wasn't always Nasty Town. Rick Kennedy, in his 1988 book *Home Sweet Tokyo*, describes Roppongi as "a quiet suburb." Yes, Roppongi was once a pretty respectable neighborhood where the upper echelon of expatriates—many of them ambassadors working at one of the many embassies in the area—hung out to talk politics and capitalism and maybe receive the odd lap dance. One such meeting place was Nick's Pizza, owned by Japan's most infamous non-Japanese Japanese citizen, American flunky Nick Zappetti, who coincidentally is buried in my old neighborhood, Fujisawa.

Then the libidinous aliens landed, and now Roppongi looks more like a futuristic neon heap of horny humanity than a place where you go to see and be seen. One fun game to play while standing and waiting for your friends in front of the Almond Café at Roppongi Crossing (allegedly the most crowded meeting place in the world) and checking out the lovely ladies in your field of vision is to try and guess who is a) a prostitute, b) a hostess, c) just a girl out for a good time, and d) a dude. You'll never determine the answer, but that's half the fun!

Roppongi as the fun-for-the-whole-family neighborhood is a thing of the past, and a laughable concept in this day and age. The Yakuza seem to like it, but I'd sooner eat fungus than spend an evening there.

As it turns out, I will have the chance to do both, since Mr. Grant has some pretty potent magic mushrooms on him, and before you can say, "God, these taste like shit," I am with Grant, Rachel, and Josephine (another teacher at Lane), and two of our party-loving students, Shunsuke and Tatsuya, in a pair of taxis heading towards Roppongi, ready to see funky colors and dance with them.

The club is tucked away on a back street, and we circle around for ages looking for it, weaving through the throngs of people, like the giant gaggle of high school girls edging out into the road, tapping away at their glowing cell phones; the skateboarding teenage hipsters with afros and basketball jerseys that appear to float on air; the wasted salarymen stumbling from their izakayas and getting a little too touchy-feely with their equally drunk and uncomfortable-looking female subordinates. We finally just decide to get out of the cab and try to find the stupid club on foot.

"That way there's a chance we'll run into someone selling mushrooms on the street, in case we need more," Rachel rationalizes, and I remember why I love her. (She thinks of everything.)

Tokyo is an infuriating place to navigate if you only have an address. Japanese addresses typically involve three numbers separated by dashes (e.g., 3-35-31). The first of these is the sub-area where the house or building is located, the second is the block it is on, and the third is the building number. And when these numbers are added together, the sum equals the percentage chance that you are never going to find the building you're looking for. Even Japanese people give directions by saying things like, "Yeah, OK, you see that Daily Yamazaki store up there on the left? You're gonna want to turn right there and then head straight on until you hit the Shinto graveyard. Across from the graveyard there's a post office, and next to the post office is an apartment building that looks like a giant Toblerone on its side—you know, the European chocolates? Anyway, between the two is an alley, and if you squint your eyes real tight you can see that a few yards up is a vending machine selling girls' panties and batteries. Next to it is a staircase. Take the staircase to the second floor. The STD clinic is right there, you can't miss it." We have an address, but no one can figure out if we are even in the vicinity of the correct neighborhood. I start to think this club is just a myth dreamed up by Grant's friend who is desperate for some street cred. We all twirl around and look high and low for any evidence of a club amongst all the anonymous-looking buildings.

The mushrooms are starting to work some magic on my brain, and I am very close to giving up and suggesting we all go to the Tower Records in Shibuya and ride up and down the glass elevator when a small pack of young Tokyo club-goers, intent on dancing the night away judging by their little backpacks, fanny packs, water bottles, and glow-in-the-dark bracelets, passes by and ducks into a building. We follow them into the elevator, and seven floors later we have found the mythical club of our dreams.

We join the queue as Grant manages to track down his friend, who is a tanned blonde Australian, and she magnanimously gives us five hundred yen off the regular entrance fee (about four dollars). I guess this is nice of her, but I'd hoped for more of a discount for being so well-connected. I can't really say that I blame her, though. Our group is six people strong, yet we have among us no whistles, glow sticks, visors, pacifiers, giant barrettes, or lollipops. Who goes out on the town without that stuff?

I suppose it always helps to look deserving if you're asking to get into a club for free. I look at my reflection in the glass: I'd chosen a semi-loose, comfortable-fitting thermal top, and now I wonder if maybe I should have put forth a little effort and opted for the painfully tight V-necked white T-shirt, the one that pits my pecs and stomach against each other in a fierce fight for people's attention and usually has me sucking in everything all evening, unable to enjoy my cocktail. (It glows in the dark under black lights real nice, though.)

Grant chats with his friend, and Rachel, Shunsuke, and Tatsuya make a beeline for the dance floor, while Josephine and I lounge around looking at the graphics bursting onto the film screen behind the dance floor and think, "I wanna live there." A cursory glance at the floor proves there are definitely some dancers here, weaving and bending and bouncing off each other like big Japanese rubber bands.

One dancing Japanese girl—Hello Kiddy?—makes me very happy I'd come out, because otherwise I would've missed the most preposterously dressed female in all the land. This being the city where I'd once seen a girl dressed in a skirt made of McDonald's drinking straws, that's saying a lot. Hello Kiddy has on a Snoopy backpack, pigtails tied back by giant barrettes with sparkling flowers encased in clear plastic globes, a pacifier and visor hanging around her neck, fifty-three glow-in-the-dark rubber bangles on each arm, oversized cargo pants, and a cut-off shirt with a clock face on it and the words "the stream of silent silky time makes you feel graceful" written under it. Yes, she was graceful. Like a student driver.

It definitely isn't the most happening place in Roppongi tonight. The crowd is about half Japanese and half non, but there are only about forty people here so far. As usual, I start feeling like there's something else far more exciting going on in the city and that's where everyone is. Maybe Fuji TV is having its annual Russian Roulette Bungee-Jumping Challenge atop the building housing its main headquarters in Odaiba. Perhaps there's a nude kendo tournament at Shibuya Crossing. Or an impromptu contest in Harajuku to see which girl can hold the most shopping bags while talking on her cell phone and hopping on one foot in platform boots. That kind of thing. Sure, I should just chill out and have fun where I am, but still, if there's something better, shouldn't we try and find it?

Thankfully, it doesn't take long for folks to start rolling in, and I am able to kick back and relax. Even if there is something better going on, at least these people are missing it, too.

Jo and I stand to the side of the main dance floor as the lights and shadows swirl around us, cuddling our mushroomed heads. "Oh yes," we think, "it has started." We lock arms, close our eyes, and allow the 'shroom surge to wash over us, riding the wave together. We look closely at each other's faces, decide that the human nose is just about the funniest thing we've ever seen, and collapse into tearful giggles.

"You know what part of teaching our lessons is really starting to drive me crazy?" I ask after our laughing fit is over. "The opening questions."

Jo nods in agreement and rolls her eyes. At the beginning of every lesson, we teachers must write three questions on the board that will dovetail nicely with what we will be covering in the lesson. If we are going to study, say, telling time, I might write, "What time do you usually wake up?" "What's your favorite time of day?" and "Why?" If we're studying making suggestions, the questions might be, "Where can I get some really good sushi?" "What's the best way to get to the station from here?" and "Why?" As the lessons pile up, though, it becomes difficult to think of new and interesting questions to pose. Sure, the last question is always, "Why?" but this leaves two other questions I have to create out of thin air using only my brain.

"I feel like I've asked every question there is to ask of another human," I say.

A powerful brainstorm commences, and for a few short minutes we are the funniest interrogators in the world. The possibilities are exciting and boundless.

If your mother-in-law were a prostitute, where would you go on vacation?

What's your favorite kind of funeral?

When's the last time you did something that brought shame to your entire family? What was it you did that upset everybody so much? Why did you do such a thing?

If you're on the train and this balls-out pimp motherfucker is jamming out wearing his headphones and his music is really loud and totally off the hook, how would you convince the little punk that he just needs to turn that shit down?

What would you do if I called your momma a bitch? Why?

We laugh and laugh and laugh and laugh. Then we stop laughing and watch the big screen on the dance floor because there are swirling paisley amoeba-type things on there and they're soooooo preeeeetty. As the techno-trance-adelic-funk-athon continues, Jo goes to find Grant and I join Rachel on the dance floor.

Rachel and I bob and weave, bob and weave, bob and weave. Then I thread my way through the people, touching heads and shoulders, saying "konnichiwa" to people I don't know, in my mushroomed mind knitting everyone on the floor into a giant tapestry of love, mutual understanding, and epileptic dance moves.

Then I see Hello Kiddy dancing like a cheerleader on speed. I sidle up next to her and attempt the same bob and weave that I was doing with Rachel, but she's having none of it. She's too busy doing high kicks and jerking her arms out and around as if she'd just regained use of them after they'd gone numb on her five years ago.

Soon tiring of dodging her flailing limbs, I decide to retire to what can best be called the Chill Out Room, a dimly lit enclave to the side of the dance floor with a bunch of black lights and couches. The room is empty, and I plop myself down on the most comfortable looking couch and assume the "chill out" position, leaning back, stretching out my legs, and opening my arms in a relaxed crucifix pose. Lifting my head and looking straight ahead, I see the only thing separating me from the dance floor is a wall of glass, so I can keep an eye on my friends and make sure Rachel's dancing doesn't take a dangerous turn. I start noticing that whenever people walk by the glass, they stand and stare in at me for a few seconds, often poking their friends to get them to have a look.

"Wow, this new pomade is really working for me," I think. I briefly reevaluate the thermal top. The public seems to like it. I see Hello Kiddy join some of her friends who are leaning against the glass; they point at me and start laughing. Hello Kiddy looks in, her eyes widen, and she slaps her hands over her mouth, the glow-in-the-dark bangles on her wrists twirling around like tiny hula hoops.

Hmm. Girls crowded together, pointing at me and laughing. This is starting to feel a little too much like middle school. What's going on?

Jo and Grant approach the glass, see me, and wave. They look above me and then back at me. They giggle.

I look behind me and realize that there is a giant photograph on the wall above the couch. What is it of? I get up and turn around to get a better look, but I still can't tell. It kind of looks like a close-up of an old woman's lips, like when they start growing facial hair around age eighty. Yeah, that's what it is. *Oh-my-god-no-it's-a-vagina!* A huge black and white photo of a horizontal vagina. The biggest vagina I have ever seen. And it looks angry.

How did I miss this? I didn't come out to this club looking for pussy, but still, if it's staring me in the face...

Feeling better that I'm not the object of all the spontaneous giggling across the glass, I begin to look around me and realize to my surprise that the room is simply jam-packed with photos of vaginas of all sizes, each one dimly lit by the blue tint of the black light. I am surrounded by ghostly, luminescent vaginas. Every gay man's nightmare. With a thrill and a shudder I gasp: I am no longer in the Chill Out Room. I am in the Vagina Room. The Vagina Room. Full of vaginas.

Vaginas.

Flushed and dizzy, I sit back down and catch my breath. Looking from vagina to vagina, I note how they differ in shape, size, and overall presentation. Here's an impeccably kept one, the hairs tended like a prized garden or perhaps just naturally minimal. On the other hand, the one over there is a veritable festival of fur tangles, an overgrown patch of briars and brambles. All of the vaginas are wet, though, which makes me wonder what they are thinking about.

"What about *him*?" one of them says.

"Hmm. Yeah, he'll do," another pipes in.

"Come on, girls," says the really hairy one. "Look at him. He's totally gay."

"You think?"

"Oh my God, yes! Look at his nose. That is one gay nose. And see how scared he is, looking at us?"

"Every guy who comes in here looks like that," the well-trimmed one suggests. (Brazilian?)

"Yeah, but not like this. He's trembling. Watch this, watch this. Hey, little man," she says to me. "Boo!"

I jump.

"What a chump."

"Maybe he's just really sensitive."

"Oh please. That's good old-fashioned mortal fear."

"そうだね," a Japanese vagina agrees. "彼はなにすればいいのかさえ分からないのね！ Ha, ha, ha!!"

"Yeah, and didn't you see him dancing earlier? No straight man dances like that."

Wait, is that a compliment?

"Shut up, all of you," the giant vagina bellows from behind me. I stand up and face her. "Sit down, little man." I sit. "Give it a rest, bitches," she continues. "Stop fucking with him. He's obviously just curious."

"Hey, Tim!" Rachel shouts, and I whip my head around to see her smiling face looking down at me. Apparently she's decided to take a break from her ferocious body-rock and join me and the vaginas.

"Oh, Rachel! Thank God! Sit down! These vaginas have been talking my ear off."

Rachel looks around at the luminous, disembodied female genitalia surrounding us.

"Wow. These are cool."

I want to tell her that a few of them are actually quite rude, but I figure they can probably hear me, and I definitely don't want the big one to jump off the wall and get all *vagina dentata* on me.

"There are so many of them," she says, lighting a cigarette. "I wonder whose they are."

With Rachel here, I start to calm down and think clearly again. Come on, Tim, these vaginas are nothing to be afraid of. They're people just like you and me. And why shouldn't I use this opportunity—access to so many good vaginas—to learn a little something. About myself and others. Mainly others. Others' vaginas. Since this is probably the last time I will ever be in a room with so many useful visual aids, and since I do have a few unanswered questions about their form and function, I should turn to Rachel and pose a few.

"So, Rachel," I say, pointing up to the giant vagina behind us, "where the hell is this clitoris thing I keep hearing about?"

I'm not likely to ever launch my own search, and this is one of the few chances I will ever have to find out without being unseemly. She gazes up at the Big Vagina and, extending her hand, points it out to me.

There it is. The elusive clitoris, peeking out from its hiding place like Nessie, saying hello to the world, confirming its existence.

"That's it? That's what guys have such a hard time finding? It's right there, for God's sake." Sure, it's about ten times its normal size in the picture, but still, if it were a snake...

"Yep," she answers. "That's it."

"But why do guys have such a difficult time tracking it down?"

She takes a long suck from her cigarette and, exhaling a cloud of purple smoke, says to me, in the tone of a mother getting tired of her son's relentless questions, "Because they just don't care, Tim."

Needless to say, this answer fails to satisfy me. There are bound to be some guys who care, some who have dedicated a decent number of naked moments searching and searching to no avail. So what's the story with clitoriseseses? Are they shy? Temperamental? Passive-aggressive?

And why am I the only person in here asking these questions? Every man in this club should be in here taking notes and plotting maps.

Rachel finishes her cigarette, gives me a little hug, and sets off for the dance floor again, leaving me to enjoy some quality time alone with the vaginas. I stand up and walk around to each of them, examining their nooks and crannies and seeing if I can pick out the clitoris. I tilt my head and zoom in and out, trying to make sense of the shadows and light and the variable contours and textures.

And damn if every vagina isn't completely different. I think I see a few clitorises, but I can't say with any certainty. Each vagina seems to make its own rules and reveal what it wants to reveal. I give up and return to the simplicity of the dance floor. As I leave I hear the vaginas behind me get chatty once again.

"Well there he goes, still blissful in his ignorance," one of them says.

"I felt him staring into my very soul," intones another.

"You were too much for him, Priscilla. Look at him, so desperate to get back to the other dicks on the dance floor."

"さよなら、ゲイちゃん。きょうつけてね！," the Japanese vagina coos.

"He'll not sleep a wink tonight," proclaims the giant one, tugging on a cigarette, sounding not unlike Bette Davis.

After a few minutes of dancing in the corner, my eyes adjust to the darkness level. I look straight at the wall in front of me and see that I've been dancing in front of an eight-foot figure drawing of a completely naked man with his completely erect penis in his hands. He has a head but no face, and it is tilted back in a pose of sexual ecstasy.

Is it an artful commentary on the objectification of the male body? An examination of the erotic nature of anonymity? Who cares?

"Now *this*, *this* is more like it," I think as I do the electric slide right up beside it. It's a beautiful drawing, anatomically devoid of mystery. And there is no tricky clitoris to complicate my life. I name him Fred and ask him to dance.

We boogie for the rest of the night as the ladies in the Vagina Room look on in extreme disapproval.

# of bowls of miso soup eaten: 414
# of pounds lost: 22
# of looks of disapproval from the natives: 1,156

CHAPTER SEVEN

The Empress of Ginza

Who proves that no matter where on God's earth you are,
crazy rich people are hilaaaarious.

Ahhh, Ginza. Tokyo's own Fifth Avenue, and the shopping district of choice for Hotlips from *M*A*S*H*. For sheer unabashed
opulence and unnecessarily high prices, no area in Tokyo can
compare to this district on the eastern side of the metropolis,
not far from the Imperial Palace, with its wide shopping avenues,
costly window displays, and surely the most gorgeously dressed
people in all of Japan. There is something about paying ten dollars
for a sit-down cup of coffee in a chartreuse café that makes one
feel strangely alive. And broke with nothing to show for it.

Where did Hotlips like to go when she went to "the Ginza," as
she put it? Ginza is home to the most expensive shopping block in
the world, so there was surely plenty to choose from. Ginza is also
home to the country's most depressed and disillusioned window
shoppers. Me, for example, eyeing some shirts at the Mitsukoshi store that I couldn't begin to fit into, much less afford. I look
down at my sleeves and am reminded of the last time I tried to
buy myself clothes in this city. I had spilled coffee on my shirt at

work, so during my lunch break I went across the street from our Shinjuku branch and bought this new one. It fit perfectly, except for the waist, shoulders, sleeves, and neck.

The world-famous Kabuki-za theatre is also here, which of course is ground zero for kabuki aficionados across the globe. (There's got to be dozens. Dozens of dozens.) I work at the Lane Ginza branch a few times a week, and the school is right down the road from the theatre. I've often daydreamed of running into some of the kabuki folk while lunching at one of my regular haunts, like Soup Friends, a café near my school that sells soups you never would've imagined yourself eating.

I'll be dipping French rolls into my tiny bowl of carrot, radish, and octopus noodle soup and cramming new Japanese verbs into my head when I look up and there at the counter I see two imposing and stern-looking kabuki actors looking at the menu hungrily, probably exhausted and famished from the lengthy double love suicide they've just committed at the matinee performance. They of course don't use conventional Japanese vernacular; they speak in antiquated kabuki verses that the counter clerks will struggle to understand.

When he places his order for, say, the vegetarian rice ball chili, the more effeminate of the two, dressed in a scarlet robe with gold trim and about thirty-seven folds and tucks, uses grand and graceful gestures and a high-pitched sing-song squeal. Ordering the green tea gazpacho, his more masculine fellow thespian, enveloped in a gray kimono with angry bulls emblazoned on it and sporting a hairstyle resembling the club symbol on a deck of cards, moves like a marionette and speaks in a deep, cranky monotone, proving who carries the sword in *their* family. When told he cannot get it without cilantro, he becomes agitated, gesticulating wildly in a fit of guttural yelping. Fortunately, his more refined companion succeeds in calming him down with a three-hour lullaby about doomed lovers who slice each other up real good on a mountaintop. At this point they saunter regally to their seats, see me, the Western sophisticate and dedicated student of Japanese, at my table, and bow. I say, "お げんきですか？" and their ears ring. The feminine one breaks into tears, and the man draws his sword, chops his companion's head off, and slices himself open.

At least once a week I go with my coworkers in Ginza, Kenji and Midori, to a café where we sit for an hour and have what is called a "language exchange." Theoretically, this involves two or more people meeting, often through the classifieds, and going to a café to converse in the languages each wishes to improve—usually Japanese and English. Half the time they speak English, then after a while they'll switch to Japanese. Alternatively, and more commonly, a "language exchange" involves a Western male and a Japanese female meeting and speaking a few words here and there in whatever language is easiest before bagging the whole thing and leaving the café to go get it on somewhere.

> White Guy: Hi, it's nice to meet you.
> Japanese Girl: Hello, it's very nice meet you, too.
> WG: Oh, darn it all, I seem to have forgotten my pen.
> JG: Oh, it OK. I have pen you can to borrow.
> WG: Oh, OK. Oh, darn it all, I seem to have forgotten my notebook.
> JG: I have a paper you if you want use.
> WG: Oh, great, thanks. Oh, shit. I seem to have forgotten my Japanese book.
> JG: Oh.

WG: I must have left it in my bedroom. Shall we just…
JG: OK.

But Kenji, Midori, and I are honest-to-God language exchangers. There is no sexual tension between us that I'm aware of, though I suppose I should never say never. Kenji, always dressed in the requisite gray suit, is twenty-eight and handsome, if a little uptight. He is an accountant at Lane and spends most of his days looking at numbers, so he looks at our meetings as a nice change of pace. It is my goal not only to have him speaking better English as a result of our weekly exchanges, but to loosen up, to relax, and to talk about his innermost feelings, his dreams, his favorite numbers, and movies. And if he wants to reach over and plant a big, wet kiss on my soft, willing lips at some point by way of a thank you, well that's just fine.

Midori might get a kick out of this. She is a receptionist at Lane. The most bored-looking receptionist I've ever seen. It's why I've taken to her so quickly. Every day she sits at the main desk listlessly waiting for the phone to ring or a student to walk in while she doodles on a big notepad. When the phone does ring, she answers in the professional, friendly, buoyant lilt so typical of Japanese receptionists. Once she's transferred the call or answered the caller's question, she replaces the receiver and goes back to her doodling. Her desk has no computer. Behind her on the wall is the giant and shiny Lane logo, veritably announcing her as company spokeswoman. Her sole function is to serve as greeter, over the telephone and face to face when people walk into the school. Saying "good morning" and "good day" and "good evening" to people all day in a pleasant and welcoming tone as they file in can really take it out of a person.

Mornings are very slow, and it is these times when she appears to be counting the cracks in the wall while contemplating grad school or joining the circus.

One morning I sat down next to her. She looked like she could use a little excitement, and I thought perhaps I could help her look for some.

"Midori-san, how do you say, 'I'm so dang bored' in Japanese?"

She laughed and asked, "What means *dang*?" From those first words grew our language exchange idea. Midori recruited Kenji after hearing that he was interested in taking English classes but couldn't really afford them, even with his Lane discount.

So we started meeting after work once a week. Since their English is far better than my Japanese, we have pretty decent conversations in English for a while on a wide range of subjects (travel, music, world events, their insecurity about their English skills) before moving on to Japanese, where the conversation tends to gasp and sputter over more basic and yawn-worthy subjects like favorite foods, least favorite foods, favorite seasons, least favorite seasons, favorite sports, least favorite sports, and my insecurity about my Japanese skills (more than justified).

Tonight we meet as usual in front of the Sony building at Sukiyabashi Crossing and then walk toward our regular café, Doutor. Doutor is a Japanese coffee chain that serves the most unremarkable, tiniest cup of coffee I've ever regretted buying. A typical Doutor store is full of dozing salarymen who always somehow manage to smoke a pack of cigarettes during their naps. But the Doutor in the center of Ginza is housed at the bottom of a swanky, ten-story cylindrical building (with the obligatory giant television screen on top), and it has the much fancier name of Le Café Doutor. Oui-*oui*, uh-*huh*. So that's where we go.

The sun is setting on Ginza. Some folks are getting off work and heading with their colleagues and bosses to an izakaya or karaoke box for some heavy drinking and awkward flirting, and the evening shopping traffic is peaking. On the street, the distinct and theatrical sound of classical music wafts through the air, and looking up ahead, we see that a small group of people have gathered in a semicircle around a gentleman with his head down as he sways to the Mozart erupting around him.

As we approach, we can see that the man everyone is watching with such fascination is actually operating a two-foot marionette dressed in a tuxedo and playing a violin, with dramatic wisps of gray hair sprouting from his head and making him look like a two-foot Strauss. We stop and watch for a few minutes, enjoying the bizarre sophistication of standing on an opulent shopping street and being serenaded on the violin by a puppet.

We continue on and huddle into le café, order some coffees, and sit down by a window, where we can enjoy our illuminating conversation while still being able to see people narrowly avoid slamming their Matsuya or Mitsukoshi shopping bags into each other outside.

We ease into the English part of the chat, with Kenji asking me what I think about our bucho, or Japanese boss, at the school. I reply that he seems really nice and always wears cool ties. Midori says she hates having to go drinking with him and all the other Japanese staff because he always drinks too much and starts hugging everyone. And sweating.

We talk about a variety of things for the next forty-five minutes: the popularity of the Seattle Mariners' Japanese outfielder Ichiro, the Japanese love of comics, scuba diving. We've just switched over to Japanese and started talking about hot tea when I see *her* walk into the café.

She wears a pink silk kimono embossed with cherry blossoms, and she walks in traditional Japanese wooden sandals that look about as accommodating and comfortable as slabs of concrete. She walks up to the counter with the clipped, restricted stride typical of women wrapped in kimono. The skin of her face is a shock of white next to her pitch-black hair and eyebrows. Her lips are painted crimson in the middle, while the sides of both lips remain light pink, eventually fading into the powder white of her cheeks. She looks to be about sixty.

She is the personification of Japanese grace and dignity: a vision of beauty, of an aging sensuality, of an over-the-top willingness to be physically uncomfortable that is so unique to Japan. I struggle trying to watch her while also keeping up with our Japanese conversation as it veers towards the topic of coffee and then to a hard-to-follow (for me) debate about the merits of hot drinks over cold drinks during winter and summer.

At the counter, the lady smiles brightly with her whole face, nodding and bowing slightly as she gives her order to the employee. I watch as she takes out her small pink money purse with her gloved hands, produces some coins, and offers them gingerly to the cashier.

I know it's time for me to put my two cents' worth into the conversation since I haven't said a whole lot since we'd switched to Japanese, so I offer a perfunctory remark.

"Cold drink good and but better than your hot drink for my summer."

Kenji and Midori nod at me and smile, wondering what I've just said, but my gaze quickly turns back to that of the regal lady, who is now bringing her tray towards us. There is an empty table next to us by the window, and she is headed straight for it, this vision in pink silk. I wonder what she smells like. Flowers? Jasmine tea? Bubble gum?

She sits down, and I notice she has a cup of Japanese green tea and a miniature brass pitcher on her tray. She takes a tiny spoon from the tray and stirs the cup before bringing it to her lips for the briefest of tastes and then replacing it on its saucer. Afterwards she puts her hands together with her elbows on the table and gazes out into the Ginza street traffic.

I am so in awe that I haven't even realized that Kenji has asked me a question.

"Tim-san! Are you OK?"

"Oh, sorry," I reply in Japanese. "I watched that woman drinking her tea. She's very beautiful."

Kenji and Midori smile a little uncomfortably, and I quickly realize why. We are speaking Japanese, and though it would have been our own secret language had we been at a café in, say, Boise or Cairo, here it is far from a secret language, and everyone has understood what I just said. I've been so used to being able to say whatever I want wherever I want without worrying about the natives understanding me, it's become second nature to just blurt it all out without thinking. Also, I think I'd spoken a little too loudly, as if I were addressing the audience at a pep rally, say.

I look over at the woman, who is still gazing out into the street. If she heard me, she has given no indication. Returning to our Japanese conversation, I apologize to my fellow conversationalists and ask if they've seen any good movies recently.

Midori launches into a rave about a movie that she saw the other day on DVD, *John Malkovich's Hole*, which I can only assume is the unfortunate Japanese title for *Being John Malkovich*. I notice that the woman, pouring herself another cup of tea from her pitcher, has broken into a tranquil smile.

I return my gaze to our table and see Kenji, who generally prefers the more straightforward movie fare offered by your Arnold Schwarzeneggers and Bruce Willises, furrowing his brow at Midori's explanation of the movie, which, if I hadn't seen the movie myself, would've had me on the floor swimming the backstroke, as it's well beyond the limits of my understanding of the Japanese language.

Then we hear a dirty, low-pitched giggle coming from the next table. Midori stops talking. I look over at the woman drinking her tea. She sits like she's been sitting for some time now, smiling serenely and stirring her tea. She does not have the appearance of someone who has just sniggered like she's been told a really good blonde joke. Midori continues in Japanese.

"And the brown-haired woman has sex with John Malkovich, but actually, she is having sex with Cameron Diaz because she's inside his head," she explains. (I'm assuming, here.) I have never seen Kenji look so conflicted. He is suspended between the erotic curiosity straight men the world over exhibit when hearing about sex with two women involved, and frustration that none of this shit makes any sense.

Then there's another giggle from the next table, this one more guttural and phlegm-shifting. Again we look over, and again the woman is stirring her tea, although this time a little more urgently. Her expression is now more an amused smirk than a smile of placid contentment, and she is nodding her head defiantly. She begins mumbling to herself as she clinks her teaspoon against her porcelain cup.

"And, um," Midori continues in Japanese, "then Cameron Diaz falls out of the sky and onto the side of the road in New Jersey..."

Clank! The woman throws her spoon onto her saucer and now sits with her arms folded around her middle, laughing mightily like an evil Santa. She picks up her spoon again and stirs like her life depends on it, all the while mumbling to herself things that I, maddeningly, cannot understand yet. I have to know.

"And her husband and she start fighting when he finds out she was in John Malkovich's head, and…"

"Can we switch to English for a minute?" I interrupt, in English.

"OK," Midori concedes.

"What is she saying? Can you hear her?"

Midori, who has been doing her level best to ignore the woman next to us, looks at Kenji, and they both smile sheepishly.

"I can't hear everything she say," Kenji begins, "but I hear her say something about, how do you say…shit of dogs?"

"Oh, I see, dogshit," I reply. "What do you think she means? Is someone eating dogshit?" I look eagerly from Kenji to Midori and back to Kenji again.

There's a bit of a pause while Midori and Kenji decide without speaking who will do the explaining. All the while the woman continues her rant, her laugh upgraded to a cackle.

"She say she, um, gonna make someone to eat the dogshit," Midori says, warming to the subject, definitely not bored anymore.

"Uh-huh," I nod sagely. "Do you know why? Did she give a reason?"

"I can't be sure," Kenji begins, also getting a kick out of our dirty topic, "but I think I hear her say a few names. And also 'God.' 神さま'と言ったでしょう？"

"Sorry, no," she says, deflating my hopes. I've never felt such irritation at my lack of skill in the Japanese language. The woman next to me is either a) having some kind of nervous breakdown, or b) already batshit crazy, and I can't properly eavesdrop. The language barrier is made of glass, allowing me to see but not understand.

All I can do is watch as she increases her volume and takes to picking up and slamming down the objects on her table. At one point, she shoves the table away from her, as if it had just told her she looks fat in that kimono. The teapot, teacup, and various condiment containers topple and crash into one another as the table teeters from side to side. She stands, her pink cherry blossom kimono still wrapped artfully around her, her face still immaculately painted, her white gloves none the worse for wear. She grabs her small bag, walks with her clipped stride to the door, opens it, and with a smile and a bow in the direction of the employees at the counter, departs into the night.

"Thank you! Come again!" they beam.

It is a suggestion she appears to take a little too seriously, as, mere minutes after leaving, the Empress is back for another cup of tea, smiling and bowing at the counter staff, looking the picture of Ginza classiness. She sits again at the same table and stirs her tea, that familiar smile on her face all the while.

"So, Midori-san, Cameron Diaz is lesbian?" Kenji asks in English, returning to our discussion.

"Only in movie, I think," Midori answered.

"Ah, in movie only. Does she make other movie like this?" he asks as he gets out a pen to write down the names of the other movies in which Cameron Diaz appears as a lesbian.

They continue discussing lesbianism as I look over at Mood-Swing Diva to see what she's up to. Sure enough, her expression has changed in the manner of that clown's face in *Poltergeist*: she looks ready to toss her teacup right through the window, pick up some shards of glass, and pick a fight with a few pedestrians. Two seconds later her face again softens and she lets out an evil laugh, perhaps having just thought of a new and exciting way to kill a person. She stirs her tea, places her hands in her lap, and closes her eyes for a few moments: a Buddha in drag. Then she screws up her face, looking like she's going to cough. Her tongue curls inside her open mouth, and her throat expands.

"Oh shit," I think, clasping my hands together. "She's not gonna cough. She's gonna puke. Yes, yes. She's gonna puke. I wish I had my camera!"

Sure enough, she starts heaving, and this being a woman who has recently screamed that she is going to make someone eat the dogshit, she doesn't engage in it quietly. Her whole body shakes in its seat, throwing itself into the task of getting rid of whatever horrible and noxious thing lives within. Our conversation stops dead, and Midori, Kenji, and I look at her with the kind of expression you have when you drive past a car accident hoping to catch a glimpse of a dead body.

She heaves and wretches and heaves, like a freshman at her first frat party. I lean closer, disingenuously hoping I can coax the puke from her stomach.

"Uuuaaaaaahhh! Oooahhhhh!! Uuuahhhh!" she screams. By this time, the entire café has gone uncomfortably quiet, its patrons wishing to God she would hurry up and toss her cookies so the staff can clean it up and we can all get on with our lives.

She wretches once more and leans forward over her teacup. Then, silence. She leans back, smiles, and as regally and serenely as she'd arrived just a few minutes earlier, she stands, carries her tray to the drop-off, and steps out into the street.

We watch as the Empress of Ginza strides by the window at which Kenji, Midori, and I are sitting. She laughs maniacally as she walks, and Kenji, laughing, says she said "dogshit" again. And again and again. Also "dick," "asshole," and the Japanese equivalent of "motherfucker."

Our conversation loses its momentum after she departs. Both Kenji and Midori seem sad that she's gone. It is certainly the most exciting language exchange we've had. We stay a few more minutes, finishing up our coffees and allowing Midori time to finish what she has to say about *John Malkovich's Hole* and for me to explain to Midori and Kenji in English what the phrase *John Malkovich's Hole* means to me when I hear it. A fresh batch of embarrassed laughter from them and we're off.

We leave and begin walking back towards Ginza Station, chatting in English about work and plans for the weekend. It's about ten now, and the pedestrian traffic has died down a little bit, though up ahead there is still a sizeable group of people gathered around the street performer and his Stradivarius-wielding puppet friend. As we pass quickly by, I can hear over the swelling of "Greensleeves" a distinct hyena-like cackle.

I look at Kenji and Midori, and we all nod in agreement.

Her majesty the Empress is in the crowd.

And she is amused.

# of salarymen witnessed throwing up on train platform after midnight: 15

# of times salmon eaten for breakfast: 7

# of times lied, said I'm from Switzerland: 1

CHAPTER EIGHT

GaijinMan and the Lady-killer

That guy you knew in high school who wore his Boy Scout uniform to school? He moved to Japan and stole everyone's girlfriends.

The western wind of Japan whispers the story of a lone white man from a tiny town in North America (or was it England?) who came to the land of the rising sun to seek his fortune, to see how they live on the other side of the world, or to simply experience his first fourteen-hour plane ride. He was a modest man, a clerical assistant at the local community college in his mid- to late twenties, with ice-blue eyes and a bright, friendly face. Also, freckles, buckteeth, a birdcage chest, and a mullet that curled up on the edges.

He had never really had a girlfriend, unless you count the poster of Princess Leia he'd had on his bedroom wall since 1977. But something deep within him told him that there was a place in this world for guys like him, and that it was probably not in any English-speaking country. More likely it was in faraway Asia.

So he got a job as an English teacher in Japan, packed his bags, and came to the great city of Tokyo to explore a country that had always held a certain fascination for him, with its famous sculpted gardens, traditions full of nuance and studied elegance, and amazing technological feats like Fujiyama, until recently the fastest and tallest rollercoaster in the world. Also because, if the Internet is to be believed, the high school girls are all total slags and really short skirts are part of their school uniform.

This mysterious stranger hoped to God he was in for a major life change. And sure enough, something magical happened when he deplaned at Narita Airport, boarded a train, and headed towards Tokyo. People took notice of him. At home he was nothing, a nobody, an eyesore. A piece of lint. A yellow sweat patch on a dirty old white T-shirt. A pocket protector. But as he settled into his new life in his new country, he became blissfully aware that he was no longer Invisible Vince from Vicksburg or Nobody Nick from Newcastle. Yes, in Tokyo, he was GaijinMan. And he had three dates this week.

There's a saying here amongst us gaijin folk, reminiscent of that proverbial "tree falling in a forest and no one being there to hear it" question: If a white guy in Tokyo is rambling on and on and on about absolutely nothing interesting and there's no one remaining at his table to hear it except for his Japanese girlfriend who can't understand him anyway, does he still need to be bitch-slapped?

Actually, I just made that up, and I've never actually said it out loud, but the more I quietly ponder this question while studying at a café or reading on the train or browsing at the record store as I'm forced to listen to the unabridged ramblings of some Western goofball explaining the Fourth of July (or was it Guy Fawkes Day?) to his newly minted Japanese girlfriend™, the more I think the answer is a resounding, "Good God, yes! Somebody shut him up!"

We gaijin are here for many different reasons. There are the lost souls like me, desperately in need of a battery recharge, who are convinced that living for a few solid years in a country that is completely devoid of Big Gulps and commercials for Plavix might just allow us to find ourselves; there are the nerds who have been obsessed with Japan since childhood and refuse to leave the country until they can properly read a daily newspaper (these are the ones who end up in Kyoto and will be there until they die); there are the artists, writers, photographers, musicians, and/or actors (not to mention architects, entrepreneurs, and other professionals) who for one reason or another have found their niche in Tokyo and feed off it for creative inspiration; there are the folks who use Tokyo as their base so they can travel easily to other parts of Asia; then there are the guys like my former roommate Sean whose number-one priority and sole reason for being in the country is to screw Japanese girls. But no matter what brought and keeps us here, we all have one thing in common, and that is that the moment we walk out of our doors and into the Japanese world outside, we are different, special, and interesting without even trying. Even if we are the most retarded people to ever emerge from our hometowns, here in Japan, where 99.9 percent of the people are Japanese, we are mysterious and exotic. And in my case, unnecessarily tall.

I saw my first GaijinMan when I was living in Fujisawa and almost stopped dead in my tracks. He had oily black hair parted on the side and combed over. He had a face speckled with acne. He had patches of beard scattered here and there. He had a briefcase with papers sticking out of it. Most amazing of all, he had an impeccably dressed, porcelain-skinned, drop-dead gorgeous Japanese girl on his arm. And she was smiling and intermittently leaning her head down on his shoulder as they walked.

"What the—" I said, doing a double take as I passed them on the street. I was deeply troubled, wondering if the earth was still round and pigs still unable to fly.

But I eventually came to grips with the fact that GaijinMan, though not nearly as prevalent, is as much a part of contemporary Tokyo as giant television screens, mangled English signs that say things like "Happy Merry Christmas Day," and cell phones that double as stereos, personal computers, porn interfaces, and best friends.

Almost every straight white guy I know has a stunning Japanese girlfriend. Every guy. Whether he looks like Steve McQueen or Steve Buscemi. These are guys who would be resoundingly dateless back home, guys who go to Star Trek conventions, guys who talk through their noses and use the word "prototypical" in everyday conversations.

Yes, sometimes it seems like obtaining a Japanese girlfriend here is about as difficult as catching a cold. If you stay out long enough, you're bound to get one. Now, this is not meant to disparage Japanese girls. I love them. They are beautiful creatures and are surely the most sublimely and ridiculously dressed girls on the planet. They must have their reasons for accepting dates from all these Barney Rubbles. But what's really going on here? Is there that much of a discrepancy between Japanese and Western concepts of good-looking? The answer is an emphatic maybe. I ask my roommate Akiko, who has a thing for black guys, what she thinks of some of the beautiful women walking around with unattractive Western men one day when we are sitting outside a kissaten (coffee shop) in Koenji. As if conjured by my very words, an absolute doll-baby of a young woman with flowers in her hair approaches holding the hand of a short white guy wearing orange shorts and Birkenstocks with socks and sporting an impressive potbelly. And a Mickey Mouse watch.

"Like them," I say, pointing to them with my big nose.

"Oh, she not so pretty, I think," Akiko replies.

"Nu-*uh*! Are you serious? She's beautiful!"

"Mmm, not so beautiful. A little cute. Looks a little stupid."

"OK, but still, look at the guy she's with, Akiko! Look at him! Isn't it amazing how brazenly unattractive he is?"

"What means *brazenly*?"

"Umm, like, you know, *openly*."

She looks back at him as they pass, adopts the expression of a disapproving aunt, and says, "Yeah, he need shower. Or, how do you say…make*over*."

Though she does admit that the guy is far from a twenty-four-hour sex bomb, I am surprised she doesn't feel the imbalance of the match as deeply as I do.

"She rebellious, I think," Akiko says upon further consideration. "Maybe want to make her parents anger."

I can see the confrontation with her mother right now. She sits at her vanity applying lipstick when her mother rushes in pleading, "Chieko, darling, why you date ugly white man?! He wear tuxedo T-shirt!"

"Shush, Mother," Chieko hisses as she applies another flower to her hair. "He take me nice restaurant! We go hot spring this weekend!"

Then the doorbell rings and it's her still-unshowered date, standing at the door in a jacket, tie, and jean shorts. Mother answers the door, takes one look at his flip-flops, and jumps out the window.

Rebellion or not, whenever I see an Asian babe with one of these schmucks, I want to take her by the hand, pull her to the side of the street, thump her on the forehead, and say, "Look, maybe you don't realize this, but this guy is a former president, vice president, and treasurer of his high school geometry team, and I think they still have weekly meetings!!"

The sensitive nerd in me at first wanted to congratulate these guys on their great luck. After all, I'm sure many of them have never been properly laid and, hey, everyone deserves a little hot loving. But my initial good wishes are turning to nerve-prickling dread and massive irritation the more I have to deal with the GaijinMen at Lane.

Yes, we have several of our very own GaijinMen haunting the classrooms, the hallways, and the teachers' room with their puffed-up egos and idiotic hairstyles. The other day I was walking through the lobby of the school, where lots of students gather between classes to chat with each other and with teachers passing through. The Lane G-Men love sitting out in the lobby during their lunch hour or whenever they have a free moment because it affords them the opportunity to chat with the lovely girlies who gather around any available teacher just bursting with questions about English.

I hear GaijinMan Brody explaining the word *freaking* to a girl and her friend who are confused by its use in the sentence, "This is freaking ridiculous!" which they heard one of the teachers saying as he stormed out of their classroom earlier that day.

Brody is a mama's boy from Vermont who probably needs help buying train tickets, putting his glasses on the right way, and eating steak. And he should definitely never be encouraged to explain anything because, as cutting off someone's head customarily leads to torrential blood flow from the neck, asking Brody a question about anything, however small and insignificant, invariably leads to a flood of unnecessary sentences, tangents, biblical references, and literary allusions that are impossible to stem. And you, the unfortunate captive audience, must ride it out until you can back out of the room far enough to make a quick getaway when he blinks.

"Well, it has several different meanings, really," the professor explains with a confident smile. "It comes from the word *freak*, which means a strange or abnormal person. *Freaking* is usually used as an adjective. Often we use it as a slangy alternative to the terms *really* or *very* when we are describing something." He folds his arms and smiles, pleased with himself. He's only just begun.

"*Desclibing*," one of the girls, Ai, says with a quizzical look, probably having understood about 20 percent of what he'd just said. "What means *desclibing*?"

"Well," he replies, clearing his throat, "for example, if I were describing, say, you ladies, I would say, 'You are really smart and beautiful.'" Then he winks. Oh my God, he winks.

Ai smiles, giggles, and covers her mouth with her hand so as not to offend Sensei Brody with the unseemly sight of the inside of her mouth. Takako, her friend, nods vaguely.

"Or," Casanova continues, "I might say, 'That's a very pretty dress you are wearing, Takako.'"

Takako smiles faintly, betraying a hint of annoyance. She isn't buying it. She knows where it's at. (Note to self: befriend Takako.) But Ai is swallowing Brody's manipulative, flimsy charm hook, line, and sinker.

"Ah, sank you," Ai says for an unimpressed Takako.

"You're very *freaking* welcome," Brody says with a cheesy grin.

The conversation continues, but I can't bear any more, so I duck into the teachers' room where I see Rachel and Josephine sitting at the table grading papers.

"I'll give you one guess as to what Brody's doing in the lobby," I say.

"Talking nothing but crap?" Rachel offers.

"Slinging a bunch of bollocks?" Josephine rebounds.

They are both right.

But I think I've come up with a satisfactory answer to this white-dork-with-Japanese-hottie conundrum which will allow me to at least get beyond the sheer bizarreness of it all: the girls want free English lessons and they probably figure that the dorky ones make better teachers. And GaijinMan is more than willing to oblige, for why not? He has the best of both worlds. First, he gets to parade around town with a stunning woman, no doubt sending digital pictures of them together back home to his old chess club buddies. Plus, due to the language barrier, he can rest assured that if his girl's going to nag, at least he won't be able to understand it.

But it wasn't until I found myself the *objet du désir* of a voracious vixen who had me cornered and was ready to swallow me whole that I began to realize—and even appreciate—the power of the GaijinMan and the mysterious magnetism of his charms.

Now God knows I'm not a full-time stud. Sure, there were a handful of broken hearts when I gave up the game, raised the rainbow flag, rented the billboard, and announced my homosexuality to the world. But I have never been a great charmer of the ladies (or the men, for that matter). So it took coming to Japan to teach

English for me to realize my potential as a potent and desirable beast. A lady-killer.

I have a fan. Her name is Yasuko, and she's a young architecture student learning English so she can study in the States. She's also a little emotionally vulnerable and needy. And has no gaydar.

I first met Yasuko when I was assigned to administer her level check, a procedure that every new student must go through so we can place them in the right class. She was a returning student, so it was my job to make sure she would be able to manage in the level she was in before.

I sit down, introduce myself with a smile, and ask her how she is. She looks at me wide-eyed, like an animal caught in the headlights of an approaching car. And what kind of car is it? Well, since you ask, it's a gleaming, sexy, cobalt-blue man machine called Tim.

She trembles a little as she replies, "Fine, thank you," and attempts a smile.

"Don't be scared," I say by way of encouragement. "I'm just going to ask you a few questions, and you answer them the best way you can. It's just like chatting."

She smiles and seems to relax a little. "Chattingu, hai," she says.

"So, why did you decide to take English lessons again?"

She launches into the story of how her longtime Australian boyfriend just broke up with her and now she has no friends because all her friends were his friends and now they won't speak to her and he keeps saying bad things about her, and she's so lonely, and now she has no one to speak English with and she thought she was going to get married and so on and so forth. So she decided to come back to English class, presumably to get another boyfriend and meet some new people to hang out with.

I feel bad for her because she seems really desperate and lonely—two emotions I have a long history with. I do my best to put forth an image of brotherly concern and sympathy, reacting to her narrative with lots of concerned furrowing of the brow and "gee, gosh, I'm so sorry."

In an attempt to steer the conversation away from her personal troubles and towards something more neutral, like what she does for a living, I ask, "What do you do?"

She sighs, and her bottom lip starts wobbling.

"Shit," I think, wondering if maybe she worked as her ex-boyfriend's personal assistant and now was out of a job, too.

Then comes a torrent of big, fat, bell-bottomed tears bursting forth from her increasingly blood-red and puffy eyes.

"God, are you OK?" I ask, offering her a tissue from the pack in my pocket lest her nose decide to spring into action.

Through a barrage of mucus and hiccups, I learn that she was just laid off from her job as an office lady at a company that publishes elementary school textbooks. Basically, nothing is going right in this girl's life, nothing at all. And then she met me. And nothing is continuing to go right.

We finish the level check, and even though her English is a little erratic and unpredictable and she said things like "I am such loneliness," and "friends don't happy for me," I place her in the same intermediate level she was in before since I can't bring myself to saddle her with any more bad news.

I wave at her as she walks away and wonder if perhaps I've found someone—a poor, friendless, frantic female—who is in desperate need of a gay man in her life. Though I'm far from a thoroughbred homo—I don't have nice clothes, I cut my own hair, I would rather go to the record store than the gay bar, and often I don't even wear cologne—she could certainly do much worse, and I have lots of pictures of my cat, which Japanese girls just love. Plus, I'm smooth and hairless like a porn star.

I could be the Will to her Grace, the flame to her unlit cigarette, the, um, Bette to her Midler. We could traipse about the city, doing all the things that Japanese girls and their sexy, gay best friends always do: chat about boys over green tea lattes, talk trash about Harajuku girls over pachinko and pizza, and crash one of the many arcades in Shibuya, where we'd saunter up to the Dance Dance Revolution game, I'd slam the machine with my strong gay hip, and she'd follow the lights on the floor, which beckon her to just say "fuck it" and dance the Charleston. As she launched into the cancan as an encore to the oohs and ahhs of onlookers, I'd fold my arms, lean against the change machine, and say to myself, "My work here is done."

Sadly, Yasuko has very different plans for us, and they don't involve pachinko, the Charleston, or even Harajuku girls. A few days later, she starts showing up to all of my classes. In very suggestive clothing. At the first class she attends, she wears a tight, navel-baring pink sweater and an ass-grabbing skirt. Trying to avoid looking at her small but admittedly perky and friendly-looking breasts, I say hello and ask her how she's doing.

"Much better," she beams.

The next time I see her in class I start to get a little worried. Not just because it was only a few hours later in my afternoon class, but also because she's changed into an outfit that shows more skin than I am prepared to handle in my capacity as her gay English teacher. I struggle to avoid her amorous gaze, feeling like I'm lost in the wrong fantasy. Is one of the straight male teachers down the hall fending off the advances of a wayward and totally fit male college student and amateur aikido competitor named Takeshi who loves coming to class with his shirt unbuttoned to the navel and staying for extra help after class? In his boxers?

I start trying to behave in a demonstrably gay manner in class so as to fend off her intensifying affections. Lots of limp-wristed gesticulations and discussions of musicals. I also sink so low as to say that my favorite movie ever is *A Chorus Line*, which surprises even me. All for naught, though. If anything, it's made her want me more.

She is crazy for me. I am a manimal. A manimal.

Yasuko even goes so far as to talk to Rachel about me, I'm surprised to find out. Rachel assures me that she told her in no uncertain terms that I am as gay as the day is long and that there is nothing short of permanent hypnotism that will make me venture into a relationship with a woman. But there is one key thing that has kept Yasuko from accepting Rachel's explanation, one thing that allows her to cling to the dream that I am her knight in shining hair gel.

"She said you look at her tits," Rachel tells me, looking at me like a mother would her teenage son. "A *lot*."

I do love tits. It's a peculiar strain of gay that I have: I'm a queer who would like nothing more than to have the opportunity to squeeze a pair of pert breasts every now and again. Have I been that obvious? I guess so. But the girl wears a Wonderbra, for God's sake. And even though I've never had the desire to rip her shirt off and place my face betwixt her supple mancushions, even though I would rather she just come to class wearing a scuba diving suit, even though I have been having a recurring nightmare where I'm being chased down a dimly lit hallway by one of her nipples, I can't help but look at them when they are displayed so wondrously. It would be like trying not to notice the lightning during an electrical storm. Impossible, unless you'd had your eyes sewn shut.

I ask Rachel to please come up with a nice way to tell Yasuko that, OK, yes, I did look at her tits a few times, but I also often look at lit candles and sparkling electrical sockets—that doesn't mean I want to touch them with my tongue. Also that I can't give her what she requires. And that she really needs to quit showing up at every single one of my classes.

Rachel promises to come up with something, and I'm able to relax and get back to my daydreams about Takeshi.

A few days later, I am walking to my class and I see Yasuko standing outside my classroom, wearing that familiar tight pink sweater. I shudder, fearing the worst: that Rachel was unable to convince her of my disinterest and that I will be forever stuck on this tight pink treadmill until I manage to convince some male student to come into my classroom and stick his tongue down my throat in front of all of my students. (Note to self: something to think about.)

The time for action is now. I've got to come clean with her face to face. Sure, in a way I'm kind of loving the attention. Yes, I'm quite keen on the idea of someone planning out their wardrobe in the morning based on what they think I'll like. Indeed, if someone wants to have endless dreams of rolling around on a sandy beach with me, kissing me all over and telling me how beautiful I am and how they could never imagine living without me, that's totally fine. And of course, if a young lady wants to take me to expensive restaurants and keep me supplied with a steady stream of French novels, bonbons, and hot Euro porn and yet expects nothing in return, I'm her man. But all of that is too complicated to explain to a student of English, and I don't know how to say it in Japanese. Despair begins to set in.

I pick up my roster of students before class and sigh deeply as I read through it; sure enough, Yasuko's name is first on the list of seven students. I look at the topic of my lesson: expressing disappointment. This might not go well.

I enter the classroom and put my name and lesson number on the board as the students file in. I say hello to folks and try to remain calm as I await Yasuko's entrance. We all chat for a few minutes after the bell rings, and there is still no sign of my tormentor. After a few more minutes, I feel sure I'm in the clear and start writing some opening questions on the board for students to discuss with their partners:

When did you last feel disappointed about something? What did you do to cheer yourself up?

I would not have wanted Yasuko to answer these questions, so I'm relieved that she hasn't shown up. The students have paired up and are discussing the questions among themselves. I can relax now and go with the flow of the lesson without having to worry about—

"I'm sorry for late!" Yasuko says as she hurries into the classroom and slides into the first available chair.

Struggling to mask my utter disappointment, I say, "Hi, Yasuko, the questions are on the board; please discuss with your partner."

Because she's the odd one out, Yasuko joins another pair of students for a few minutes before I call them all back to report what they learned about their partners during their discussions.

We go around the room and each student tells the class about their partner's answers to the questions. When we get to Yasuko's group, one of her partners, a travel agent named Yuki, says in a loud theatrical voice, complete with hand gestures, "Yasuko was disappointed recently because her boyfriend broke up with her and also because she lost her job. To cheer herself up she decide to come to English school, but she think it's not working. Also, a boy she likes is not liking her."

"Thank you, Yuki," I say with an uncomfortable smile.

Some of the young girls in the class whisper to Yasuko in Japanese, asking her who she likes. She demurs and instead directs her gaze at me.

"Tim-sensei, when did *you* last feel disappointed?"

Crap. I can't say that it was last week when my Internet connection froze right before it started downloading Brad Pitt's naked holiday photos. What can I say?

"Oh, it was something very similar," I fib. "I was disappointed that someone I liked didn't like me the same way."

"Really?!" Yasuko says, using the opportunity to dig deeper. "What girls you like? Blonde? Or Asian? Or tall?" Each student leans in to hear my answer.

"Oh, you know, I like the classic beauties: Grace Jones, Cher, and, of course, tennis great Billie Jean King." If she knows any of these ladies, maybe she'll give me a freaking break?

Yasuko's face slowly falls as she probably remembers seeing *A View to a Kill* as a child.

Yuki chimes in with the follow-up, "Tim-sensei, what did you do to cheer yourself up?"

After thinking for a few seconds, I shrug my shoulders and say, "You know, nothing chases the blues away like a few hours of baton twirling!"

Yasuko's eyelids dim.

The next day, I wait outside my classroom as the students walk in. I see Yasuko in the lobby chatting with some friends, and I assume she's here once again to get in her daily Tim sighting. She says goodbye to her friends and then spots Brody walking out of the teachers' room with his roster and some teaching materials. She taps him on the shoulder and waves a cutesie hello.

"Hi, Yasuko-san," he says, winking. "That's a very nice sweater." Yes. *Freaking* nice. As she follows him into his classroom, Yasuko looks over at me. I want to tell her all the things I really think she needs to consider: that this guy most certainly has an Oedipal relationship with his mother; that his haircut is featured on at least thirty satirical websites; that in high school he was voted Most Likely to Marry a Xena Warrior Princess Avatar at ComicCon. But what am I thinking? This is my chance to make a clean getaway. Whatever Brody has done to charm her into his classroom, it has clearly worked. And though I'm less than happy to learn that I can be so easily traded in for a guy who wears Tasmanian Devil ties, I have to admit it: I owe him one.

Thank you, GaijinMan. You've saved the gay.

*# of times heard Tokyo movie audience laugh
while watching Hollywood comedy: 0
# of times seen man on train looking at
porn on his cell phone: 17*

CHAPTER NINE

Problem Student

*The story of a woman unafraid to make her classmates weep
in her brave pursuit of smutty English excellence.*

I teach twelve to fifteen two-hour classes a week, ranging from
the basic-level world of irregular past tense verbs to the mid-level
challenges of phrasal verbs and past-perfect tense to the sophisticated and colorful realm of telling jokes and debating. Ever since
I started at Lane Language School many months ago, I've tried to
be a dynamic and inspiring instructor, empowering my students
with a more solid grasp of the English language and the confidence to stand tall and release their barbaric yawps to the world,
even daring to say controversial things they would never dare to
say in their mother tongue, things like "I don't really like sushi"
or "Meg Ryan is totally overrated." I recently had a long overdue
meltdown in the classroom. It was nothing I didn't see coming.

If I do say so myself, I've excelled at this job, at times. When
I came to this city, I was a recovering wallflower paralyzed by the
idea of standing in front of a group of people, however small, and

somehow summoning the confidence to say something interesting and persuade them to repeat it after me.

My lessons have developed from stilted, forced affairs with conversations beginning and ending with unanswered questions like, "Did anyone do anything interesting this weekend?" into frenzied free-for-alls with instructions like, "OK, Miho, you are a reservation clerk, and Aki, you want to book a flight to Brazil, but Miho, you don't have any tickets to Brazil. None! Sold out! So you have to suggest alternatives and come to an agreement. You have one minute! And…action!"

There have been good times. I've had my pet students who have made teaching both rewarding and hilarious. They usually tend toward the aged and slightly senile. I just relate to them the best. There's 150-year-old widow Reiko, for example, with her cropped and slightly off-center wig, heavily powdered face, and crimson lipstick that gives new meaning to the term "coloring outside the lines." She takes English classes because she wants to keep her mind sharp. Her favorite thing to say in English is "I'm very old," which is always followed by a squinty giggle and appreciative laughter from anyone else in her basic-level class who had understood what she'd said. Once a week, she says, she goes to Ginza with her dog and has tea and cakes at an outdoor café. She has never invited me along, though I have longed for a washi paper invitation to arrive in my mailbox complete with calligraphied Japanese characters and a small watercolor of her and her Chihuahua. I could bring the doggie biscuits.

Then there is Fumiko, who is about sixty and roughly half my height, with fat little fingers and huge tombstone teeth, which she flashes constantly in a giant smile that takes up nearly half her face. She paints all of her clothes herself with swirling floral designs or wispy animal figures with huge eyes, and she goes to visit her dog's grave every Wednesday. Though she's been coming to Lane for years, her English remains horrific. She's at an intermediate level, which she arrived at solely because the teachers felt bad that she'd taken all the lessons in the beginner level about five times each.

I knew I loved this woman the first day I taught her. I was teaching a lesson about expressing obligation—e.g., "I have to go to the store" or "I somehow have to come up with five grand for my dealer before midnight or he's gonna kill my cat"—and we were doing a listen-and-repeat exercise in which I make a statement that the students then turn into a "why" question, in order to practice those treacherous interrogative forms.

Turning to Fumiko, I prompted her with "He had to go visit his mother." She replied, "Why did he have to go...bank?" So I repeated the sentence again, and she said, a bit thrown off and confused, "Why...bank?" I smiled benevolently, sage-like, and said, "Visit his mother," while rolling my head to coax the correct answer out of her.

"Why did he have to go to..." she began, looking around at the other students nervously. (Come on, you're almost there, oh my God, Fumiko—just say it, say it and save us all!) "Bank?" (Argh!)

Now there comes a time in a lesson when the teacher realizes that no amount of correction is going to help. Too much will make her nervous, distracted, and may embarrass her in front of her peers.

"You really want him to go to the bank, don't you?" I smile, walking over to her and lovingly tapping her shoulder with my hand. "OK, let's just send him there. He can visit his mother later."

Right on cue, she said, "Why did he have to visit mother?" I want this woman to move in with me and paint all my clothes.

Over the past year of teaching, I've had to contend with the extreme shyness of Japanese students in an English conversation class. Forever concerned with maintaining equilibrium, they have an almost pathological aversion to speaking out of turn, disagreeing outright, or giving the wrong answer. It can make for a precarious environment for teaching English conversation since in order for my job to be performed with any degree of success, I need to get the students speaking without scaring them away.

To teach English as a foreigner in Japan, one must do daily battle with the complex and often frustrating elements of the national psyche that don't exist in the American mind. For one thing, in the school system here, the classroom atmosphere is one of absolute deference to the teacher. Their word *sensei* has connotations that our English word *teacher* does not. *Sensei* communicates respect and acknowledges the teacher's role as imparter of wisdom and knowledge. (By contrast, our *teacher*, to many American students, is just a fancy word for *target*.) Students are discouraged from speaking out without first being addressed, and if they do speak out, they'd better have the right answer or they will be reprimanded. It's all about one-way instruction, teacher to students. The student is not so much taught as indoctrinated.

It's the exact opposite of the American school system, where children are encouraged to speak too much, the result being that we Americans never know when to shut up. Just look at our talk shows, our love of using cell phones while driving, our chatty reality shows, and our obsession with bumper stickers expounding our beliefs in God, political candidates, the genius of our honor students, the righteousness of guns, and living simply so that others may simply live. We Americans excel at giving too much information. The Japanese excel at not giving nearly enough. So the idea of a classroom where students are not only encouraged to speak out but required to do so leaves many of them confused and scared. And not just due to their fear of a foreign teacher. They are also dealing with their fellow Japanese, who will most certainly judge them. If they speak too enthusiastically or answer too many questions, they will be seen as arrogant and a show-off, a protruding nail in need of a good whack-down.

At first it didn't bother me that it took a good fifteen to twenty minutes of my asking questions to a deadly silent classroom before they would relax and start talking. But when you deal with this lack of responsiveness day in day out, it starts to make you a little touchy. It's not that they don't want to talk. It's that they don't want to talk to *you*. Slowly, my insecurity has crept toward mild and now pronounced paranoia, and silence has become my albatross. If I have to sit through another miserable eerie quiet brought on by a question I've asked at the start of class ("How are you?"/"What did you do last weekend?"/"What's your problem?"), there's no telling what I might do. Then, one day in a basic-level class, the meltdown.

Things began promisingly. When I first looked at the attendance sheet before class started, I was surprised and thrilled to see the name Maria Gonzales listed among all the Yoko Omimuras and Naoki Moritas. After asking around, I'd learned that she comes from Mexico and is married to a Japanese man.

"Wow...Maria Gonzales," I said to myself with a sigh, my brain racing with exotic and stereotypical images of forbidden dances, all-night fiestas, and tequila shots passed around the classroom. It had been so long since I'd considered a name like "Maria." It sounded so zesty, vibrant, full of life. My classes could certainly use some color, some spice, some Marrrrrrrrrria.

The only time I'd had a Mexican in my class was a few months earlier. Boy was he a stud. His name was Diego Martinez, and he couldn't speak much English, but it didn't really matter because none of us were listening. He had the sex appeal of several South Pacific Islands. I think the word is "smoldering." He'd made my classroom hot to the touch. For two hours we swooned, hanging on his every mispronounced and misused word. We didn't get much done in that class, but we all definitely learned to love Mexico.

Now, what of this Maria? Would she enter the class wearing a tight red dress, her bronze skin glimmering like gold in the artificial light, her voluptuous curves and hoop earrings swaying from side to side as she sauntered to her desk and pulled out her bright red pen, spiral notebook, and maracas? Would she bring the other students out of their shells and show them that there's nothing to be afraid of, nothing at all, "so just to speak the English and dance!" Would she?

No, she wouldn't.

I walk into the class as usual, write my name on the board, and give a bubbly, if forced, hello. There's no answer. I turn around, face the class, and give a somewhat more aggressive, even scary hello. The students look at each other nervously.

"Hello," a few of them mumble.

I take attendance quietly, a chance to scope out our Mrs. Gonzales. She is a pretty conservative and serious-looking woman of about fifty. But I still cling to the hope that bubbling under her stern veneer is a Mexican madwoman who is ready to party.

"How's everyone doing?" I ask.

No answer. From anyone. Not even Maria. I realize then that the next two hours are going to be absolutely excruciating. I'm going to have to pull every answer out of them like a dentist. An evil dentist with a big pair of bloody pliers.

I decide to target people for my answers.

"How are you, Akira?"

No answer. Only fear.

"Maria?" I venture.

"Ehhhh," she stammers. "No...me...to speak...to...on top... take...the class."

OK, so it turns out Maria speaks the absolute worst English I've ever heard in my life. There will be no one to save me, after all. I'll drown in a sea of introversion.

But though my classroom is silent, I can hear the teacher in the next room loud and clear. It's McD, the ex-marine tough guy with a head shaped like a cardboard box. He sounds like he's speaking into a bullhorn.

"IN AMERICAN FAST-FOOD PLACES, YOU CAN MAKE ANY ORDER BIGGER FOR AN EXTRA, LIKE, THIRTY-FIVE CENTS! THAT MEANS YOU GET MORE FRENCH FRIES AND A BIGGER DRINK! YOU CAN'T DO THAT HERE! BUT YOU CAN DO IT IN AMERICA!!"

I want to bite off my hand and throw it at someone. I feel like I'm losing my mind. My class refuses to talk to me, and the only sound bouncing around the room is McD's ode to American fast food.

"How are you, Akira?! Eiko?! Akiko?! How are you?!"

"AND IN AMERICA, YOU CAN FILL YOUR OWN DRINK! THEY HAVE FOUNTAIN DRINK STATIONS THAT THE CUSTOMERS CAN USE TO FILL AND REFILL THEIR DRINKS! IT'S REALLY CONVENIENT! BUT YOU CAN'T DO THAT HERE!!"

Then I lose control.

"Talk to me! Say anything!!Anything! I don't care! Just speak! Please, *speak*!!" I slam the dry-erase marker onto the tray, making an embarrassingly loud noise that I immediately apologize for.

They remain silent. Maria takes notes. I excuse myself and walk out of the class to take a short breather in the teachers' room. I sit down and inhale deeply before going back in a little calmer. This time I skip the small talk and get straight to the topic of the lesson—giving directions. Resisting the temptation to give them all directions to my ass so they can kiss it, I make it through the class, but I start having real doubts about my ability to continue this job.

Something is wrong with me. I am not the same champion teacher I was before, one who can handle the weird neuroses of his classes with grace and humor. Someone has swiped my mojo, and I need it back.

Other teachers have started to notice my slip in enthusiasm for the job.

"What's wrong? You look nauseous," says Grant, whose limitless gusto in the classroom I've always admired.

"I'm out of ideas," I weep, looking down at my roster of students, fearing the worst. "I can't bear the thought of facing another classroom full of blank stares. My self-esteem can't take it."

I have an advanced discussion class coming up, and I have no idea how I am going to jump-start it. So Grant tells me something he's been doing in his classes lately.

"You should just walk in, say hello to everyone, then clap your hands together and say something like, 'OK, someone give me a good topic to start things off with.' Usually someone will pipe right in with something from the news or about a movie they just saw or something."

I look at him, dubious.

"That actually works?"

"It does for me, I swear to God. But you have to make sure that your tone is the perfect mix of friendliness and authority. You can do it, I'm sure. You're really tall."

I'm not so sure it will work. In a perfect world, one that I'd created, someone would suggest something like "bad TV shows" or "hideous fashion trends" or maybe even "most unique forms of suicide." But this is far from a perfect world.

Grant senses my apprehension.

"Listen, in a discussion class like that, there's always at least one person who wants to talk himself silly. If all else fails, just sidle up to that student and ask him for a suggestion. Once they're forced to speak, they'll give you something good you can use. Then you should clap your hands again and say, 'OK, everyone please get together with the person next to you and talk on this subject for three minutes, then we'll all come back together and share stories.'"

I look down at my list of students. All the usual suspects. Shizue and Takehiro, an old married couple, both in their seventies, who lived in England a long time ago and still take English class together once a week. There's Kumiko, a college student who checks herself in her pocket mirror at least six times every class. There's sweet Kayoko, a young travel agent who looks exactly like Minnie Mouse. And Tomo, a surly, aloof, soon-to-graduate high school senior who is intensely obsessed with J. D. Salinger. But there's one name on the roster I've never seen before. Naomi. Hmm. She could be just the wild card I need. I decide to take Grant's advice.

I walk in, say hello, write my name and the class number on the board as always, clap my hands, and say, "OK, let's get started. Someone give me a good topic."

Silence. A tumbleweed rustles past the open door.

"Anything's OK, you guys. Someone just give me an interesting topic."

I look around the room at each student. The students look around the room at each other and then me. I feel a lip wobble coming on.

Just when I'm about to collapse on the floor at Kayoko's feet and offer her money just to recite her ABCs, Naomi the new student chimes in. She is very slim and stylishly dressed and has the severe facial angles of a hard-nosed businesswoman or perhaps a television executive. The world seems to hang off her cheekbones. She also has a blank, completely unreadable expression on her face. She could have just killed someone, or she could have just baked a chocolate cake. Who knows? She is a femme fatale, a Japanese Marlene Dietrich, and a stunning contrast to the rest of the class, which is stubbornly cute. Naomi, in her charcoal-gray pinstriped pantsuit, occupies a world of her own, one of film noire ambiance, long white cigarettes, and women in dark glasses with secrets for sale. Yeah, like that.

"You said anything is OK, right?" she asks in a husky voice.

Now, that is a dangerous question in this job, one that can lead down paths you'd rather not tread. But there's no saying no to a dame with this much moxie. I want to hear what she has to say. Plus, she's the only one offering to speak. So I nod and say, "Sure."

"Well," she intones enigmatically in nearly flawless English, "I was reading the newspaper this morning, and it was interesting, an article I read. It was about a group of women who were drinking in a bar, and they saw a guy and, how do I say, surround him and make him to take his clothes off and they assault him."

I look around uncomfortably at the pensioners in the class, poor Shizue and normally unflappable Takehiro, but it is impossible to read their expressions. Tomo, the catcher in the rye, looks at Naomi and rolls his eyes like he's never seen such a total phony in his life. I look back at Naomi and brace myself for the rest of her story.

"At their court, they were punished, but it was much less than if the same thing was done by men to a woman. I thought that was interesting." She smiles in the manner of Cruella De Ville.

I ask her, "Do you think their punishment should have been more severe?"

"I'm sorry, *severe*, what means *severe*?"

"*Harsh, serious*," I explain. "Occasionally *merciless, inhuman*, or *brutal*."

She pauses and looks around the class that she holds transfixed.

"No," she says with a giggle and another quick look around the classroom, gauging the reaction.

Wow. Now here is a woman who clearly likes to bait people. Japanese folks are generally quite loath to speak about contentious topics like, say, public sexual assault. Naomi-san is obviously not. What she wants, it is becoming increasingly apparent, is to get a reaction from her fellow countrymen.

She is a troublemaker. A breath of fresh air. I love her. I am afraid of her.

"OK, anyone have a comment?" I ask. No one has a comment. I am uncomfortable because, even after teaching over two million lessons, I still never know exactly how to read a class of Japanese students. They like to preserve the appearance that nothing is wrong, while underneath that polished surface likely lurks irritation, fear, loathing, dread, and/or arousal.

I don't feel comfortable giving the class this topic to discuss for three minutes and report back on. Naomi wouldn't mind, but I will not fall into her trap, no, no, no. As much as I appreciate her left-field suggestion, we will talk about civilized things in this class, like good ways to stay cool in the hot Tokyo summer or favorite amusement park rides. Not reverse-gender gang rape. Definitely not reverse-gender gang rape.

"OK, great, thank you, Naomi. Anyone else have an interesting topic?" Shizue quickly comes through with the lifesaving—if boring—suggestion of favorite restaurants in Tokyo. The next three minutes go by without a hitch.

After this warm-up activity, I broach the topic of the first hour of the lesson, which, in our appalling textbook, is "Expressing Thanks." Now, the good thing about these high-level classes is that, once the class gets warmed up, the students should be doing most of the talking, making the teacher's role that of advisor and confidante. Just give them some things to discuss and let 'em go. But don't be fooled. It's harder than it sounds. After all, these students have taken a lot of lessons by the time they reach this level. So the threat of repeating an activity that a student has done recently with another teacher is very real. There's nothing worse than being informed by a student, "We talked about our most embarrassing moment in my last class."

I pair them up and then write a few questions on the board to give them something to talk about: "What is something that someone did for you recently that you really appreciated? How did you show your thanks?"

Innocent enough questions. I envision answers involving taxi drivers who are nice enough to help their passengers get their heavy bags to their apartment on the second floor or young boys helping old women pick up the change they dropped at the station ticket machine. They all begin talking, and I sit my chair in the middle of the small classroom and begin listening in on what they're saying.

Shizue is telling Kumiko about her husband cleaning his own rice bowl the night before, while Takehiro sings the praises of a shop assistant who was so instrumental in helping him choose the right suit (and, consequently, relieving him of about a hundred thousand yen).

Naomi is partnered with the aforementioned Minnie Mouse look-a-like, Kayoko, who in every class is sweetness and light, always has a smile for everyone, and always wears extremely fashionable shoes. Naomi eyes her with suspicion and annoyance; might she feel the need to shake up her world and rearrange it a little bit?

"So," Kayoko begins, gesturing to the question that I wrote on the board, "what is something that someone did for you recently that you really appreciated?"

The whole class is alive with broken English conversations, but I have my ear pricked in the direction of Cruella and Minnie, dying to hear what they'll come out with.

"Well," Naomi begins. Ideally, at this point, the lights would dim, the spotlight would cast its dramatic glow, the strings would begin to flutter, the rest of the room would fall silent, the saxophone would sing, and Naomi would take center stage, a Benson and Hedges Deluxe Ultra Light 100 poised between her fingers, ready to tell the cold, cruel world her story. Thankfully, none of this happens, because her chosen subject is even less appropriate than I could have ever possibly hoped.

"Ever since my husband and I were married, we've agreed never to fart. In front of each other."

My God. She said *fart*. This is soooo not an answer to the question.

Kayoko's face tilts questioningly. "*Fart?*" she says, with the same blissfully innocent tone a young girl might use to say the words "flower petals?" or "Reese's Pieces?" "What's *fart*'s meaning?"

I'm paralyzed. I know I should perhaps intervene and suggest to Naomi that her answer is kind of inappropriate. But I don't wish to anger her. Plus, I'm desperate to see where this is all going. I bow my head and hope for the best. As the other students' conversations continue to fill the classroom, I listen as Naomi tries to explain to Kayoko in English what a fart is.

"It's a noise we make. When we eat some foods, especially Mexican food."

In American middle schools this would've done the trick, but Kayoko still isn't clear.

"Shout?" she guesses.

"No."

"Clap?"

"No."

"Laugh?"

"No."

This goes on for far too long, until finally Naomi has mercy and whispers the word in Japanese into Kayoko's ear. Kayoko promptly turns an impressive shade of red and looks as if she wishes she were dead.

So let's recap. Naomi is grateful that her husband has never farted in her presence, and this is the inspirational story she has chosen to tell her partner, the poor, quivering Kayoko.

Naomi is an enigma. Everything that comes out of her mouth is meant to rile people, to stir them up and make them wriggle in their seats. So far she has used every opportunity she has been given to force us to see the world as she sees it. It's a dirty, blood-red piece of fleshy, sexually violated pulp. I want to see more.

In the second hour of the lesson, I ask for someone to give me an example of a restrictive relative clause (because I have no idea what one is), and she quickly chimes in with, "My mother-in-law, who is very particular about housekeeping, drives me crazy and makes me want to vomit."

At the end of class I ask if anyone has any questions. She raises her hand and utters the words I've now begun to simultaneously dread and hope for: "Anything OK?"

"Sure, why not?" I say.

"Well, is it true that when men go into the toilet for the purpose of performing a bowel movement, they first spit into the bowl?"

Tomo looks at her wide-eyed, like maybe, just maybe, Naomi's not a phony at all. She might just be the real thing.

Up until this point I've pretty much gotten off scot-free, but now I'm the target. Obviously Naomi wants her teacher to share in the atmosphere of unease that she's created in the room. What does she want me to say, I wonder. I really don't think she cares about the answer. She just wanted to ask the question, to just toss the sludge against the wall and see what would happen. Should I just laugh and say, "Oh, Naomi, you're so funny. OK, see you all next week!" and then run away? Something tells me this won't let me off the hook.

"Yes, it is true," I say. "Sometimes twice. You know, depending."

I begin to look forward to my Wednesday afternoons with Naomi. Without fail, I am shocked, embarrassed, and mortified at the things she comes out with. But I am never bored. And that, in the end, is the bottom line. After teaching for so long, I am nothing if not bored stupid. And just when my fire was about to expire, Naomi came into my life. She is giving me what I am in desperate need of: fear.

The next week Takehiro and Shizue are both absent from class. The rest of the students file in, Tomo sitting next to Naomi, Kayoko choosing a seat over in the corner, Kumiko between them.

"So, hello everyone. Let's get started. Someone give me a topic."

Ever since Naomi reared her tawdry head in my class, I've noticed the other students are much more eager to suggest a topic at the beginning of class. This is probably so they can avoid discussing anal warts or assisted suicide at the suggestion of Naomi, but it's progress nonetheless.

"How about difference of Japanese and American culture?" Kayoko says.

"OK, that's a great suggestion. Thank you, Kayoko. Everyone, please get together with your partner and let's talk about it!" Good Lord, I'm turning into Oprah.

As usual, I allow the students to do their talking while I go write the grammar points we'll be covering on the board. When I'm finished, I pull my chair up to Kumiko and Kayoko to have a listen. They are both giggling and covering their mouths with their hands.

"I so surprised! I no understand why they say!" Kumiko manages to say through tears and quiet chuckling.

"I know!" says Kayoko. "I go to post office in New York and lady was talking so fast I, あの, can't understand, so I say, 'Please speak slowly,' and she scream at me and I still not understanding, so she calls next person and not talk to me again!"

Confident they are enjoying their conversation, I stand and carry my chair over to Naomi and Tomo. Naomi, of course, is speaking, while a wide-eyed Tomo, who has never looked so engaged, hangs on her every probably disgusting word.

"I just think it is very stupid, don't you, Tomo-kun?"

Tomo doesn't answer. He smiles uncomfortably and then looks at me, desperate for me to help him say the right thing.

"What are you guys talking about?" I ask, desperate to know the reasons behind Tomo's horror/arousal.

"I was talking about the difference between Japanese and America pornography," Naomi begins. "I explain to him about how in the America they show everything, but in Japan, they cover the private parts with those little blocks, you know Tim-sensei?"

"Yes, pixels," I say a little too quickly.

"Pixels," she says, writing the new word down in her note-book. "They cover with pixels, and you can't see very well unless you look careful. It stupid. Japan treat us like children. Don't you think that, Tim-sensei?"

I do think that. I've said this before. I'll say it again. The pix-elation of Japanese pornography goes against the very thing that makes pornography great. But should I say it now? In class? In front of impressionable Tomo, who is looking more and more like he wants Naomi to walk him home on a leash?

"Yes, it's strange, but..."

"So you have seen Japanese porn movie?" she asks, her lips curling into a smile on one side.

I look over at Kayoko and Kumiko, still laughing about being completely shat on by cranky New Yorkers, and look back at Tomo, who is composing his marriage proposal to Naomi in his head, and I think, "Oh, screw it."

"Yes, of course. Hasn't *everybody*?"

Naomi nods her head and smiles. Tomo makes a mental note to educate himself about the world of American porn. Kayoko and Kumiko laugh and snort.

And as mysteriously as she appeared in my life, Naomi was gone. Was she just a vision? A figment of my desperate imagination? A guardian angel sent from heaven's red-light district to do the community service she was sentenced to for flashing Jesus and the Buddha at last year's Christmas party? Nah, she was promoted to the next level, which I don't teach. The next week, when I look down at my class roster and her name is not there, I die a little inside.

But though I'm saddened by her departure, I know that her legacy will live on. Naomi changed the atmosphere forever with her constant indecent proposals. She stirred things up and made seemingly straightforward questions like "What's the best drink to have with ramen?" dangerous.

Now there will be no more talk of menstrual cycles and their effect on one's cooking; no more impromptu speeches like the one about that country in Africa that, allegedly, had outlawed sex for two years because of the AIDS epidemic ("I think it would be impossible," she said); no more sexual harassment; and no more manipulation of the text for her own nefarious ends. No more piss, no more vinegar.

And just like that, it's back to conversations about Japanese society, vacations, and dreary answers to appalling opening questions like "If today were your birthday, where would you be, who would you be with, what would you be doing, and why?" Of course, I could follow Naomi's example, throw caution to the wind, and offer questions like "Why is it that in Japan, it is horribly rude to blow your nose in public, yet sniffing, snorting, chewing, and swallowing, or spitting out one's own snot with the forcefulness and volume of a morning radio DJ is perfectly all right?" But that would cause more problems than it would solve. And I'd probably be asked to repeat the question more slowly.

So my classes have gone back to being placid affairs, with the occasional bit of accidental rude language. ("My son is a really good cock," Shizue would say, meaning, of course, "cook.") Tomo has lost his innocence and has probably moved on from Salinger to *The Story of O*. Kayoko comes to class unafraid, knowing that, until she herself is promoted to the next level, she won't find herself on the wrong end of Naomi's sadistic gaze. Kumiko still checks herself in her mirror six times per class.

But even though Naomi is gone from my class, her spirit can sometimes still be felt. One day, Shizue suggests we discuss our thoughts on Japanese tabloid newspapers, and another time, Kumiko proposes the topic of "sexiest Hollywood actors," neither of which would have been possible pre-Naomi.

Naomi is now wreaking havoc in the next level, no doubt trying to get people to discuss the prime minister's favorite sexual positions or whether or not adult incest is a victimless crime. I envy the teacher of that class and would kill to be sitting there as he or she naïvely replies, "Sure, why not?" to those two magical words that are guaranteed to open up a world of smut and disorder: "Anything OK?"

# of teriyaki burgers eaten: 13
# of Saturday nights spent on mushrooms watching
the three competing giant TV screens at
Shibuya Crossing: 1

CHAPTER TEN

Too Cute

In which our hero/Christ figure realizes with a shudder that
Hello Kitty could be spending her nights stalking and anally
raping Disney characters with baseball bats and no one
would care as long as she still wore a wide-eyed expression of
pure innocence and a cute pink dress the next morning.

It's early morning, and the sun is only just beginning to consider poking its way above the jagged Tokyo horizon. Giant black pterodactyls scavenge for scraps from the trash bags lining the concrete outside, dwarfing the trash collectors who are doing their best to remove the millions of pounds of waste and sludge left for them the night before. And me, I'm on my bed shivering, having just woken up from a horrible, horrible early-morning dream in which I was being brutally attacked in my bed by Tare Panda, the wide-eyed, oval-faced character from the Hello Kitty School of Aggressive Cuteness who's weaseled his way into every corner of Japanese popular culture, from advertisements to greeting cards to cell phone accessories, threatening to usurp Miss Kitty as the national mascot. It was trying to cute me to death.

Admittedly, I'm not just irked because of the panda attack. It's that it happened to occur simultaneously with an early-morning earthquake tremor deep beneath the city. I wake to the bed shaking. Also the bureau, the television, the sliding wooden door that opens out on the kitchen, and the walls. And since Tokyoites are expecting "the big one" any day now, I quickly jump to the conclusion that that day is today and the panda in my dream was just an adorable li'l angel of death.

I sit frozen on the shaking bed for a few moments, praying for everything to stop wobbling, hoping there isn't a bigger tremor to come. After a few minutes, I stop writing goodbye e-mails to friends and family in my head and start to calm down. I've experienced these tremors before, and it's always the calm after the shaking stops that is the eeriest; it's still within the realm of possibility that something has been jiggled loose (a nearby house, a telephone pole, Tokyo Tower), something that will soon come crashing down on my bed without warning.

I gather myself together, clamber out of bed, and slide into the chair at my desk. I figure I may as well watch television while I'm waiting to be crushed, so I switch it on and go out to the kitchen to make some tea and toast. When I return to my room, I'm greeted with a horrifying image on the television screen, one that will emblazon itself on my memory for weeks, maybe years, to come.

It's a commercial for the Japanese language version of *Annie* currently running in Tokyo, complete with a freckle-faced, curly wig-wearing Japanese girl squeaking out the words to "Tomorrow" in Japanese.

I. Am. Aghast. There are many things that should never be allowed to leave America's borders. Adam Sandler movies, for example. Fox News. The McRib Sandwich. But number one on the list, I feel sure of it, is the musical story of that nauseatingly precocious and cherubic red-haired orphan who, whenever she has a problem, is bored, or just has some time to kill, thinks it necessary to sing songs through her nose in a voice that could wilt plants, crash airplanes, and bring about worldwide famine.

"The horror...the horror," I murmur, convinced I will never fall asleep again.

Later, on the train on my way to Shibuya to do some record shopping, I am still feeling the aftereffects of unprotected exposure to Jap-Annie. As it happens, I'm sitting across from a young office lady holding in her lap a tiny blue purse with a pastel drawing of two dancing bunnies, a chicken, a strawberry, some flowers, and the words "Something Pretty" on it. I think of Tare Panda. I think of little orphan Jap-Annie. I want to vomit.

Looking around me, I see the train is dense with commuters with their heads buried in a variety of reading material. Many read comics full of characters with glistening eyes half the size of their heads. Women read fashion magazines, like *Cutie*, one of the most popular. In its pages, young ladies can find useful tips on how to wear oversized bracelets, pink barrettes, fluffy scarves, tiny handbags, wacky hats, flowery shoes, pastel nail polish, futuristic headphones, bubble gum lip gloss, sparkly eye shadow, tight/bright T-shirts saying things like "Sweetheart" and "Kissypoo Sugar," wide-eyed girl-next-door expressions, and countless other tried and tested ways to optimize their cuteness and make sure they're never the last sweetie on their block to have that completely necessary YumYum brand, bunny rabbit-embossed makeup kit.

Considering my panda dream again, I decide that my sub-conscious is desperately trying to tell me something. It is this: the Japanese obsession with all things cute is becoming a little more than I can handle.

I think back to when I opened my first Japanese bank account. I had two choices of bankcard designs. The first one was a lovely drawing of a small boy on a fishing boat staring at the setting sun against a beautiful auburn sky. Elegiac and elegant. The other choice was a picture of a cartoon bunny named Miffy who looks like Hello Kitty with bunny ears and no nose. He was licensed as the bank's mascot. The friendly bank teller told me it was the most popular choice. After a few moments of quiet reflection, I chose the fishing boat sunset one, ignoring the devil inside me scream-ing, "Give me that bunny!"

"Tim, really," I lectured myself. "Calm down. You don't need the bunny. You want the bunny, but you don't need the bunny. Yes, he's cute. But is that really what you need in a bank card? Choose the sunset background and walk away."

Cuteness is of utmost importance in this country. It's why the films of chipmunk-faced Meg Ryan have always been infi-nitely more popular than those of giant-jawed Julia Roberts. It's why adorable Audrey Hepburn's image is used to sell products from bottled jasmine tea to English lessons at Berlitz. It's why Tokyo Disneyland exists, why there are giant Snoopy Stores in Tokyo and Yokohama, and it is, I will forever believe, why Cher never became a superstar in Japan. With her long narrow face, dour expression, Medusa-like tendrils of hair, and overactive serpentine tongue, she is the antithesis of cute. She's the stuff of nightmares. The Japanese would much rather be entertained by Michael J. Fox.

At the giant RECOFAN record store in Shibuya I go to the Japanese section to see what's on offer. No shortage of cute over here. One of the most popular pop bands in the country in the past few years is an all-girl troupe going by the name of Morning Musume, which translates, worryingly, to Morning Daughters. They are the female Japanese Menudo, an ever-changing roster of pubescent—sometimes prepubescent—young ladies brought together by a record company to help satisfy the Japanese public's demands for endless gallons of teenage squeakpop. They sing (off-key), dance in formation (like drunk beauty pageant contestants), and wear brightly colored costumes (the kind seen in Southern American parades). They're horrendous. They sell millions. They're fucking everywhere. And each one is probably set to embark on an equally cute solo career during which she will tour the country dressed in a tutu, holding a fluffy pink baton and singing nursery rhyme–like songs that will provide her with a bit of cash flow before it all comes to a crashing halt when she reaches the cutoff age of twenty-five. Because twenty-five, my friends, is not a cute number.

There's nothing like the sound of a group of Tokyo girls gathered around a store window display featuring whatever character is the It cutie of the moment and screaming their approval with a bloodcurdling "KAWAIIIIII!" It means "cute," but it also implies "in," "we like," and "that would look really good on a handbag, a T-shirt, a cell phone screen, and a pair of underwear!"

"Kawaii!!" If you hear that word directed at you, you're in there, man, you're hot, you've really got it. You are officially cuddly. I've not had that word directed at me.

Whereas in America the number-one preoccupation is being thin (eating french fries being a close second), in Japan, they don't generally have to worry about the bloat factor. They do, however, have to worry about not being kawaii enough.

Recently, while on my way to work, I ran into one of my students, Ryoko, a basic-level student in her late forties who was always a joy to teach, and though she was typically insecure about her English abilities, she was never shy about giving it a try. I saw she'd gotten a haircut, and I complimented her on it.

"Oh, you've had a haircut," I said, pointing to her head with one hand and mimicking a pair of scissors with the other. "It looks really nice!"

She smiled and said thank you. She looked pensive, though, as if she wasn't ready to move on to a different topic. As if what I'd said was deficient in some way.

I started to worry that maybe I had not complimented her enough. Perhaps "nice" was too neutral an adjective.

"Thank you," she began, "but...is it *cute*?" She slapped her hand over her mouth as soon as she said it, perhaps realizing the inherent ridiculousness of a woman her age asking such a question. Or maybe she was afraid of the answer. Or thought she was going to cough.

"すごいかわいいですよ！" I said with a big smile. "It's really cute!"

At hearing this, she relaxed and we walked to the station together, the initial awkwardness dissolved by the magical "c" word.

I should have a very strong appreciation for that which is cute. My country invented Mickey Mouse, after all. And the Snuggle fabric softener teddy bear, which never fails to give me an ice-cream headache. And I do like cute things. My best friend when I was a kid had been my Snoopy doll, but that was less because he was cute and more because he was the only one in the neighborhood who didn't throw things at me. As far as I'm concerned, though, when the eyes get too large, when the heads become too round, the smiles too aggressive, the voices too squeaky, and the bodies too puffy and squeezably soft, this is when it becomes a problem for me, and I struggle to turn a blind eye.

At the same time, in spite of myself, I have been won over by some of the cute ephemera around me. When McDonald's recently sold stuffed Hello Kitty dolls dressed in pink kimono for two hundred yen with the purchase of a combo meal, I took the bait. Twice. Hello Kitty needed a friend, and who better for her to share her time with while lounging on my bedspread than Dear Daniel, her male counterpart dressed in an adorable blue yukata robe? And yes, when Mister Donut launched a campaign where customers could get miniature bed pillows with precious dog and cat faces on them with the purchase of two-dozen donuts, you bet I bought two dozen donuts and took them to work just so I could have those pillows and take them home for Kitty and Daniel to cuddle up against. Who wouldn't? And, looking down at my phone, OK, I do have a cute little pudgy blue elephant hanging from a little chain connected to the antennae. And, well, yeah, I guess I do have on a T-shirt with a perfectly round monkey face that says "Everything Ya-Ya." So? Oh, and I suppose you're going to ask me about the little Miffy figurine I have on my keychain, and the Pikachu stuffed animal I bought for my nephew but then kept for myself because everyone needs a little stuffed Pikachu to help them sleep at night. And I can't forget the Hamutaro hamster toy that has the cutest little nose and a smile to melt the heart of the devil himself and OH MY GOD WHAT HAS HAPPENED TO ME?!!

I have crossed over. I've never wanted cell phone accessories before, never needed daily calendars with smiley-faced mice and rabbits on my desk when I was of sounder mind. I recently bought a shoulder bag so small that the only thing I can fit into it is a paperback and my iPod. Why did I buy it? Why do you think? And, oh dear Lord, look, I'm carrying it right now. And you know, if I'm really being honest, I'm more likely to buy one bag of rice over another if there's a dancing koala vouching for it on the label. My world has changed, and I'm just now realizing it. This has got to stop, and now.

Standing there on the Shibuya street, I see an advertisement in a store window replete with a smiley hamster, a mouse, a chicken, a duckling, and a few other small furry mammals I can't identify. My eyes widen, and I involuntarily smile at the sight. Then the most unexpected thing happens: one by one, each jumps off the advertisement and onto my shoulder. The hamster snuggles into the nook between my neck and shoulder and starts cooing. The chicken and duckling hop onto my head and start juggling the smaller furry tufts of fluff. The mouse scurries over to my other shoulder and pecks lovingly at my neck. I stumble back, look over, and what should be approaching me from in front of the HMV but a gaggle of girls from anime movies, all bending down with their hands coyly on their knees and blowing kisses at me. There are about twenty of them, and they are coming for me. ("One of us! One of us!") There's a schoolgirl with long brown hair swept back and held by an ungainly green bow. She's dressed in a sailor suit top and a short skirt that keeps billowing up à la Marilyn Monroe. There's a white-haired sorceress in a body-hugging black gown carrying a wooden scepter that she keeps pointing at me with a wink. There's a blue-haired cutie-pie in what appears to be a female stormtrooper uniform, and, most bone-chilling of all, a girl in a blue leotard, long pink leggings, blue and white space shoes with robotic wings attached to her arms, and, swinging from those arms, a furry white mammal giggling and occasionally jumping up to her shoulder to whisper something in its mistress's ear. All of these cloyingly cuddly cartoon hotties have eyes the size of American footballs and are fixing me with their red triangular smiles. They hop closer and closer, giggling and clucking, ready to pounce and drown me in the pools of their gigantic and horribly cute eyes. The hamster nestled in the space between my neck and shoulder has his claws dug into my skin and is purring up toward my ear. Oh my God, he's so *precious*! No! Not precious! Manipulatively adorable! Get thee away!

As the cute anime sluts come nearer, I grab the hamster and toss him at them. I shake off the mouse, the duckling, the chicken, and their furry little friends and start running for my life. I run past game-center arcades with electronic images of teddy bear/bunny rabbit/kitty cat mascots dancing blissfully around the sign at the entrance; past amusement park advertisements like the one saying "Let's Summer!" showing a cute little girlie surfing with a cherubic snowman and a toothy squirrel with a Mohawk amid lots of pastel pinks, oranges, and blues; past the Tsutaya CD and video store, on the steps of which a group of round-faced girls dressed in what look like Tiger Lily costumes are smiling, waving, and handing out promotional packets advertising the new SMAP album. As I near the Shibuya Crossing intersection in front of the station, Astro Boy, the first-ever anime character, shoots out of the sky and fires the cutest little laser beams out of his fingers toward me. I duck and dive and run across the street and am almost to the threshold of Shibuya Station when who should block my path but Hello Kitty herself, standing before me, fixing me with her static gaze, staring into my very soul.

She's much taller than I would have thought (seven feet at least) and, I gotta say, I see a most beguiling, loveable evil in her small black eyes and li'l yellow nose. She smacks me in the face. Her open hand is sooooo soft. She smacks me again and again, alternating slaps with soft caresses of my face and, wow, honestly, it's like being made love to by a giant feather pillow.

"Hello Kitty, I wanna be your dog!" No! No! Must...be... strong! Think of un-cute things: Evil clowns! The Cuban Missile Crisis! Ann Coulter being interviewed in a bikini on *Larry King*!

I click my heels together three times, open my eyes, and Hello Kitty is gone. I discover I am in absolutely everyone's way as they push and shove me aside to enter the station. I come back to myself, look around to make sure I'm no longer being followed, and step into the station.

On the Chuo Line train home, I keel over in my seat, my hands clutching plastic CD bags. I begin to sink into sleep, ready to dream of more exquisite abuse at the hands of Miss Kitty, when my sinking eyes catch a glimpse of a familiar English word on the T-shirt of a woman sitting opposite me.

She is an elderly woman, maybe sixty-five, with a stoic and inscrutable face, sleepy eyes, and a faraway gaze. She is dressed casually in high-water slacks and a Bermuda hat. Her T-shirt says "Bitch." I swear to God.

She looks adorable.

# of glass elevators taken in that look like space pods: 5
# of advertisements seen using English word
"happy" with at least one exclamation mark after: 49

CHAPTER ELEVEN

Survivors

*A chapter that pits teacher against teacher in a thrilling
and bloody fight for job security.*

I have recently come into possession of a videotape with very dark powers. This video could wreak unspeakable havoc if it fell into the wrong hands, which it did when I got it from Rachel the other night. We were sitting around on the floor of her small flat in Ogikubo desperately trying to get stoned off some really, really weak weed and talking about things we missed about our homeland.

"Pop-Tarts," I sigh.

"Antiperspirant," she coos.

"Squeeze cheese."

"Jon Stewart."

We look at each other wistfully and say, in unison, "Mexicans!"

"You know what?" Rachel starts, sheepishly. "I'm embarrassed to admit it, but I really miss *Survivor*."

"Oh, Rachel," I respond, shaking my head with profound disappointment.

I've always considered myself free of certain curious traits shared by a good number of my fellow Americans: a high tolerance threshold for precocious children in television commercials, sitcoms, and movies; the biological need to wear baseball hats; the tendency to order sandwiches bigger than one's head—these kinds of things. And I know for a fact that the same would be true of the need to see people fighting tooth and nail, embarrassing themselves, putting their lives in danger, and offing each other one by one on prime time.

It's not that the idea of people flung together on television to make each other's lives miserable doesn't appeal to me. Of course it does. I am human, after all. Humiliation television is a staple of Japanese TV, and I've enjoyed watching some of the late-night shows that deal with this very issue. I can't really understand what's going on, but I'm able to catch on with the help of Akiko, my roommate and interpreter. One of the best I've seen gathers together a different group of four or five up-and-coming female teen "idols" every week—always cute models or pop stars—and makes them choose who among them is a) the bitchiest, b) the least talented, c) the ugliest, and d) the stupidest. The announcer reads the results of each vote, people cheer, and the camera zooms in on the unfortunate winner, who does her best to save face and laugh it off, bowing her head repeatedly.

"She just voted ugliest girl," Akiko would explain, completely straight-faced.

One time there was one girl who won all four. All four. Yet when the camera zoomed in on her face, she may as well have just been told she would have to wait thirty minutes for a table by the window. She nodded, looked a little disappointed, and quietly waited for the camera to leave her the fuck alone. Then she probably went home and threw herself belly-first onto her pink sword with the satin trimming on the sheath.

I guess the reason I enjoy watching the Japanese get up to all this foolishness is because they're generally so pathologically shy, their reactions to such awful circumstances as being hung upside down by their toenails and whipped with udon noodles or forced to mud-wrestle a businessman who happens to be wearing only Speedos and a wristwatch make for compelling viewing. The contestants, who often appear to have found themselves on television by accident, nod answers to questions and explain slowly and thoughtfully their feelings about what has happened to them as the sadistic laughter of the audience and panel of hosts roll in. Americans, on the other hand, believe in the manifest destiny of stardom. We'll do shocking things to get noticed, we relish the spotlight we're given, and we don't really know when to shut up once we have it. We love to talk about absolutely nothing important and to cry while doing so. We enjoy the attention way too much. The Japanese just seem to endure it.

"Oh, please, don't be such a snob," Rachel chides. "It's really cool and totally addictive. It's like a drug, I swear, especially when you have a tape and you can watch them all back-to-back."

The two magic words: addictive, drug.

"Oh my God, you have a tape?!" I shout, tapping my arm, looking for a vein.

She reaches into the cupboard under her television and pulls out an old-school videocassette labeled on the side, "Survivor Season 1: Chronic." She hands it to me, and I can feel myself already surrendering to its sweet, sweet oblivion.

You see, I know my tendency to get sucked in by appalling television shows. I get my emotions tangled in their ridiculously threaded and highly unlikely plotlines and find it impossible to tear myself away. I watched one Friday episode of *General Hospital* when I was thirteen and ended up addicted for three years. I take the videotape home to Koenji and slide it into the VCR.

Though I try to keep an emotional distance from the proceedings, it's not easy, what with my attachments and aversions to certain people quickly forming and the hand-wringing uncertainty of the outcome. It's frightening, but I quickly find myself seduced by the show. All my previous dismissals of it fade more and more with each new immunity challenge. I am an expatriate obsessed. And I am able to indulge my obsession uninterrupted, for I have the entire series on video, from start to finish. No commercial breaks, no waiting long weeks to find out who will be the next to be crushed under the weight of all the backstabbing, allegiance switching, and general inhumanity. It all happens in an action-packed, two-day holiday from work. By the end of the videotape, my eyes are swollen and blood-red, my mouth is covered with potato chip crumbs, I'm inadvertently blowing drool bubbles when I exhale, and I've lost the ability to move my toes. I stumble bleary-eyed out into the kitchen and out the front door. I don't know where I am or how I got here. I catch a reflection of myself in the neighbor's kitchen window. Wow, I look horrible. Like a ninety-year-old woman. Then I realize it is a ninety-year-old woman I'm staring at. Grumpy old Miss Ueno, doing dishes, gazing out the window, and giving me her obligatory daily look of suspicion and disapproval. I wave to her and quietly vote her off the island.

"I need the next tape!" I say to Rachel calmly. "Give it to me! Where is it?!"

"I knew you'd love it," Rachel sings.

"I don't just love it. I *need* it. Please tell me you have another season on video."

She doesn't. I gasp.

"You know what, though?" she offers. "Just watch the same season again. It's really fun because you know when everyone's going to be kicked off and you can look forward to it."

So, like any junkie, I go back for sloppy seconds.

I again watch the episodes straight through in a marathon effort that tests nothing more than my ability to sit down for long stretches of time. But it is only in the following weeks that I realize the huge impact that *Survivor* has made on my life.

The world around me has become my own personal tribal council. I am now fixated on the idea of voting people who are in some way undesirable out of my life. On the train late on a Saturday night, sitting next to a drunken salaryman keeling over into the about-to-throw-up position, I find myself looking around to see who might be encouraged to join in an alliance with me to get him voted off the train.

Or standing in line at the invariably long lunch-hour ATM line at the bank, the machines already occupied by customers engaged in every form of banking transaction possible by machine in Japan—withdrawals, bankbook updates, transfers, deposits, movie tickets, laundry, pap smears, and so forth—all taking up precious time. "The tribe has spoken," I grumble to myself, gazing at the tiny lady who shows no signs of giving up her position at the machine.

And of course in class, on those days when a student—for example a young female university student named Noriko, eyelashes curled, lip gloss immaculately applied, mobile phone ringing repeatedly—is too scared to speak to me, too embarrassed to speak to her partner, yet too dedicated to say "screw English" and walk out, I relish the idea of being able to just close my eyes, cast a vote in my head, and exterminate the weakest link from the room.

Soon I start to think about the English teachers here at Lane and how the *Survivor* rules could be applied to us. If for some reason we were forced to vote other teachers out of the school, who would be the ultimate survivor?

"It would totally be me," my roommate Eric says without a moment's hesitation. I admire his self-assurance, but I smile at the thought of voting him off at the tribal council just to thwart his plan and take him down a few pegs. To the camera, I'd say, "Eric, you're a good guy and a great roommate, and I love listening to you and your boyfriend have sex upstairs, but your overconfidence is a real drag." This all given I haven't been voted off yet.

"'Twouldn't be me," Will from South Africa imagines aloud. "Jdddiengkcmd wowiuet cuirtios oourdke todlsh mwlekeri, and dkeiwpo wojdap wieorot woeikd ih sowheiwo rowierhs." I'm not sure what reason he's giving, but I tend to think it has something to do with the fact that no one can ever understand a goddamn word he is saying. Ever. No, it 'twouldn't.

So who would it be? Definitely not Brodie and his mullet. No reasonable teacher would allow that hairstyle to survive and prosper at this school. And what about everyone's favorite ex-military man McD? He has the deltoids and abs to survive in the real *Survivor*, certainly. But that will get you nowhere here. Recently he put a sign on his shelf reading, "THE STUFF ON THIS SHELF IS NOT PUBLIC PROPERTY. HANDS OFF," which I think somehow alienated the majority of the other teachers. It was completely unnecessary, since none of us want his Listerine, razors, cologne, or collection of muscle tees, and we definitely aren't interested in pilfering his lesson plans, which we imagine contain multiple-choice exercises like:

Please write the correct choice on the line. If you circle the answer and don't write it on the line, the answer is wrong. Sorry. I can't help you if you don't follow directions. Pay attention next time.

1) McD gave his girl a dozen roses and took her out to Applebee's _____(to celebrate/for celebrating) their one-week anniversary.
2) McD beat up the guys trying to scam on his girl _____ (with/by) his bare hands.

I'll hazard a guess that he and his shelf would be two of the first to go, though the shelf might last longer depending on how badly we needed to shave.

And how about yours truly? How long would I last in this game?

"We'd get voted off at the same time," Rachel says with absolute certainty. "Everyone would write both our names on that little paper with exclamation marks after them once they got sick of hearing us talk about stupid shit. We don't have any other role here. We have nothing else to contribute."

I think back to the last few no-doubt very loud conversations Rachel and I had in the teachers' room. Let's see, we covered 1) the screw-ability of Japanese heartthrob Masaya Kato (extreme), 2) the lameness of the sandwich choices at the Daily Yamazaki convenience store (potatoes on white bread is not nearly as good as it sounds), and 3) how Madonna rates as a lyricist (verdict: not great but better than Björk). Yeah, I'd vote us off, too.

My *Survivor* obsession begins to subside a bit, and I try and return to some semblance of a normal life—the carefree life I had before that odious videotape—until I'm shaken back into survival mode after a curious twist of fate at our busy conversation school.

PLI and Wyndam, the two companies that until recently co-owned Lane Language School, are constantly at odds with each other, the former being PR-based and the latter concentrated on curriculum development. It is a marriage made in hell. As teachers, we are actually contracted to and paid by Wyndam, but this is all about to change. The two companies are dissolving their partnership, and PLI will take over the entire school. For most of us teachers, this is not good news. Why? The PR people.

The job of the PR people is to bring prospective students into the school, show (sometimes drag) them around, and convince them that really expensive English lessons are just what they need. During their tour of the school, the PR person will joyfully tell them as many lies about the greatness of the school as they can fit into thirty minutes. To a young, homely male college student—"Most guys your age usually find girlfriends here." To an elderly, blue-haired obaasan—"Do you like my Japanese? I learned it using this school's method." (Our school doesn't teach Japanese.) Lies, lies, lies. And then they come to us and ask us to do a "level check" on the student, hoping we don't manage to ruin the momentum they've got going and scare him or her away with our loud Western speech and pronounced gestures.

The PR people are an enigma, and they wear very strong cologne. They're kind of like "the TV people" that Carol Ann is so spooked by in *Poltergeist*: disruptive, creepy to be around (as salespeople usually are), and possessed of evil clown faces. They also never take on the same form twice, and the smile you saw yesterday may turn into something much scarier if you don't watch yourself. So we're less than thrilled that they will now be overseeing every aspect of the school, lording it over us with what we can only assume will be a firm hand, a steady grip, and, perhaps, a swimming pool full of dead bodies.

But the real poignant moment comes when we're told via office memo that as a result of the switchover in ownership, the Ginza school will close and the entire Lane School will become concentrated on the two floors we now occupy in Shinjuku. Which means that some of Lane's one hundred teachers will be let go.

Upon hearing the news, each of us feels a surge of vulnerability course through our bodies.

"Oh shit, if I lose a job as a freaking English teacher in Japan, I'm going to gouge my eyes out," Rachel said. And I must say I am right there with her. It's about as hard to get fired from a teaching job in Japan as it is to be mistaken for a native Japanese. As my former employer so clearly demonstrated, some schools seem to import village idiots from across the English-speaking world to come and try their luck teaching in this fair country. As a result, some poor Japanese folks are probably walking around saying things like "Jerry, he a lazy, good-for-nothing mama's boy and he deserve what he get. I'm *glad* I fucked his cousin!" So what does it say about one if one is actually sacked from the easiest job to get in the country?

I shift immediately back into *Survivor* mode, making a mental list of all of those who are more likely to get the sack than I am. The word on the street is that there are certain teachers who have numerous complaints in their file already: Fran, who is always putting his name and phone number on the board at the beginning of every class and has been heard encouraging a few unimpressionable young girls to use it; Brad, who has offended a few with his chronic sweating problem; and of course Will, whose file allegedly overflows with accounts of students unable to follow anything he said in any of his classes, ever, in his history as an instructor. And this is only what Tami knows. Rachel is bound to know more.

"So Rachel, what's the story? Who's gonna get the axe? Give me the lowdown, the 411, the in-fo-ma-shun."

"Well, I don't know. I've heard a few rumors about Fran, Brad, and Will, but not much else."

Drat. The one person I thought I could count on to have her finger on the pulse is no more clued-in than I.

Work becomes a little unsteady. It's kind of a dramatic time, each of us teaching our classes as if in a matter of weeks we will be peddling English lessons door to door. All of a sudden, our lives have turned into *Survivor: Tokyo Smackdown*. Will we start engaging in sabotage against each other, planting incriminating evidence in each other's classrooms? Will I walk into a class one day soon and find that my students have already been given a handout with a paragraph at the top detailing the order in which I'd like to see them naked and the reasons why followed by a fill-in-the-blank exercise at the bottom? Will I retaliate against this unknown trickster by replacing all of his or her worksheets for students with a positive chlamydia test result made using the Roppongi Hills Clinic letterhead? Will embarrassing dirty laundry start being aired, like what so-and-so did with a student in the restroom of the club the other night that's not really true but would really make tongues wag if announced in the lobby where everyone can hear it? Will friend turn against friend and colleague against colleague in a ruthless race to see who will be the ultimate sensei? Sounds fun.

Unfortunately, some folks have already decided they're not up for this kind of cutthroat competition. They are happy to pack it in, to give up like a bunch of gutless Democrats. Pam takes this company upheaval as a sign that she should move herself, her Japanese husband, and her little girl back to mighty Canada.

"We went home last summer and visited my sister, her husband, and their two children. Their combined income is just a little more than ours and they have a house in Vancouver that's so big they have rooms that don't get used for *weeks*."

"But Pam," I say, "don't you want to see who gets taken down in all this? Aren't you the least bit curious to see how popular a teacher you really a—"

"They also have a sailboat and a little getaway cabin on the Puget Sound!"

"Wow, that's pretty cool, Pa—"

"And they have a nanny helping her with the kids. A nanny, for God's sake!"

"But, Pam, your students need you!"

"Oh, fuck the students! All we have to show for our income here is a two-bedroom place two hours outside of Tokyo and my daughter's print club collection! It's time to move!"

A few other craven souls have the same idea. At least three other teachers are packing up their Japanese spouses and getting the hell out of Dodge. Greg is going back to Detroit, Lyle is moving to LA, and Rich is returning to Australia to buy a house and settle down and marry his girlfriend. It is a time of soul-searching and uncovering what one really wants out of life. Pfft. Obviously some people would rather leave and do something substantial and rewarding with their lives than stay and play *Tokyo Smackdown* for a prize they're not sure they even want anymore. Pussies.

The number of teachers is already dwindling, and nobody has even gotten fired yet. Thankfully, there's a good number of us who have decided to stay and fight. Or at least stay and keep teaching until we get the axe, at which point we will beg on our knees for our jobs back. None of us is foolish enough to think that we're in the clear. After all, we really have no idea what the students say about us. I assume I'm a well-liked teacher, but who's to say I don't have a long list of complaints from students offended by my statuesque frame, undeniable and distracting sex appeal, intimidating intellect, impeccable taste in music and hair products, and enviable sock collection? The drama of knowing that not one of us is safe is absolutely delicious.

Of course, the big talk around the shop is about the prize that will be bestowed upon the chosen ones, namely, what kind of compensation we'll get from Wyndam for breaking contract with us, because essentially they're firing us and another company is hiring us. There have been whispers about three months' salary, the prospect of which makes me weak in the knees. That sweet cash could completely clear me of all my debt and also pay for something new and completely unnecessary, like that giant, gold-flecked piggy bank I've had my eye on at that shop on Omotesando Dori in Harajuku.

"Oooh! I could also get that five-foot statue of that drag-queen Buddha for my room!" I think as I Photoshop a picture of McD from the Christmas party to make it look like he's lifting the skirt of one of our elderly students, a picture I plan to leave on the floor of the lobby.

The whole takeover thing takes on a new light. For those who survive the downsizing, it's beginning to look like getting fired will be the best thing that's happened to us since all that high school graduation money. We'll be paid for doing absolutely nothing, an idea that has always appealed to me but never seemed all that realistic.

School spirit lifts. We begin teaching our classes with enthusiasm and verve once again, knowing that in a few short weeks we could be going shopping.

Finally, after weeks and weeks of hand-wringing, the decision is handed down. The tribe has spoken, and sure enough, Fran, Brad, and Will have been unanimously voted off by the new management. And there's one surprise. Keith Brady—cute, sweet, cuddly little Keith; gentle, soft-spoken, sensitive little Keith, and, at five feet two inches and 130 pounds, just plain *little* Keith—has also gotten the can. Apparently little Keith had a little problem with sleeping with almost every little student under the age of eighteen (the age of consent in Japan is sixteen) and then never speaking to them again, even in class. Little Keith was a little pig.

The remaining teachers will be paid in full next month, and there will be much celebration all over the greater Tokyo area. We have indeed been the ultimate survivors, and we haven't had to eat cow brain, sleep in the rain, or wipe our asses with leaves. And though I would have preferred to watch my colleagues engage in a little more backstabbing and shit throwing, you can't have everything in this world.

I may not be the ultimate survivor, but I did survive, even if ultimately I'm not sure how badly I really wanted to. But the bottom line is this: I survived, and I have a giant tranny Buddha with a gold-flecked piggy on a leash standing in the corner of my bedroom to show for it.

But will I survive the PR people?

of "X-large" T-shirts bought that cut off blood
circulation to wrists and hands: 4
# of kanji characters studied: 120
# of kanji characters forgotten: 104

CHAPTER TWELVE

Gay Agenda

A deeply personal chapter about the transcendental
pleasures of artfully drawn dirty pictures.

Being in this country what the French call a *homosexuel* is an
interesting study in comparative queerness. I've always had
trouble in my day-to-day life deciding if a certain gentleman on
the train or in the noodle bar might have un-Christian desires
toward his fellow man. Not least because Japanese men, with
their prominent cheekbones, narrow noses, tailored suits, impeccably moussed hair, and spot-on fashion sense, are often prettier
than their female counterparts. I've always had incredibly faulty
and unreliable gaydar, and to complicate matters, since I've been
in this country I've had to adjust its settings to allow for straight
men who check themselves in pocket mirrors on trains or pluck
their eyebrows in the locker room.

Like almost every other aspect of life in this country, the
"gay" thing isn't easy to get to the, er, bottom of. There is no big
dramatic coming out for the vast majority of Japanese gay people.

Newly out of the closet queers don't all of a sudden start wearing T-shirts that say, "Nobody knows I'm gay" or "I'm not gay, but my boyfriend is," prancing around in pride rainbow colors and tight Lycra shirts, and forcing their same-sex lovers on their families at holidays.

Coming to terms with one's homosexuality is a much more low-key and much less public affair. None of the gay guys I know in Japan have told their parents about their gayness, and none have plans to. I think this is a tragedy. If gay men in civilized countries have only one right to speak of (having relinquished all hope of ever having biological children, getting into a decent fistfight, or being tough on defense), it is the right to make a big cathartic announcement at an inopportune (preferably public) moment and force their friends and family to visualize them (1) engaging in sodomy and (2) marching half-naked in a parade. If a gay man has that right taken away, what on earth does he have?

Gay Japanese men who wish to maintain relations with their families will largely live as bachelors for the rest of their lives, and though their families will probably eventually figure it out from their love of shlocky pop radio, their coterie of hopelessly platonic female friends, and their love of gladiator movies, nothing will ever be said.

(Also, much to my displeasure, I've yet to meet a Japanese lesbian. Where are they hiding? How do they dress themselves, and more to the point, how do they style their hair?)

I ask my friend Shunsuke, who has a close relationship with his mother and brother (his father left when he was young), if he will ever high-kick his way out of those familial closet doors.

"My family have no doubt who I am," he says.

"Oh, really? They know?"

"No, they always ask when I to get married."

I exclaim that surely they realize that something is different about him. Like that he's never had a girlfriend and always matches the color of his handbag with the color of his socks. Also, that he carries a handbag.

"Yes, but they no think about it. My grandmom don't think gay people exist."

"If you are different from the others in Japan, it is a really big burden on your life," another gay friend Takahiro tells me. Taka's reliably negative view of his countrymen never fails to make me feel happy not to be Japanese. "For many people, still, it is not really understandable that there are Japanese people who are gay. It would be much easier for Japanese people to accept and understand that you, Tim-san, are gay. Because, you know, you are weird anyway."

Interesting. "Weird meaning non-Japanese, right?" I ask as Taka looks at me with furrowed brows and gives the typical Japanese response when the answer is no: "Mmmm…maybe."

I get his point, though. It is much easier for me, a weird gaijin from another planet, to get away with being gay. We're expected to be strange. It's part of our culture. We also wear our shoes indoors and happily bathe in the same room we take dumps. It is much harder for a homegrown Japanese to get away with it. Unless, as Shunsuke points out, he works in the fashion industry.

"My mom think all gay people work in fashion. I no work in fashion. So, of course, I not gay."

Once, a few weeks after I'd moved to Tokyo, I was on the train riding home to Koenji from Shinjuku. I was tired, and like everyone around me on the train, my eyes were rolling around beneath sinking eyelids and my head was beginning to bob and sink into the familiar sleeping-while-sitting-up position.

I woke myself up snoring, looked around to make sure nobody had noticed, and then decided to take out my book, which happened to be Haruki Murakami's *Underground*, the uplifting and life-affirming story of the Tokyo sarin gas attack of 1996. I hadn't been reading for long when I detected eyes on me. This is of course not unusual. With the number of pairs of eyeballs in this city, a few are bound to land on you and perhaps linger for a moment at some point, especially if your eyes are a piercing baby-blue like mine. I looked up and noticed that the eyeballs belonged to a young man sitting directly opposite me. He looked to be in his early twenties and was wearing a brown zip-up sweater, blue jeans, silver laceless sneakers, and on his head one of those trendy knitted hats that fit squarely on the head like an oversized yarmulke. He gazed at me nervously and darted his eyes around the carriage as if checking up on the other passengers.

I looked around the train also, fearing that he had heard me snoring and that perhaps I'd caused a disturbance in the carriage. I looked straight ahead again and our eyes met. He then winked his left eye as fast as the wing flap of a hummingbird—so fast that I couldn't be sure it was a wink and not simply a nervous twitch—and once again darted his eyes in a different direction.

Am I being wooed? I wondered. What an interesting way of going about it. Normally in this situation I would prefer a potential suitor to smile at me handsomely and ask, "Is that a good book?" "Gosh, those are cool pants, where'd you get 'em?" or "I can kiss my own butt, how about you?" How would he have me answer this wink?

And was it actually a wink? God knows I've made horrible mistakes before when faced with an ambiguous gesture from an attractive male. Like the time in college when I was reading on a sofa in the library and became convinced that the frat boy making friendly faces and eyebrow wiggles at me was going to up and leave the girl he was sitting with, come over to me, and either propose or ask me to join him in the bathroom. (Turns out he was making those faces at someone sitting at a table behind me.) As is so often the case, I couldn't be sure if this guy was flirting with me or simply having a spasm. I gave an uncomfortable and silent laugh in answer, his eyes dropped to the floor, and he scampered off the train at the next station, no doubt filled with shame for himself, his family, and his ancestral lineage.

So it *wasn't* a spasm!

It makes cultural sense that homosexuality is not the most comfortable of subjects for the Japanese public to confront. There is a definite history of hot man-on-man action amongst the samurais of the Shogun era. But those times are long gone and do not really gel with life in modern Japan, with its belief in the importance of homogeneity, its dwindling birth rate, its aging population, and its preoccupation with safeguarding oneself and one's family from any kind of public shame, like the kind that comes of being caught dancing to house music in a muscle-T at the club and singing into a hairbrush in one's bedroom.

Overall, gay culture in Tokyo holds few surprises for anyone familiar with gay culture anywhere else. The gay district is called Ni Chome—"Second Street"—and is famous for being the best place in the city for a horny businessman to go to give and/or get a blowjob. Most places I've been to, like GB—the most popular bar for gay gaijin and the men who love them—really seem indistinguishable from any other big city gay place. Lots of useless diva dance music and power balladeering on the speakers, sinfully tight T-shirts on the bodies, and the smell of overpriced cologne mixed with cigarette smoke on every floating molecule of air. I don't know exactly what I was hoping for, but I guess I wanted Japanese gay bars to offer something that I'd never before thought possible. I've always been frustrated with the mind-numbing predictability of the gay scene in general. The Japanese always take things and tweak them until they're just weird enough. The mind boggles at what they could do with gay culture, already weird by definition. Like, instead of the obligatory gay uniform being tank tops and tight jeans, wouldn't it be fun if it was hula-hoops and little pup tents? Or see-through kimono and banana hats? Fun, right?

But just when I'd written Japan off as having nothing new and jaw-dropping to contribute to Gay World, what should I come upon while browsing around a manga café one day but a certain genre of Japanese comic books that deals very openly and—to my infinite delight—graphically with the subject of love between men. Even more shocking is the fact that these comics are not written by gay men for gay men. No, gaywad, they are written by women for a target audience of teenage girls.

Manga comics are to the Japanese public what sitcoms, police dramas, and *Dateline* are to the American public. Here, comics are not just for thirty-five-year-old men who still live with their mothers and blush when asked about having a girlfriend. Comics are for everyone. They are an essential piece of contemporary Japanese popular art, as important if not more important than movies and television. There are comics for teenage boys, which includes stories on subjects such as sports, delinquent high school students (who invariably hang out with doe-eyed schoolgirls who can't think of a good reason to keep their clothes on for more than a few pages at a time), the occult, martial arts, and motorcycle gangs; comics for adult males that offer stories involving hired assassins, samurai, big-breasted stewardesses, hapless office workers, and war; comics for adult women with lots of romance and period pieces; and those for young girls featuring schoolkids solving mysteries, grappling with the supernatural, and flirting and falling in love. But curiously, a growing number of young girls, who range in age from preteen to late twenties, wish to read stories from a genre of comics called yaoi, tales filled to the brim with the high drama and star-crossed romance that is best portrayed and appreciated when presented in the form of a gay male love affair.

I never would have thought I could have so much in common with thirteen-year-old Japanese girls, but the world is a very strange place, and I guess it just goes to show that there are indeed some needs that span cultures, genders, and generations. One of those, apparently, is the need to see and read about wispy, beautiful men with impossible cheekbones falling in love and passionately screwing around with other wispy, beautiful men with impossible cheekbones.

This is not simply animated gay porn. It's more like an animated, all-male *The Young and the Restless*. Characters are developed and emotional, and often fatal conflicts are introduced. And the men's bone structure, hair color, and wardrobe are infinitely more important than their equipment below the belt. These men are beautiful, their physiques patently unattainable. Broad shoulders, tiny waists, faces so angular they're in danger of cutting themselves every time they swish their hands upwards to move their golden/purple/silver/magenta locks out of their eyes, all to achieve the perfect pose of pensive angst.

And these guys like to mess around. It could be a tormented university student lying with his equally tortured history professor, or a profoundly unhappy young banker making it with his best friend's brother, but no matter the pairing, the sex is going to be dramatic, ecstatic, and often. The drama inherent in storylines involving men expressing their long-repressed desire for each other is the attraction for the girls, it seems. These stories offer for their female audience the ultimate tales of forbidden love. It's Romeo and Romeo. And Juliet gets to watch.

Needless to say, I have now developed a mild obsession with these comics. And I'm hell-bent on learning more, to the point where when a young female student says in class that she loves comics, I wonder if there's an appropriate way to ask her if she enjoys stories involving two guys getting it on, and if so, what the turn-on is, which positions she really likes to see them in, and by the way, can she recommend some good titles because I have a friend who's interested.

When I first discovered yaoi comics at a manga reading room in Shinjuku, I pulled a few dozen off the bookshelf, retreated to a remote corner of the café, and thumbed through them greedily. Of course, I couldn't understand what I was reading, but the pictures did help fill in quite a few gaps, if you know what I mean. Here are two college friends sucking face and getting to third base in their university library. And here is a mob boss giving one of his young charges an offer he obviously can't refuse. Oh, and here are two long-haired warriors taking a break from all the chaos on the battlefield to vanquish each other in a cave. And they just happened to bring along their leather harnesses and candle wax. Great!

I emerged a few hours later bleary-eyed and thinking I really could have used those comics when I was thirteen.

In my research on the topic, I've discovered that the word *yaoi* is actually an acronym in Japanese meaning "no climax, no purpose, no solutions," which is kind of a creed for the genre. A gay agenda of sorts. And though the appeal of such nihilistically themed stories does have its limits (many of them end with some sort of self-mutilation or terrible tragedy) and somewhat offends my American need for some type of reasonably workable resolution, any comic book series that offers spectacular scenes of wild, passionate, and otherworldly homo-sex is worth a second look in my book.

I now look at all the young ladies around me—in my classrooms, on the train, at the makeup counter—in a very different light. Are these girls, beneath their cotton tops and cardigans, behind their cherubic, innocent, immaculately painted faces, just mad for a peek at a lusty all-male hump-a-thon? Do they long to be a fly on the wall in the men's locker room? Do they lose sleep palpitating over the divine clash of lips, cheekbones, and sinewy male flesh that fill the scenes in their precious comic books?

Your typical Japanese Joe finds it difficult to say the word "gay" without giggling, as if by uttering it he is professing to believe in mermaids. I sit on the train again and watch four young inebriated professional men stumble onto the train. They are impeccably put together, their skin polished to a fine shine, their hair sculpted in tight waves, their tailored suits pressed, their rock-solid masculinity melted by alcohol into a fluid and suggestible ambivalence. I look at the ringleader of the pack, the loudest one to whom the others obviously defer. He rubs his face languorously with his perfectly moisturized fingers, stands with his legs far apart and his crotch tilted out. He is telling a story and repeatedly putting his arm around his drunken colleague next to him to stabilize himself as he sways back and forth. I wonder if he realizes how often the young girls on the train gaze at him as he banters with his be-suited colleagues—joking, laughing, snorting, back-slapping—and how more than a few of these girls really wish that the guys would just shut up, unbutton their tailored shirts to the navels, whisk their hair out of their eyes, and start making out.

I know I do.

 # times used Japanese-style squatting public toilet: 1
 # times used Japanese-style squatting public toilet backwards: 1
 # times wished to God Japanese
public toilet offered toilet paper: 1

CHAPTER THIRTEEN

Jim-zilla Attacks!

In which the resilient city of Tokyo is once again under siege
and the city's citizens must run for their lives from a giant
foreign monster who has brought his own eating utensils.

"Just don't forget," Jimmy coos over the phone as we discuss the
details of his upcoming trip to Tokyo on my dime. "You owe
me."

Normally that is no way to talk to someone who's just spent
over a thousand dollars on a plane ticket for you, but I can't deny
he has a point. I've been away for over a year now in one of the
world's most neon cities while he's been back in sepia-toned
Raleigh living the life of a starving artist, dealing with a cocaine-
obsessed roommate, and constantly fielding questions about me
from friends that he has trouble answering, like, "How's Tim
doing?" and "Is he ever coming home?" and "When is that cheap
fucker gonna fly you over there?"

I do owe him. He's been very accommodating of my oat-
sowing. He deserves a vacation, and he's going to get it. There

will be temples, there will be shrines, there will be many, many Japanese pancakes.

"I know, I know. Listen, you're coming, and we're going to have a blast. I'm so excited!"

"No you're not," he deadpans.

"Yes I am!"

"Whatever. Anyway, is there anything I can bring? Do you need deodorant or magazines or anything?"

"Yeah, can you bring me a Cajun chicken biscuit from Bojangles? And some of the spicy fries? Oh, and some Pillsbury strawberry cake icing?"

"Sure."

I can't wait to see him holding that sweet, sweet pink frosting.

I remember fondly our last night together, the night before I left Raleigh. We'd gone for a romantic dinner at the Waffle House, the one downtown on Hillsborough Street where people go to get shot. We sat, ordered our burgers, and then I had a nervous breakdown. Have you ever cried and eaten greasy hash browns at the same time? If you ever plan to, bring extra napkins.

But though I was seriously losing my shit, my brain aflame with last-minute panic, Jimmy was holding up pretty well. When we first got together two years before, he quickly figured out that I had a bit of wanderlust in me that would eventually need to come out. (I think it might have become evident when I said, on the morning after our first night together, "I hate this fucking town; God, I can't think of anything worse than staying here for the rest of my life!") An army brat, he'd had his share of moving around the world, uprooting his life every few years, and was now completely uninterested in pulling up stakes again. Like me, he was desperately poor with no health insurance, but he liked being in one place. He was working on his art and enjoying his new job at a frame shop. Leaving Raleigh made no sense for him. So he'd resigned himself to the idea of my leaving. But because we'd drifted so effortlessly into each other's lives, we both knew we wanted to stay together through my Tokyo jaunt.

So there we sat at the Waffle House, two years down the road, and I was leaving the next day. I don't think either of us was convinced that it was realistic to try to maintain a long-distance relationship since I'd be gone for over a year. But that night we vowed to try. With the help of regular phone calls and some good porn.

As I sat sobbing and causing a scene like a toddler who hadn't had his nap, a group of painfully upbeat teenagers in hipster garb walked in, sat down, and then one of them, presumably their leader, headed to the jukebox.

"Oh my God, Jimmy, if that skinny bitch puts on the 'Waffle House Song' I'll just die!" I blubbered.

"I'll slap her. Are you gonna eat your pickles?" Jimmy said, comforting me.

"Nmph. Tkmh," I said, my mouth full of mucus, soggy red eyes bulging. I hadn't touched my cheeseburger. He'd cleaned his entire plate.

There was an understanding here. He was being strong for both of us. He was holding it together because he knew I couldn't. My system was too overwhelmed. And though his was too, he'd decided to take the reins and not allow us to sink into maudlin dramatics.

"You need to wipe your nose...God, get a napkin or something," he said, laughing. His emotional bravery was heartbreaking.

The waitress arrived with our extra order of scattered, smothered, and covered hash browns. No doubt she cast her sympathetic eyes over us as we struggled to keep it together, our last night together, our farewell banquet of grease and butter.

"I'm gonna enter some stuff into the New American Paintings contest next month," he said, trying to remain strong.

A fresh harvest of silent tears burst from my exhausted eyes. I began to make embarrassing noises when I inhaled.

Jimmy let my tears run their course, deciding at this point that silence was probably golden.

"Your burger's getting cold."

A few oceans of tears and mucus later, hunger finally gripped me and I downed the thing in three bites. As I chomped, he sat staring at me, his gaze a mixture of love, irritation, and acid reflux.

When Jimmy and I got together, we had both pretty much given up on finding a guy to spend our lives with who wasn't a complete disappointment. We'd both been around the block several times. Jimmy came out when he was fourteen and was promptly sent off to a mental institution by his loving, hysterical mother who makes Piper Laurie from *Carrie* look like Barbara Billingsley; he then developed into a serial monogamist, having one unfulfilling long-term relationship after another. And me? I'd been around the block more in the sexual sense. (Is it considered a one-night stand if they kick you out of their bed before day-break?) By the time our paths crossed, we pretty much immediately realized we were two potential peas in a pod: we shared a mutual love for *Purple Rain*–era Prince, tuna noodle casserole, Gore Vidal's bitchy smugness, and Pedro Almodóvar's use of primary colors and trannies.

Even better, we hated many of the same things (giant poodles and local gay bars being the first two among many). When I was able to convince Jimmy that Siouxsie Sioux could wipe the floor with Grace Jones if the two were ever to come to blows, our relationship was taken to the next level. I had a feeling it was true love when Jimmy, describing Alanis Morrissette as she performed on *Letterman*, uttered under his breath one of the finest and most apt similes I'd ever heard: "Plain as homemade soap." And I knew I'd found the man I'd spend the rest of my life with when he smacked me in the face with his dick one morning—not as an overture for sex but just to say "good morning" as he was leaving the bedroom to make coffee.

Always a man of very few words and an effortlessly agitated artistic temperament, Jimmy, when he does speak, tends to create the wrong impression when he meets new people. He just doesn't try that hard to make people like him. Not because he's an asshole; he just doesn't think about it. He once told my friend Dani that her quiche was "delicious, almost as good as mine." He complimented a friend's band one time by saying they "sounded so much better than the last time I saw you guys." And when he first started coming to family dinners at my parents' house, he would sit quietly and respectfully through dinner and then as soon as he was finished, he'd get up, wash his plate, put it in the dishwasher, and then plop himself on the living room sofa with my parents' *Parade* magazine before anyone realized he'd left the table.

"They have lots of good drugs—you know, medicines—for depression now," an aunt visiting from California who came to one of these dinners once said. She was convinced Jimmy was clinically depressed. But she'd never had the opportunity to see how his face lit up when talking about Almodóvar's *Women on the Verge of a Nervous Breakdown* or *Law of Desire*. She'd not witnessed him singing along to Prince's "Pussy Control" in our living room. She didn't know that sometimes he laughs and says the word "turd" in his sleep. He's not depressed. He's just artistic.

But I have to admit I'm worried. I've been away for a year, and while Jimmy's getting on with life at home, I'm living a completely separate life from him now, and it's a life I'm really enjoying. Worse still, I'm smitten. Yes, I've been seeing someone behind his back, and though I think he knows, I'm dreading the talk we're going to have to have about this third wheel. My new lover is complicated, schizophrenic, unwieldy, fast, and furious. In short, I'm in love with a crazy bitch named Tokyo. And she takes a back seat to nobody.

Over the past year during out periodic phone calls I've tried my best to convince Jimmy of my baby's otherworldly charms.

"I saw a bunch of young girls dressed up as Victorian England–era prostitutes in Harajuku today!" I'd say.

"Interesting," he'd reply after a long pause, during which he's sucking in a massive bonghit.

"Oh my God, I got groped by a gross old man in a rush-hour train in Shinjuku!" I'd beam.

"Uh-huh," he'd reply after drinking down a couple spoonfuls of NyQuil.

"Vitamin drinks in tiny cans are really popular here! I just drank three and chased them with vodka and then ate a big sushi!" I'd rave.

"Yeah, can you send me some money?" he'd respond. "I need paintbrushes."

Tokyo is a hard sell for Jimmy. At least on the phone. He's jealous of her. To him she's nothing more than a home-wrecker. A harlot, a vixen, a temptress in a foreign land with her restless arms all over his boyfriend. He knows that every day I'm walking her streets, slurping her noodles, shoving my big feet into her tiny bathroom slippers, pushing myself onto her trains, sliding in and out and in and out and in and out of her underground tunnels.

And yes, I am doing all of that. But when I get Jimmy over here, he'll do it too. And he'll love it. He'll fall for her just like I have.

Oh yes, it will be an epic, sexy, disgusting ménage à trois. Two charming men. One hot city.

I sit breathlessly at the arrivals gate at Narita Airport. After waiting for a while for him to deplane, I decide to go get some coffee from a nearby kiosk. After paying, I turn around, take a sip, and burn my lip, for down the ramp comes Jimmy, his shiny head sweating and shining like a beacon, his face a desperate shade of gray, his huge tote bag slipping slowly off his shoulder. He weaves in and out of the people in his way, and once he reaches the arrivals lobby, I rush up to greet him as he passes me by and walks out the automatic doors and into the fresh air, the first he's felt on his face in probably about seventeen hours.

"Jimmy!" I yelp as the doors open for me to exit. He finishes lighting his cigarette and looks at me with an exhausted smile. I give him a hug. He sure is clammy.

"Sorry. I really needed one."

"That's fine. How was your flight?"

He looks at me as if to say, "How do you *think* it was?" and then he takes a very long drag on his cigarette.

I start pinching his cheeks and lightly slapping them because that's one thing I do to show my affection. He rolls his eyes, exhales a bunch of smoke, smiles, and squeezes my butt, which is what he does to show his affection.

He finishes his cigarette, puts it out, and in full view of all the other desperate smokers standing outside with us, we engage in a proper public display of affection. (No tongue. We're not animals.)

"I'm really happy to see you," he says.

"It's great to see you too. I've missed you so mu—wait, did you bring me my Cajun chicken biscuit?" I ask.

"I brought two," he nods, his eyes brightening.

I grab and squeeze his hand. "I've missed you so much!"

We get on the train from Narita heading into the city. Since Narita is a town well outside the city limits of Tokyo proper, it's a long ride and gives us a chance to catch up and for Jimmy to see some of the Japanese countryside. As we chat, I can see that Jimmy's head is spinning as he gazes out the window at the landscape gliding past us.

"Them's *artistic* wheels be turnin'," I say to myself in my best North Carolina drawl as he sits quietly, his eyes passionately drinking in the view.

After a few minutes of silence, I ask him what he thinks of what he sees. He appears to have recovered somewhat from the twilight zone of the trans-Pacific flight and could very well be prepared to offer some solid criticism.

"Well," he begins, "the airport was, honestly, kind of plain. I was disappointed. Light yellow walls accented with blonde wood panels? Beige carpet? I expected better from Japan. And the place was way too well lit."

"Hmm. I suppose you make a good point," I chime in. "Although I didn't notice any of the stuff you just mentioned. The walls were yellow? Please continue."

"You've lost a lot of weight," he continues.

"Really? So have you!"

"Drugs and loneliness. But that shirt is way too tight. I'm surprised you can breathe in that thing."

"Jimmy, it's the biggest T-shirt I've been able to find here."

"You should have told me. I could have brought some. Anyway, you should probably throw that shirt away before you come home. It'll scare the cat."

"How is Stella?"

"She's been talking a whole bunch of shit about you."

"Really?"

"Yeah, she said you treat her like a redheaded bastard cat and you need to at least send her some Japanese catnip or something. She also called your momma a bitch. She's pretty pissed."

"Aw, bless her. So, have you got anything positive to say about your trip so far?"

"Actually, yes," he begins, looking out the window. "The quality of light is just brilliant, and the trees actually look exactly like they do in the Japanese watercolors I've seen."

"Good, good."

"And the way all these rice paddies and fields are laid out, it kind of reminds me of a painting Van Gogh did of the French countryside."

"I'm sure the French would slap in you in the face for saying that."

"Whatever. I'd slap them right back."

We get to my apartment in Koenji and unload all of Jimmy's stuff. Then we spend a manic ten minutes having gay sex and then we take a big gay nap. When I wake up, Jimmy's rifling through his bag searching for something.

"What're you looking for?" I ask, rubbing my eyes.

Jimmy pulls a fork out of a balled-up pair of socks. "Found it. Can we go eat?"

We eat at a local Yoshinoya restaurant, a cheap fast-food chain where the specialty is what is called "beef bowls"—thin slices of seasoned beef over rice. Jimmy cannot hide his enthusiasm for the ordering protocol, which involves very little human contact and admirable efficiency: you walk in, put your money into a machine, push a button, get a receipt, sit down at a semicircular counter, and hand the receipt to the enthusiastic worker behind the counter. Your beef bowl and miso soup will be with you in a matter of seconds.

"Is Jimmy impressed?" I ask as he digs in with his fork.

"Yes, he is. Pass me the ginger."

One point for my mistress Tokyo: she makes a quick, sensible, delicious meal.

After our late lunch we take the train to Shibuya because I want to show Jimmy Tokyo's crazy side, the side that cakes its face with panda makeup, bleaches it's hair until it looks like a pile of straw, and slips on its pencil skirt, rainbow knee-socks, and foot-high platform boots and thinks that's a perfectly reasonable state in which to face the world.

We exit Shibuya Station along with 2.3 million other people, 90 percent of whom are at least ten years younger than us. Shibuya is where the young people of the greater Tokyo area come to play videogames, smoke cigarettes, visit "love hotels," and, in a financial pinch, sell their underwear to appreciative and deep-pocketed salarymen. I ask Jimmy if he feels like doing any of these things.

"You know," I prod, "to try and fit in with everyone else."

"I might be willing to sell my underwear," he says after a minute of reflection, "but let's wait till Thursday and see how my money's holding out. I'd like to get a few more days' wear out of it."

"Gross."

As we pass under the three giant television screens the sole purpose of which appears to be to give the nation epilepsy, Jimmy breathlessly gasps, "It's like *Blade Runner*."

"Isn't it? Or at least *I, Robot*."

In Shibuya we do what the both of us were put on this earth to do: record shop. Tokyo has the best record shopping any indie pop-grime-jazz-krautrock-acid fusion-dream-pop-dub-trip-hop-afrobeat-grunge-eurotrash-neujazz-freakbeat-hip-hop-electro-glitchpop-freak folk-old school-electro-minimalist-reggae-dance-hall-girl group-lounge-punk-goth-new wave-house-new world-old world new world-shoegazer-noise pop-new wave revivalist-folk-electro-folk-rhythm and blues-Jpop-gospel-French pop-Bulgarian noise opera fanboy could hope for. That band from Perth from the eighties that only released one single but it's the best song you ever heard? It's here somewhere. And you know your friend who is in that god-awful band that somehow found the time in its busy schedule of totally sucking to put a CD together? Tokyo's got that CD. That song you've been kicking around in your head for a few years but have never committed to tape? Also here. And it's expensive.

We go to my favorite store, Disk Union, where the narrow aisles present a tough but rewarding challenge for any customer with a waist over thirty inches. We wade in and look around, twisting and angling our heads so as to read the titles and allow people by, but Jimmy ultimately succumbs to a crippling claustrophobia before even getting to the Momus and David Sylvian sections, and he takes his leave after just forty-five minutes of browsing. I reluctantly put back on the shelf a Madonna twelve-inch on skin-colored vinyl and follow him out.

"Well," I say, trying to assuage Jimmy's guilt over forcing us to leave the record store so prematurely, "there's a CD shop for big fatties just around the corner."

"Great, let's go there."

We browse in a few more spacious record stores, and Jimmy excitedly finds something. He gasps, holds it up, and walks determinedly toward me. I look at it and realize that this find is something that could mark a turning point in his trip: a Japan-only release of a best-of by Japanese electro pioneers Yellow Magic Orchestra.

"We wants it," he hisses in his best Gollum. "We neeeeeeeds it!" He nudges my shoulder over and over with his head.

"OK, but if I buy this for you, you have to use chopsticks at our next meal. And greet the waitress in Japanese."

"Whatever."

"And you have to eat whatever I put in front of you."

He considers this last point with a pensive and dreamy glare.

"OK," he finally agrees. "But don't get pissed if I puke in your lap."

We meet my friend Shunsuke and his friend Chieko for lunch at an izakaya in Shibuya. It doesn't take long for the two of them to start chatting like old friends, even though Jimmy keeps calling Shunsuke Shinjuku, as in:

"So, Shinjuku, how long have you lived in Tokyo?"

or

"Shinjuku, have you ever been to the U.S.?"

or

"So, Shinjuku, you like Celine Dion. Why is that?"

"Jimmy, his name is Shunsuke!" I finally correct him. "Shun-su-ke! Shunsuke."

"It OK," Shunsuke says, laughing. "I just make new name for Jimmy. I call him Miami. Is OK?"

"Sure," Jimmy says. "Better than Kernersville."

Our waitress arrives, breathless, stressed, and with no time for small talk. A perfect candidate for Jimmy to bludgeon with his newly acquired Japanese.

"Jimmy," I say, holding up the expensive CD I just bought him and nodding in the direction of the waitress.

"Cone nishy wa," he says with a big smile.

Shunsuke translates for her.

"こんにちはと言おうとした," he says. "He's trying to say hello."

She smiles, bows slightly, and says "sank yuu" to Jimmy. He looks at Shunsuke.

"Thanks, Shinjuku."

"You're welcome, Miami."

We order a number of small dishes to share, the way real Japanese folk do. I make sure that one of these dishes is the one on the menu that looks like a plate full of fried popcorn shrimp from Red Lobster. Jimmy loves popcorn shrimp, as do I. I've had this dish before, two weeks into my Japan odyssey, and it really altered my perception of what I can voluntarily put in my mouth, chew, and swallow. It was fried chicken gristle, and it felt like eating deep-fried knuckle. As an American Southerner, I stand firmly behind any food that is deep-fried. It's part of who I am. So even though I had a profound distrust of this new dish, I continued popping those little suckers into my mouth and negotiating them into my stomach. Ick. I couldn't stand it. But I ate more. So gross. Then I ate more. Revolting and unequivocally foul. I couldn't stop eating. Wanted more. What a horrid culinary delight! Disgustingly delicious! I finished the plate myself. No food had ever filled me with such a fervid ambivalence. I haven't tasted that crunchy gristle since, but I am dying to witness the awakening of Jimmy to its existence. He's a Southern boy too, born with a fried drumstick in his hand. I'm going to test his limits.

When the plate arrives, I place it in front of Jimmy and hand him a pair of chopsticks.

"Go for it, little man."

He takes the chopsticks, separates them, and positions them in his right hand just like any red-blooded American would who is recovering from a horrible accident during which he was stabbed repeatedly in the right hand.

Using both hands, he manages to get a piece of fried kernel between the two sticks and lifts it to his mouth.

Crunch.

Crunch.

Grating of teeth.

Crunch.

Grimace, furrow of brow.

Grinding and then grating of teeth.

Crunch.

Wonderment.

Crunch.

Swallow.

Picking of teeth.

"You like it?" Shunsuke asks, doubtful.

"I like the fried part," Jimmy responds. "What's inside it?"

I can't hold it in any longer.

"It's chicken gristle!" I hiss excitedly. "Chicken gristle! Gross, right?!"

"Hmmm," he says.

"Don't you love and hate it?! Doesn't it make you want to throw up and eat some more?! Isn't it just immorally appetizing?!"

He picks up another piece, this time with his hand, and tosses it into his mouth. His crunching is less reticent now, his grimaces and brow furrowing more often giving way to thoughtful expressions of acceptance and, after a few more nuggets, unconflicted, decisive satisfaction.

"Actually, it's not bad. But it needs better dippin' sauce."

Jimmy and I circle Tokyo, and she does her best to show him what she's got. And what does she got that Jimmy might like? She's got the Rainbow Bridge that takes you to the Odaiba district on Tokyo Bay, voted the best place for a date in the city, with its miles of shopping, street performers, amusement parks, game centers, and even a fake Statue of Liberty. She's got the crazy kids dressed in their finest gothic threads and having a pose-a-thon next to Harajuku Station. She's got the dancing Elvises in Yoyogi Park. She's got the serenity and heart-stopping beauty of a hidden Japanese garden just off of the bustle of Omotesando Dori. She's got the tallest building in the country in Ikebukuro and the glass capsule elevators running along the outside of the Mitsui Tower building in Nihonbashi. She's got the labyrinthine underground malls and subway paths, which are a really fun place to hide behind a pole and watch Jimmy get confused and then a little worried. Best of all she's got lots of food and, to Jimmy's delight, an abundance of forks.

"Look, Jimmy! Isn't it beautiful?" I ask Jimmy as we stare wide-eyed at one of Japan's most marvelous sights, the majestic Mount Fuji, which on a clear day is visible from Tokyo.

He doesn't answer. He looks impressed and awestruck, but more than a little scared, like a child sitting up in bed, eyeing his bedroom closet door, fearful of the hideous monster that lurks behind it. But why? Why does Jimmy look so pale, so panic-stricken, so pop-eyed? Is it the experience of looking at something so beautifully formed by nature and nature alone? Is it due to the vertigo one gets sometimes when seeing in person a sight normally only seen in pictures and postcards? Or is it because he's currently at the Fuji-kyu Highlands amusement park just outside of Tokyo, strapped in beside me in one of the world's fastest and tallest roller coasters, the Fujiyama ("Mount Fuji"), from which Mount Fuji is clearly visible, and which is currently at the beginning of its great initial ascent of eighty meters? We'll probably never know.

We clamber up towards the summit, and when we reach it, the coaster momentarily straightens out, allowing us a brief respite from abject terror before nose-diving back to the ground at warp speed. Jimmy's gleeful screams fill my ears as my cheeks flap in the wind and spittle splashes upon my chin and neck. We drop and drop and drop. Then we twist, turn, twist, ascend, nose-dive again, and finally, finally the carriage slows down and pulls back into the boarding area. The ride is over. With exhilaration, we realize we've survived, that everything will be OK, that we'll live to eat another Japanese pancake. Though just a few moments ago we were tasting our own mortality in the back of our throats and were very close to puking it up, we managed to keep it down and make it through to the finish line. This calls for some green tea ice cream.

"How about it, Jimmy?" I ask.

"Yeah, but while we're here, we might as well visit the haunted insane asylum. Get that out of the way."

You know how, in the first blush of romance, you spend so much time with someone because you don't want to be out of each other's sight and it's all great for the first few days because you're all excited and you start mapping out your future together in your head and then the magic wears off a little bit and a few days later you kind of get sick of the sight of them especially after you catch them using your toothbrush—your toothbrush!—and you start to wonder when oh when they are ever just going to go away and sleep in their own freaking bed? I didn't want that to happen between Jimmy and Tokyo. So after spending a few days locked in a passionate three-way with this fair city, we decide to take a trip south. It's preemptive day trip time.

So it's off to Kamakura to show Jimmy my friend the Big Buddha and then to the small rocky island of Enoshima, just off the coast of Fujisawa city, my old stomping ground. We walk across the bridge from Kamakura and onto the island on a beautiful sunny afternoon. We hike up the narrow, winding paths of the island village, visit small neighborhood temples, and sip green tea at little old-fashioned tearooms where the staff are simultaneously fascinated and horrified by us and our big, ungainly American ways. We follow the paved paths as they cut through thick greenery and eventually find ourselves heading down toward a rock outcropping on the side of the island where the land meets the water. I follow Jimmy down, and we alight on the flat rocks, pushed along by the determined Enoshima wind whispering in our ears, "Hurry up, gaywads, it's beautiful down there!"

We walk to the edge of the rocks and stare down as the water from Sagami Bay licks at the hard edges of the island, and we wordlessly sit for a rest after our long walk. The cold water laps against the flat rocks and into the deep gaps between them. The sun and wind work in perfect concert, ensuring we are neither too hot nor too chilly as we lie back on the rocks and allow the surroundings to lull us into a brief catnap.

I open my eyes a half hour later and feel a bit of a chill. The sun has fallen behind the clouds, though its rays still pierce them in a few narrow, jagged lines. I look over and Jimmy is lying very close to the edge, dipping his hand in the cold water. I realize that we haven't really talked much about our relationship since he's been here, and I get the feeling we're about to. We've managed to avoid the topic for a few days, busy as we've been with entertaining ourselves. Now that we're away from Tokyo and in a place where we can actually hear each other, the time seems right. He needs to know when I'm coming home. And I need to decide.

The setting sure lends itself to a good, deep conversation about where our lives are going. "Jimmy, our love is like this water," I might say, waxing poetic on our future. "It's deep, it's cleansing, it's salty. And it covers three-quarters of the earth. Yes, Jimmy, our love covers three-quarters of the earth. It leaves Sagami Bay and flows out into the Pacific into all sorts of amazing places like Australia and Poland."

"Our love flows to Poland via the Pacific Ocean?" Jimmy might wonder.

"It's just a metaphor, but, you know, our love is deep and blue and has the power to sink many ships."

At this point Jimmy might sigh and say, "Spare me the double-talk. I need dates. When are you coming home?"

"But…what will Tokyo say?" I wonder. "She loves me. Or at least tolerates me." (OK, she finds me quite irritating.)

I go over and sit down next to Jimmy on the edge of the rocks.

"This is the most amazing place I've ever been," he says.

"Wow. And *you've* been to Kraków."

"I feel like I'm in one of those Kuniyoshi paintings."

"Me too. Who is he?"

"A painter."

"Oh, yeah."

"You're coming home, right?" he asks. "Soon, right?"

"Yes."

"I need to know when."

I struggle to figure out what to say.

"I really need to know when."

"OK. How about five months? Can you wait five more months?"

He sighs, dips his hand in the cold water, and flicks droplets with his wet fingers.

"Yeah, OK. I can do that. But I want a kimono. And not one of those cheap ones we were looking at at the Grand Asia Plaza. I want one that feels like flower petals against my skin. Got that? Flower petals."

I do some quick calculations in my head and try to remember the name of that cheap, secondhand kimono shop in Kichijyoji a student once told me about.

"OK."

"OK."

"What if I found one that—"

"Flower. Petals."

"OK."

Our Tokkaido Line train glides back into Tokyo's Shinagawa Station, and I snap Jimmy out of the daze he fell into thirty minutes ago as he watched an old man across from us reading a big fat manga comic and picking his nose. We change to the Yamanote train, then to the Chuo Line, and finally reach Koenji. We slump back to my tiny room and collapse onto the bed.

I awake slowly the next morning, wondering groggily what we should do on Jimmy's last day. I know he's had a great time, I know Tokyo has shown him her best, but his visit is still lacking that transcendental moment when the world explodes into a widescreen Technicolor and people start dancing around you Busby Berkeley–style. Hmmm. What could we do? Where could we go? Who could we see?

"Oh my God! Fucking Itoya!" Jimmy cries, popping awake and jumping out of bed.

"Who?"

"Itoya! *Itoya!*"

I stare at him with big dumb eyes.

"The goddamn washi paper store! We've got to go there!"

Itoya, of course. Everyone who knows anything about washi knows Itoya. What? You don't know what washi is?

Well, dummy, washi is a traditional Japanese paper made from rice or bamboo or some such type thing and then dyed and used to make things like art and stuff. Jimmy loves washi paper, and pretty much the only thing on his to-do list when he came here was to go twirl around Itoya, the famous washi paper store in Ginza, a plan that had completely escaped his mind once he'd gotten here and had his mind blown by how thin I am.

So we scuttle eastwards to Ginza on a mission to get Jimmy some artfully made, tradition-bound transcendence.

The first floor of Itoya is your standard stationary shop. (For me, it's a big pile of "meh," but those who are into stationary had better fasten their seatbelts.) It's the second floor where the magic really happens, when the strings start to flutter and the horns start their low burbling. There, for the world to see (if the world could be crammed into a five-hundred-square-foot room) is roll upon roll upon roll, sheet upon sheet upon sheet, of wild, wonderful washi. All different colors and designs. And as soon as Jimmy sets foot in the room it's like *Charlie and the Chocolate Factory*. Except it's *Jimmy and the Washi Paper Store*.

Upon our entrance, the floor staff immediately goes on full alert, nodding to each other that there's a big whitey in the room and he may want to dirty up the place with his greasy American hands. Jimmy doesn't care. Humming the love theme to *Romeo and Juliet*, he starts flipping through all the sheets on the closest countertop while I dedicate myself to explaining his behavior to the staff in my serviceable Japanese:

"Don't worry! Washi is his favorite paper!"

"He came from America to see this washi!"

"He is an artist with the washi!"

The young male floor manager, looking exceedingly worried, starts following Jimmy around to make sure he doesn't compromise the washi and its proud Japanese tradition.

"He won't drop the washi!" I assure him. "He is very famous in America for loving washi!"

The manager asks Jimmy in extremely hesitant and uncertain English if he can help.

"Do you have a darker blue version of this?" Jimmy asks, holding up a piece of blue washi, not bothering to adjust his vocabulary or speaking speed for his ESL audience. "Like something a little cloudier and ominous, like a storm is about to break out, you know, like there could be some thunder and lightning coming? That kind of blue."

The manager's face falls.

"He ask any darker blue washi!" I translate, and while the manager starts looking for a darker shade, I shadow Jimmy, making sure he's careful not to breathe too hard on any of the paper.

"Jimmy, you've got to speak more slowly and use easier words," I tell him. "Also, look at him when you're talking. And open your mouth a little wider."

"Oh," he says. "Can't you just translate what I say for him?" he says.

As much as I want to tell him that my Japanese skills are indeed up to that demanding task—even though just a little over a year ago it had taken me the better part of two weeks to understand the grammar structure of the sentence, "The notebook is on the desk, and the pen is on the notebook"—I don't think I should commit myself to it. But pride and the instinct to show off beg me to give it a try, so I do.

"Uh, yeah, I guess I could do that."

"Great," he says. "Can you tell him that I'd like to see the different types of green he has? With Japanese symbols on them."

"This is OK?" the manager says, holding up a sheet of dark blue.

Jimmy nods.

"Yes, that is good," I venture in Japanese. "He also has an interest in seeing green things that you have here."

The manager smiles, sensing that, for the first time since he began helping us, he just might have the upper hand.

"Green? Green washi, right?" he says, continuing our Japanese tête-à-tête.

"Yes, kanji green washi."

"Also," Jimmy interrupts in English, "ask him if they have paler colors with little flecks of other colors in them."

"Also," I continue, "do you have bright colors and small various colors on the washi at the same time?"

"And," Jimmy continues, "do they have any with that little waving cat on them or like one of those demons you see at the temples? Or like those old crazy Noh masks! Ask him if they have Noh masks!"

A single bead of sweat pierces through the skin of my left underarm, thus opening the floodgates for an all-out perspiration celebration.

The manager hands Jimmy some green sheets decorated with various kanji characters and then starts trying to find some bright colors and small various colors on the washi at the same time. He hands more samples to Jimmy and waits expectantly for more instructions from me. He's not ready to let us browse freely.

"Are you going to ask him?" Jimmy persists.

This charade really shouldn't be allowed to continue. My ability to say where I am and where I want to go in Japanese is pretty flawless. My ability to request different kinds of washi paper according to Jimmy's whims—for which I would have to remember the words to all the colors as well as come up with ways of saying "flecks" and "demons" and probably eventually "Arabian sunset" and "mother of pearl"—are negligible. There's a bunch of washi here, and we are perfectly capable of sorting through it ourselves. But the Japanese are sometimes infuriatingly unwilling to let foreigners touch and pick things out for themselves. Sure, sometimes gaijin break things or stain them or set things on fire, but only the clumsy ones. I really want Jimmy to search around, find what he wants, and proceed to the checkout. I just need this guy to relax and leave us alone.

"He says," I begin, addressing the gentleman assisting us in a conspiratorial tone, "that you are really handsome."

It turns out that if you ever want a pushy male shop assistant who strikes you as a little bit repressed to back off and leave you in peace, all you really need to do is tell him your boyfriend finds him physically attractive. No sooner do I say this than his face turns bright red and he launches into a series of short, nervous bows as he backs away and heads for the safety of the cashier's counter.

"Jimmy, just pick out what you like and let's get it," I say. "I've just sent a poor guy into a tailspin of homosexual panic."

"Oh shit," Jimmy sighs. "Did you at least ask him how much these are per sheet?"

Jimmy's full-to-bursting bag shivers and shakes on the floor of the train from Ueno Station to Narita Airport. He flips through a copy of *Vogue Nippon* that someone had left on a bench at the station and comes to a page full of beautiful kimono patterns. He looks at me pointedly and starts circling ones he likes with his index finger.

"You're dreaming," I say.

"No," he replies, sure of himself. "Predicting the future."

When we get to Narita, we walk slowly to the security checkpoint, trying our best to slow down the time and delay the inevitable goodbyes. In spite of himself, Jimmy has fallen for Tokyo, in his way. I don't know if it was when we ate takoyaki octopus balls while walking through the smut district of Kabukicho, when we'd been photographed by excitable out-of-town junior high school students at the Edo-Tokyo Museum as if we were Brad and Angelina, or when we basked in the afterglow of a good, long karaoke session during which we'd taken on Chaka Kahn and Sheila E; but at some point, Jimmy began to look at the city as less of a threat and more as a great dream from which he would soon wake up.

"This place is insane," he said once as we passed a man walking his monkey in Yoyogi Park. "I see why you like it. It kind of suits you."

When we get to the security gate, we hug, and both of us tear up.

"Come home," he says.

"I will."

He lets go, grabs his bag, and scuttles off to explain to passport control that, yes, he looks like a terrorist child molester in his passport picture, but no, he is neither of these things and nobody can prove anything. Just before he's out of sight, he turns to me and mouths the words "flower petals" one last time. He slides through security and is on his way home.

I slump in my seat on the train from Narita with a heavy heart. I'm headed back into Tokyo's arms and feeling more conflicted than ever. My days with her are numbered now, I know. I've got to make our time together count. I've got to make her show me the things she's been holding back.

"I really need to see a Japanese lesbian," I say to her when we are together again and I'm once again riding her Yamanote train westward. "You've never shown me one, and I think it's about time. I'm not afraid. I feel ready."

She ignores me, and as the train rolls on toward Shinjuku I look at the teenage girl sitting across from me with an electro-shock hairstyle she has obviously achieved with the assistance of a hot iron and a fork. She's a rebellious little thing, probably worrying her parents sick with her bad attitude, her mismatched socks, and her imprecisely applied lipstick and eyeliner. As she manically texts someone on her cell phone, I notice she's carrying a fashionable tote bag embossed with a generic black stick figure standing next to a tree, like the figures in those traffic signs designating a crosswalk. Under the picture it reads, "It is forbidding to urinate here."

That'll do for now, I guess.

# of pounds lost: 28
# of rumors heard about straight-as-an-arrow fellow
teacher who went to Thailand, accidentally hooked up with
a she-male, and now is very, very confused: 1

CHAPTER FOURTEEN

Lego My Ego

Is there no end to our hero's talents?

Jimmy's visit changed me. Yes, after coming to the realization that, for the sake of my relationship, my days here are numbered, I saw that I've become too comfortable, too relaxed in my daily life. I've decided I need to branch out, that I haven't tested these polluted Tokyo waters enough. I came here to make things happen for myself, after all. Great big things that will pay large emotional dividends. More and more I'm feeling the need to spread my wings, to escape from the daily grind of teaching the same lessons at the same school week after week, day after day, hour after hour. I want to fly, to explore, to see what else is out there for me in that vast Tokyo jungle. To follow its trail, capture it, clasp it to my breast, and proclaim triumphantly, "I know now what God wants for me!" Also, I want more money.

Lucky for me, the opportunities are boundless for an enterprising young(ish) English instructor in Tokyo, especially if you know the right people. I've just gotten a job teaching English to corporate clients because I know the friend of a friend of the ex-boyfriend of a former associate of a guy named Mr. Takeda who has been put in charge of setting up and developing an English program for the employees of a famous Japanese maker of electronics, and the first thing he needs is a teacher. This friend of mine, Keiko, who knows the friend of the ex-boyfriend of the former associate of Mr. Takeda, told her friend to tell the ex-boyfriend of the former associate of Mr. Takeda that I was a very good teacher, very friendly, extremely competent, and that I speak a little Japanese. Mr. Takeda liked what he heard, so he told his former associate to tell the ex-boyfriend of the friend of Keiko to tell Keiko's friend to tell Keiko to tell me that Mr. Takeda would be getting in touch with me to set up a meeting. I'm in a network!

Mr. Takeda and I meet in Ginza one afternoon and go to a swanky Chinese restaurant where everything on the menu is more than I would typically pay for a pair of shoes. We discuss some of the broad ideas he has about the class. They include twice-weekly sessions with a specially designed English program involving both grammar instruction and real-world role plays like how to order a beer in an American bar. I will be responsible for choosing the text and planning the classes. Then he brings up the question of remuneration. Now, God knows I'm not a hard-nosed negotiator, and I usually have a really hard time answering this type of question. But I surprise myself with my forthrightness. Greed is the mother of motivation, and I am the big fat pig suckling at her enormous breast.

"Six thousand yen an hour plus travel is my usual fee," I say, as if I am in demand all across the city as one of the best English conversation teachers the great country of America has produced in years and am doing him a favor by even lunching with him in this dump. I steel myself for his reaction, expecting him to spit his half-chewed wanton back into his bowl.

"OK, I just have to checking some numbers at office, for seeing if that is OK for with our budget." As usual, I have probably undersold myself.

We leave the restaurant and take a taxi to his office, where we discuss the specifics of my contract. He does some number crunching and figures out that my fee fits within the budget, so I have the job. We will have two classes a week, both beginner level, and each class will have about nine students. Mr. Takeda writes all of this information on the dry-erase board, numbering each point so as to maintain a semblance of order in this unknown territory into which he is stepping.

"Oooo-kaaaay. Twooooooo begiiiiiiin-ah claaaasses. Niiiiiine stuuuuuudents to eeeeeach. Eh?" He stops writing and looks at me quizzically. "'Nine students to each?' Correct?"

I smile and, with humanitarian gravitas, correct him. "Nine students *in* each."

"Oh, OK," he says, making the correction. Then he starts making different lists, enumerating things I need to do, things he needs to do, things he needs to get his secretary to do, and things he will ask the students to do, all in preparation for the class. Then he makes another list that he titles "Salaly," where he writes the specifics of my payment. Once he's satisfied that he's made as many lists as he can reasonably be expected to make, he presses a button at the bottom of the white board and out comes a printout of all the lists he just made on the board. He hands it to me and says, "Please."

I take it, and when he turns his back to erase the board, I kiss it.

A few days later, Mr. Takeda e-mails me, saying he would like to introduce me at the next company meeting. It will be on Friday at ten a.m. Imagining that I will be introduced in a board meeting–type room with free-flowing green tea and tiny, semi-sweet doughnuts, I reply with no reservations that I am looking forward to meeting some of the staff.

Friday arrives and I'm with Mr. Takeda in his office. He greets me with a smile and a firm, very un-Japanese handshake, and then we leave the building and walk to the head office building a few blocks away. Meetings are held every Friday, he tells me. The sign-up sheet will be posted later in the day, so he figures it's a good opportunity for everyone to see me.

"That's great," I beam.

Wait, did he say "everyone"?

Then he says he'll be asking me to say a few words to the group—introduce myself briefly. "But," he says, "no people can't understand English, so maybe you can just talk in Japanese."

"Oh, OK," I say calmly, trying not to drop to my knees, grab his hand, and beg him not to make me do this.

I talk myself down. "You can do this, Tim. You've studied Japanese for over a year now. Sure, you never have to use it except when you're ordering food or asking directions, and sure, you've had very few conversations in Japanese lasting longer than a few minutes, and yes, usually when you do have those conversations, the person you're speaking to starts finishing all of your sentences for you, but hell, you can introduce and say a little about yourself in front of a few company bigwigs."

We walk into the meeting room, and it is much larger than the boardroom I was expecting. In fact, it's the size of your typical school cafeteria. We enter from the back, and there are no less than a hundred employees standing up and facing the front of the room, where one man, presumably very important, is talking into a microphone and writing numbers on an overhead projector. All the employees look very sleepy. Many are holding themselves up with their hands against their chairs or on their desks. Mr. Takeda gestures for me to sit at an empty desk off to the side. I feel awkward sitting since the rest of the room is forced to stand, but I am a native English speaker, so I guess I have the right.

The meeting seems to go on forever. Several speakers take the podium, each bringing his own overhead projector sheet onto which he writes his main points. As my head bobs and I and the rest of the listening audience begin to slip into eternity, the chief speaker calls Mr. Takeda over to talk about the new English class he's spent so much time organizing.

Mr. Takeda takes the stage and enthusiastically explains these new classes. Then he pulls out some of his own overhead projector sheets, and I begin to wonder if I was supposed to bring some. The first one gives the days and times for the classes, and the cost. As he speaks, people glance coyly over at me and smile, embarrassed if I catch them looking. Mr. Takeda quickly moves on to the next sheet he has prepared, which gives information about me, the teacher. I continue watching Mr. Takeda as he talks until I begin to hear tiny eruptions of giggles coming from the audience of shirts and ties. I look up at the overhead and see why.

Up on the screen is an information sheet about me, including some personal details like teaching experience, nationality, and hometown. But it is the accompanying photo that has people giggling. It is not a picture of me; Mr. Takeda never asked me for one. (I swear to God it wasn't on my list of things to do.) No, the black and white image staring out at those sleepy-eyed company folk is, spectacularly, Bruce Willis, circa *12 Monkeys*. Admittedly, it's a more appropriate choice than, say, Posh Spice, but I am a little sad that Mr. Takeda didn't consider a full-color glossy of a shirtless and oiled-up Brad Pitt circa *Fight Club* to be the logical substitute.

"So," Mr. Takeda says to the audience, switching to English, "I would like to present you to Mister Tim Anderson-sensei!"

There are a few lonely claps as I take the stage, the ghostly, sweaty, and shell-shocked face of Bruce Willis shadowing me in the background. It's been a long time since I last stood in front of this many people, and it's been absolutely forever since I stood in front of this many Japanese people. I stammer a bit and say, in Japanese, "This is a little scary," which gets me a few chuckles. Actually, I'm not sure if I said, "This is scary," "I'm scared," "I'm scary," "You're scary," or "This is scared." But I get a few chuckles.

Then, continuing in Japanese with sweat beads covering my face and body, I introduce myself, make a few short statements about how long I've been in Tokyo ("I've lived in Tokyo first year"), how much I love Japan ("I love Japanese things!"), and at Mr. Takeda's request, I say one thing in very basic English using words and phrases I think everyone will understand: "I'm looking forward to having exciting English lessons and making a special program for nice conversation and enjoyment!"

This country is ruining my English.

Classes start the next week. The students are chosen in a company lottery, and the lucky winners for my first class are seated with notebooks open, and pencils poised and ready for action when I walk in, sweaty and breathless from my dash from the train station through the soupy humidity of the city.

I generally like to open the floor to questions at the beginning of a new class. Mr. Takeda has told me that, for most of the students, this will be their first time meeting a Westerner; consequently, they're very curious about me and bursting with queries.

I pretend I'm Carol Burnett telling the A/V guys to lift up the lights at the beginning of her show.

"Anybody have a question? Yes, you. Please say your name and where you're from."

"Yes, hi, I am Hiroshi from Tokyo. Why do you come to Japan?"

"You know, I'm really glad you asked that. I came because I love noodles and weird skyscrapers with fast elevators. [Laughter.] Anyone else? Yes, you. Hi."

"Hi. I am Kobayashi. I am from Kawasaki. You like the women?" There are some questions I'd rather not be asked by straitlaced, straight-faced Japanese men in the first five minutes of class, and this is one of them. Hmm. Let's see, now. How do I answer this convincingly?

"Yes, of course!" I say with a wink.

"What kind of the women to like?"

So Kobayashi from Kawasaki wishes to continue his line of questioning.

"Well, I like beautiful women." Everyone nods in agreement. "But I like strong and smart women too," I add, pointing to my brain. Kobayashi looks unsatisfied. I think he wants names.

"For example?" one of the students, Yukihiro, asks with a mischievous grin.

Ugh. Now I have to think of someone famous who embodies these very qualities. I wrack my brain.

"I like Angelina Jolie," is what comes out. How can you go wrong with Lara Croft: Tomb Raider? There are a few nods.

"Me too," said Yukihiro. "She has very big mouth."

Everyone nods again, a little more enthusiastically this time. I'm not even ten minutes into the first class and already I've created a sexually charged classroom—funny, because, in my heart of hearts, I really wanted to say Dolly Parton, but I hadn't wanted to make things too weird on the first day. (And then we'd just be talking about boobs.) And anyway, the important thing is that the gentlemen are all at ease and comfortable, and one certainly must be relaxed when one is learning how to order alcohol in a hotel bar in New York, which is the role play I have planned for today.

Class continues with no major screw-ups, and each student successfully orders the cocktail of their choice by the end, with me as their bartender. I throw in a few curveballs ("I'm sorry, we're all out of martini glasses; can I put that in a paper cup?") just so they don't get too comfortable, and I think everyone enjoys the supreme discomfort of having to sit in front of the class and pretend to order booze in front of their fellow students, who are all laughing at them.

Naturally, we go drinking after class, and I teach them drunk English. ("Highball me!" "Lite beer is for losers!" "Dude is *wasted*.") They treat me with an interest and respect that is strange and undeserved, yet really addictive. Sometimes it seems like they ask me all the questions they've always wanted to ask an American but never had the chance, like "Do you have a gun?" and "Do you love Meg Ryan?"

Junichiro, a fifty-something silver fox of a man who plays guitar and is a huge Led Zeppelin fan, asks my favorite question of the evening. During the lesson I explained to them that some verbs we rarely use in the progressive ("-ing") form—verbs like "have," "like," and "love."

"For example," I said, "we don't say, 'I am having a pair of glass slippers.'"

This declaration seemed to bother Junichiro and, after a few beers, he's lubed up enough to address the topic again.

"Excuse me, Tim-sensei, I have question," he says.

"Junichiro!" I rejoin as I put my arm around him, my belly filled with three beers and quickly absorbing a fourth. "Call me Tim-san! We're friends!"

"OK," he laughs. "Tim-san. In Led Zeppelin, Robert Plant is saying 'since I've been loving you.' But you say we no can say 'loving.'"

"Wow, that's a really good point, Jun. Can I call you Jun?"

He tilts his head as if to say, "I'd rather you didn't," and laughs.

"Well, I'll tell you, and not many people know this—Mr. Plant had to get special written permission from the queen to do that."

Junichiro tilted his head again as if to say, "You're shitting me" or "Speak more slowly and less slurry."

"But," I continue, taking another swig of Asahi Super Dry beer, "you know, she was a really big Zeppelin fan, so, you know, it was cool."

After a few more rounds of drinks (none of which I have to pay for) and innumerable toasts made in my honor, I declare to my students that our next lesson will be at a karaoke box and that everyone should be sure to bring their tambourines. And I promise to sing "Goodbye Yellow Brick Road."

Meanwhile, my classified ad has borne fruit. A woman contacts me about teaching her children. Being deathly afraid of children, I was at first reluctant to take on the job. They—children—are always plotting against me and/or making inappropriate comments about my hair, my glasses, my clothes, my speech patterns, and/or my sexual preference. But then I reconsidered, thinking I could charge a nice price for private at-home instruction. So money talked, and my ears were pricked. Besides, though I fear them, I'm pretty good with kids. They like it when I cuss in front of them.

I experience a rude awakening on the first day of the job. You see, though I am a revered and admired superstar at my business classes, basking in my students' unshakable interest in me and all that I have to say, the children I will be teaching couldn't give a good goddamn that I am a native English speaker from the exotic country of America.

Their names are Kai, age thirteen, and Daisuke, age eight, and they have just returned from the U.S., where they lived for about three years while their father was on an assignment for IBM. They know a good bit of English already, but their parents are worried about them losing their speaking skills now that they're back in a completely Japanese environment. Kai and Daisuke do not share their parents' concern.

Since they have just returned from spending three years in the U.S., having an American tutor isn't so exciting for them. In fact, I can say with complete certainty that I am of absolutely no interest to them whatsoever. For three years, they went to school with Americans, lived next to us, ate our food, watched our television, played with our toys, read our books and magazines, and wore our clothes. They went to our ugly strip malls and Walmarts and realized how fat we actually are. To them I am not an entrancing enigma, a handsome stranger from the West. I am just another white guy. So when I try to get them to ask me questions about myself during their respective lessons, a warm-up technique that never fails to work with students who haven't spent much time away from Japan, it falls flat.

"Who are you?" Kai asks.

"Why do you come to here?" asks her brother.

And since they spent a lot of time with American kids, they have also picked up some expressions that I am not used to hearing from my other Japanese students. For example, "give me a break," "that sucks," "aw, *man*," "you suck gorilla butts," "what's your problem?" "no fair," and Daisuke's personal favorite, "that's gay." One time Daisuke even called me a "nasty old Yankee," which I would have reprimanded him for severely had I not been crying tears of laughter.

I teach them three afternoons a week. We spend a lot of time reading and working in the grammar workbooks their parents bought from the Kinokunia bookstore. Actually, the first few lessons I spend trying to get them to talk to me without rolling their eyes.

Daisuke at first seems only able to communicate with Legos. Every time I walk into his room he's on the floor making cars, houses, aircraft carriers, and alien colonies with his beloved Lego set.

"What's that you're making?" I say in my kindly teacher voice.

"I no tell you. You no need to know," he grumbles.

"Come on, tell me, what is it?"

"You have to figure out."

Towards the end of my hour with him, I'm eventually able to coax him up to his desk to do a bit of reading or grammar, but he always huffs and puffs the whole time, and he usually brings at least two of his Lego creations with him to play with.

Soon his uncooperativeness starts to bug me and I decide to put my foot down.

"Put the Lego robot down, Daisuke," I command him.

He slams it down and breaks it, then picks it up and puts it back together.

Ugh, I'm not getting anywhere with this kid, I think. I've got to show him who's boss. Looking down at the floor on my side of his desk, I see a Styrofoam gun that shoots out little Styrofoam missiles when you squeeze it. I pick it up and point it at him.

"Drop the robot, Daisuke."

He puts the robot down, reaches over to his side of the desk and picks up a big-ass toy rifle, points it at me, and pulls the trigger. It goes "*rickety ricket rick*" and shoots out a rubber ball, which bounces against my forehead. Then he puts it back, picks up his pencil, and does some grammar, every so often looking over at me with a little Japanese smirk on his face.

He finishes two whole pages of grammar exercises, and, elated that I now have some actual proof of work that I can show his mother, I tell him that if he does better next time, I'll bring him some candy. He promptly writes down for me what candy he likes and hates. I bring treats the next time, and he spends the entire hour on the floor with his Legos. I tell him I'm not going to beg him to do his work.

"Look, Daisuke, I'm totally fine with sitting here and reading my *Vanity Fair*. I'm not going to beg you to do your work. It's up to you. I'm not going to beg."

Forty-five minutes later I'm begging Daisuke to do some work.

"Please, Daisuke, we've got to show your mom that we've done something, OK? Come on! Just five minutes! Five minutes!"

Thankfully, Daisuke seems to respond to near-nervous breakdowns. He sits in his chair and finishes his vocabulary worksheet.

"Can I have some candy now?" he asks.

"Um, no, Daisuke, you can't have any candy. You worked for five minutes."

He picks up his worksheet and makes like he's going to tear it in half.

I take some candies out of my bag and put them on his desk. Then I swipe the worksheet from his hands and pick the candies back up.

On my way out of the room a Styrofoam missile hits me in the back of the head.

Kai is a little more mature about things, but no more excited about having to spend an hour and a half after school with an English tutor, no matter how tall and handsome he is. Every day she sits at her desk listless and bored. If I don't constantly prompt her to answer or move to the next question, she will happily sit silently staring at the page until I slowly disappear from her life.

"OK, what do you think about number two?" I ask, to which she shrugs her shoulders, to which I say, "Give it a try," to which she then answers with something like, "Had been watching," to which I say, "Exactly, very good," to which she says nothing, after which there is a pause, and then, "OK, what do you think about number three?" and the cycle continues.

A few weeks in, I have a breakthrough. Extremely hungover from my previous night's lesson with my business students, I can't bear the thought of teasing English out of Kai for an hour and a half. I take the easy way out and ask her about her print-club pictures, the instant photos you can have taken at shopping plazas and game centers all over Japan and that are decorated with titles of your choosing, generally messages like "Happy Camping!" or "Laughing Party!" and always feature at least one cute animated creature waving at the camera from the corner of the photo for good measure. When I ask her if she likes taking print-club pictures, it is a watershed moment. Immediately she is seized with a new energy. Her face lights up, and she seems to float across the room to get her pocket organizer, where she keeps all the stickers. She returns to her desk and opens the organizer.

"This is me and Kumiko at game center in the Shibuya," she beams. "And this is at mall near to my house. Oh, and this is mall in Shinjuku." That's just the beginning. We spend the rest of our time that day looking at and discussing photo stickers of her alone, her and her friends, her and her boyfriend-who-isn't-really-her-boyfriend-really-but-they-kissed-once, and her friends alone and with their boyfriends-who-aren't-really-their-boyfriends, all taken in malls and game centers throughout West Tokyo. She never asks to see my print-club pictures, even when I offer to show them to her (I only have two), but I don't push it. I have just successfully moved our awkward teacher/student relationship to the next level, so I can hardly complain. Plus, I get to learn that Kumiko smokes cigarettes sometimes, plays the guitar, and has talked about going to a tanning salon.

One day, she asks me a peculiar question. "What's a cinder-block?"

"Why do you ask?"

"Because my friend Denise told me this joke at the summer camp in U.S., and I never understand it."

"What's the joke?"

"OK, a girl named Rose ask her father how she got her name, and he say, 'When you were born, rose petals fell onto your face while mommy was holding you.' Then his other daughter Violet ask same question, and he say, 'When you are born, violet petals fell onto your face while mommy was holding you.' Then his third daughter asks same question, and he say, 'Shut up, Cinderblock!'"

I explain to her what a cinderblock is, and she covers her mouth and laughs. Then she gets on the Internet and starts translating the joke into Japanese for all her friends.

Seizing on this moment of lighthearted fun, I say, "OK, and after you finish doing that, we can finish this worksheet!"

She pretends not to hear me, and I sit in silence as she click-click-clicks her fingers on the keyboard, telling the sad story of poor, lonely, unloved Cinderblock.

This job leads to another job with a little first grader named Ryuji. His mother works for IBM and knows Kai and Daisuke's parents, which is how I get the job. Since I'm now on a mission to make children like me, I gladly accept another tutoring gig. Ryuji, his mother, and his grandmother have also just returned from a stint in the States, so Ryuji is continuing his study of English in the same fashion as Kai and Daisuke.

The first day of class, I show up at his house, ring the doorbell, and Ryuji answers the door with a puppy in one hand and a paper airplane in the other.

"Teacher?" he says.

"Yes," I smile.

"*Bark*," the puppy says.

Then he pivots around and launches the paper airplane down the hall, hitting his grandmother in the forehead.

I am very happy to find out that he is not nearly as averse to continuing his English as Kai and Daisuke. Though I am still not the international man of mystery to him like I am to the business folk, he doesn't resent my very presence like Kai and Daisuke, and he usually even looks happy to see me when I arrive. In fact, I often have trouble shutting him up; he has an amazing ability to stray from any topic and involve me in complicated discussions that his English is not sophisticated enough to handle.

"Spiderman's Batman," he says once when we are talking about the difference between subjects and verbs.

"Huh?"

"Spiderman's Batman."

"Spiderman's Batman?"

"Yeah."

"Um, I know Spiderman and Batman."

"Yeah."

"What about them?"

"He have gun."

"Spiderman?"

"No."

"Batman?"

"Batman."

"He has a gun?"

"But Spiderman have wings."

"Wings?"

"Yeah."

"You mean he can make a spider web."

"And he go *kssshhh! Powwww! Ffffghhhsh!*"

"Yeah."

"Do you like more Buzz Lightyear or a Spiderman?"

And so on. When it comes to studying, he has the attention span of a gnat. Often he'll become bored or frustrated with the task at hand and stop what he's reading or writing to draw a crude picture of what is happening in the story or the sentence. One day we're reading a story about two guys, Jack and Dave, who are fishing on a boat in a lake. Ryuji, clearly not riveted by the story, picks up his pencil and draws an interpretive study of Jack and Dave in the fishing boat. Actually, it looks like Jack going down on Dave on a surfboard, but I know what he's getting at.

His favorite device for spicing things up during the writing exercises is the exclamation point. He uses it to innervate sentences that in his opinion are lacking in action and drama, which, of course, is every sentence without an exclamation point. Thus, we constantly end up with sentences like, "Jim ate pizza for dinner last night!!!!" and "The bird was flying high in the sky!!!!"

And at the end of every lesson, he makes me read to him from his favorite book, *Captain Underpants and the Curse of the Wedgie Woman*, which gives him his fix of innocuous toilet humor for the day. But before I read to him I always make him recite to me the Pledge of Allegiance, which he learned when he was at school in the States.

> *I pledge lesions to the flag*
> *On night states America*
> *And to recoldic*
> *Which is sand*
> *One nation*
> *On the guide*
> *Invisible*
> *And seventeen justice graw.*

Just like I used to say it.

So now, as part of my extracurricular schedule, I work with children, something I never thought I'd be doing and something that is allowing me to build useful future social skills, like patience, empathy, and the concocting of unique punishments for not doing what I ask. When I first imagined having to teach children, I thought of Medusa, the tattered redhead from Disney's *The Rescuers* who in one scene has a helpful exchange with her sidekick Snoops regarding a young girl, Wendy, whom they've just kidnapped. It goes something like this:

> Medusa: Snoops, you don't have a way with children. You must gain their confidence, make them like you...
> Snoops: Yeah? How do you do that?
> Medusa: You force them, you idiot!

But though Japanese adults are much easier to convince of your likeability, especially after a few beers, you can't force their children to like you. It just happens, either by happy accident or after a gradual wearing down of their steely willfulness. But even though it involves much less adulation and alcohol than my business classes, it's a nice change of pace, especially when Kai insists on lecturing me, telling me that I'm old and I should already be married and that I might end up alone for the rest of my life if I don't do it soon, especially if I don't stop biting my nails and picking the dead skin off my fingers; or when Daisuke cross-examines me about my homeland with questions like, "Why America doesn't have bullet train and only cars? It's stupid. And why American people so fat?"

But my heart really belongs to Ryuji, who the other day successfully got me to say the word "sex" by telling me to say the letter X five times fast. I knew where he was going with this, but I did it anyway to humor him and myself. He laughed at me for "saying bad word," then asked me what it meant.

"Um, it's a little hard to explain," I said.

"Is it like 'poop'?" he asked as he folded the phone bill into a paper airplane.

"Yes," I answered. "I guess sometimes it is."

# of times shoes taken off before entering room: 841
# of times reprimanded for not taking shoes off before
entering room: 1

CHAPTER FIFTEEN

Karaoke Queens

Pat Benatar and Ann and Nancy Wilson's favorite chapter.

If there's one thing I've learned I can count on during my time on Planet Tokyo, it's that every day I step outside my door provides me with a new opportunity to sit in judgment of an entire nation of people. Sure, I did that back home in the States too, but it's a richer and more rewarding experience here because there's no way I can be mistaken for those I judge. Most of the time.

The Japanese, like yours truly, are a beautiful, counterintuitive symphony of contradictions. They are responsible, anal-retentive recyclers, yet each day one Japanese person probably goes through an entire continent's worth of plastic because they are completely obsessed with packaging: i.e., putting things in bags, then putting those bags in bigger bags, putting those bags in one final climactic bag, and so forth. They are hesitant to speak about contentious or embarrassing topics, yet I hear the word "diarrhea" used in conversations in my classroom with mystifying frequency (usually after someone asks, "How are you?"). And as is well-documented in these pages, they are painfully shy and try their best not to draw attention to themselves, yet they are the same people who invented and made immensely popular an arcade game called Dance Dance Revolution where the player must, in full view of others, gyrate and wiggle his body to electro music, mimicking as closely as possible the figure dancing on the screen, thereby gaining points and perhaps beating personal records. And my students shift uncomfortably and turn red when I ask them what they did last weekend?

The other night in the front of a Shinjuku sidewalk arcade I saw a man in shirtsleeves dancing on the Dance Dance Revolution platform as if his very life depended on it, face sweating, armpits drenched, expression determined. He stepped, twisted, kicked, and jumped like a kid on ecstasy at his senior prom. A crowd of people was gathered around to watch him dance and marvel at his high score. I wouldn't say he danced with any inborn sense of rhythm or flair, but he knew the steps and could put his feet and arms where they were supposed to be at any given point in the dance. When he finished, folks clapped, a person handed him his suit jacket, he bowed graciously to everyone, tried his best to re-fashion his hair into its former slicked-back style, and walked down the street by himself, briefcase in hand, a slight spring in his step. He was probably off to English class, where he'd sit in the corner and not speak above a whisper for two hours.

The quintessential embodiment of this contradictory element of the Japanese character is their love of karaoke. There are few events in Tokyo that are announced with as much fervor and enthusiasm as the opening of a new karaoke venue. I was on my lunch break in Ginza one day and happened to pass by a karaoke place that was having its "Grand Opening Fun," and I had to swerve to avoid the men dressed in giant blue bear costumes beating on drums, shaking tambourines, passing out flyers, and shouting the good news at the top of their lungs. There were also glittery dancing girls waving, as well as an accordion player.

We've all done karaoke. It's an addictive and idiotic but fun thing to do while drunk, and a reliable way to publicly humiliate oneself/give the world a small taste of one's undeniable talents. Most importantly, it's the best way to prove once and for all that those countless and friendless hours spent in my bedroom listening to Top 40 radio during middle school when I should've been learning how to not fall off a skateboard were not wasted hours. Not at all. I know lots of lyrics!

My former MOBA colleagues and I used to go out karaokeing regularly to let off steam. Sometimes a Japanese worker would come along, but more often than not it was just us gaijin looking for our moment in the spotlight. One time, Donna had gotten enough beer in her to think she could take on Kate Bush's "Wuthering Heights." If you're unfamiliar with this particular song, it may assist your understanding to know that Ms. Bush's extremely high-pitched voice makes Betty Boop sound like Bruce Springsteen. She hit notes not scientifically proven to exist before this song scaled the heights of the British charts in 1979. In short, I didn't think Donna was up to the challenge, and as it turned out, she wasn't. It was like hearing Jennifer Lopez trying to sing Maria Callas. It was like hearing Jennifer Lopez trying to sing. One of our fellow teachers, Pete, picked up the other microphone and started singing along, obviously feeling that, well, somebody had to do something. But Donna, eyes closed, face shining, voice creaking, was having none of it, and with a flick of her dainty wrist, she knocked the microphone out of his hand and whispered in a tone of voice usually indicating demonic possession, "Shut up, it's my song!"

But we couldn't fault her. We all had the same agenda, i.e., to sing the song we wanted to sing and make everyone else listen.

Next up was Big Bob from Wales, who always picked whatever Tom Jones song was in the songbook, especially if it was "The Green Green Grass of Home." This night he surprised us by bogarting the remote control and programming in "Sex Bomb" followed by "God Save the Queen." There he was, this huge white man standing up in a tiny room singing "and I am the antichrist!" while the television screen showed a short film of two Japanese lovers at an amusement park, twirling around, laughing, hugging, kissing, and then crying after their star-crossed separation.

As for me, I am probably the worst when it comes to using my time at the mic to make a dramatic personal statement and force everyone to sit and watch, awestruck, as I unfurl my very essence. My song choices naturally tend towards power ballad territory. I strongly believe that there is something deep within us human beings, a profound, inexplicable, emotive force that drives us to do things that we know may hurt other people, maybe even hurt ourselves. But life is full of such dilemmas, and I find it's best to follow your heart wherever it may lead you. And if not your heart, then your beer buzz. And my karaoke beer buzz always leads me, coincidentally enough, to Heart. Not the biggest muscle in the human body; I'm talking about the legendary rock band led by siren sisters Ann and Nancy Wilson, the queens of the rock torch song, the mystical madams who helped get me through sixth grade. There isn't an emotion too naked, an anger too vitriolic, a love too conflicted, or an animal metaphor too far-fetched for them to sing about atop a glassy piano refrain or a nasty guitar lick. I can't help but respect that and to do my best to stay true to the original spirit of their songs when I grab one microphone for myself, turn the other one off and kick it on the floor, and open my vocal cords like a flower greeting the rising sun to push out the opening verse to "Magic Man," "What About Love?" "Dream-boat Annie," or "Barracuda."

For a few precious minutes, these songs written by two big-haired girls from Seattle are my own, because no one in the room (or in their right mind) knows them like I do. Not even needing to read the lyrics on the television screen, I can close my eyes and devote myself totally to creating an atmosphere of naked inti-macy and flawless grace for my audience. And unlike Bob, I'm not afraid to use a falsetto if I have to. Which I do. Often.

It's not Carnegie Hall, but it's not the size of the arena in which you sing, it's the motion of the emotion when the notion hits your ocean. Or whatever. Anyway, no one really cares when you're finished. I'd like to say they're stunned and breath-less when I reach the end of my song with a fist in the air, my head back, and the microphone held upside down above my gaping mouth as it wails, "How do I get you alone?! Alone! Aloooooooooooooooooooooooone!" It would be a lie, as every-one is already scrambling for the song directory and the remote control like a bunch of attention-starved Mariah Careys, ready to enter in their next musical choice.

In short, I'm comfortable with being a selfish bastard in a karaoke box. I'll swipe the song catalog out of a bitch's hands if I have to. But, of course, this is Japan, so one should never get too comfort-able. And sure enough, when I go to karaoke with my business students, I learn that, sadly, just because you're blissfully drunk doesn't mean everyone is dying to hear your interpretation of Juice Newton's "Love's Been a Little Bit Hard on Me" without at least joining in with a little percussion or backing vocals, *even when they don't know the lyrics!* Yep, in this curious country—or at least among my business students—karaoke is an activity for the group to enjoy together, not one at a time, like God intended. People can all join in the fun, unwind, relax, get drunk, laugh at each other's vocal shortcomings, and, as one of my pro-karaoke students once put it, "be very too happy." This is surely how they'd done it in Eastern Bloc countries during the cold war, in their communist karaoke labor camps.

It all happens one night after class. We're drinking at a company party for a few hours, and once everyone is lubed up enough to start suggesting, nay demanding, that we proceed immediately to a karaoke box, we make a break for it. We all pile into a room, sit down, and order some drinks. Mr. Takeda immediately punches in "Twist and Shout," one of the easier Beatles songs for Japanese to sing, and he and Yukihiro begin belting it out ("Shek eat shek eat shek eat bebe now!! Tsuist-oh and shout-oh!!") while Mr. Yamamoto backs them up on tambourine and everyone else heaves glasses full of beer into their mouths and cheers along.

Next comes a Japanese song by Utada Hikaru. A few of the guys sing this one, often passing microphones and swapping instruments with each other. I smile and laugh, but inside I'm wracked with disapproval.

"Why isn't Junichiro demanding that everyone else shut up so he can sing the song by himself?" I wonder. "Does he not know how you're supposed to do it?"

Mr. Takada asks me what I want to sing, and I start looking through the book for something good, ready to show the room what I can do. Though I see many that tickle my fancy, like the Eurythmics' "I Need a Man," Pat Benatar's "Hell Is for Children," or Madonna's "Like a Virgin," they don't seem terribly appropriate, and I don't want to bring the festivities to a crushing halt, so I settle on "Piano Man" and bring the house down with my amazingly accurate (to them, at least) imitation of Billy Joel. Problem is, they all sing along (three of them into microphones!), jingle their tambourines, click together their drumsticks, and generally make a huge racket. So even though it is my song, really, since I chose it, the entire room felt like they could just barge in at any moment like this was some sort of hippie jam session. Soon, Takada starts plugging in songs for me to lead them in, from the Rolling Stones' "Wild Horses" and the Monkees' "Daydream Believer" to Bette Midler's "The Wind Beneath My Wings." And everyone backs me up. Folks who just a few sober hours ago stared at me blankly when I asked them a question in front of the class, not even able to bring themselves to say, "I don't understand," are now fully outside their classroom shell, passing the microphone, shaking the maracas, clapping their hands, and "whoop whooing" like it's showtime at the Apollo.

And wonder of wonders, by the time we get to David Bowie's "Let's Dance," I am totally digging it. The selfish, attention-starved diva in me retreats into the background and I become just another member of the gang. The only white guy, yes. With better pitch and melodic sense, sure. And a native understanding (more or less) of what Bowie means when he says "under the moonlight, the serious moonlight"—absolutely. But whereas before I wouldn't have been happy without my moment in the sun, now I'm grooving with this ecstatic communal experience. No one is the center of attention, and nobody feels embarrassed, because each of us understand the deep-seated human need to sing our favorite songs into a microphone and be backed up by a decent sound system and some swirly lights.

After sipping from this cup of cooperation and collaborative energy, I decide that perhaps the group therapy of Japanese-style karaoke is not so bad. But can I really leave the "me first" mentality of my previous karaoke outings behind? With a group like my fellow teachers, you might try to sing along, but it's someone else's solo you're stealing. And the threat of violence is real. With my business class, the microphones would be passed, the tambourines traded, and the choruses sung, anthem-like, by everyone. It's an arrangement I'm just not sure I can ultimately be happy with. I've turned Japanese a bit, yes. But have I turned *that* Japanese?

I think we all know the answer. The lure of the spotlight is too great for a deluded fame whore like myself. Yes, though we can sometimes come together over a good Beach Boys, Elvis, or Madonna tune, we selfish gaijin tend to use karaoke as an opportunity to stand out from our peers rather than harmonize and clap along with them, and to assert our sometimes offensive individuality. We want to sing our lives and justify our existence. We sit and wait expectantly for each person's song to hurry up and finish so we can stomp a stiletto on the carpet and announce ourselves to the room, if not the world. We want to show what we know and prove unequivocally to ourselves and to everyone else in that tiny soundproof room, "Dammit, I exist, and I'm gonna fucking sing about it, so hand over the goddamn microphone, bitch. And cool it with the backing vocals, please. We're not Martha and the friggin' Vandellas, for God's sake!"

Final Summary:
Total # of pairs of chopsticks used
(for eating): 1,261
Total # of food items dropped on floor
(while eating): only 19!
Total # of times waitress brought me a spoon or fork
unasked: only 3!
Total # of visits to Tokyo Disneyland: only 2!

CHAPTER SIXTEEN

Look Homeward, Gaijin

In which our hero's adventure reaches its musical climax and then everyone goes home with their ears bleeding.

—

Concert for Viola and Piano
Music by
Johannes Brahms

Tim Anderson, Viola
Toru Miyazaki, Piano

Sunday, July 22
3:30 p.m.

Steinway Salon, Tokyo
1-6 Kanda Surugadai, Chiyoda-ku

—

The flyers are all printed; the studio space rented; the sheet music dog-eared, ink-blotted, and bloodstained. It's time for my great Tokyo debut—as part of a recital given by my friend Toru and me. It took a fair amount of cajoling on Toru's part to get me to agree to this public performance, as standing on a stage in front of a roomful of sober people ready to get all judgy gives me the flop-sweats under normal circumstances. Standing on a stage trying not to drop my viola in front of a roomful of blank-faced Japanese people who are probably expecting a competent viola player, having seen the fancy font on the flyer—now this really puts the fear in me. And facing these same people after I choke, throw my viola onto the floor, and scream, "I can't do it! Everyone knows it! My thesis advisor was right! I'm a fraud!" and then jump stage left, get tangled in the curtain, fall over, and pee in my pants—this could be a real career killer.

But one evening as we drank Asahi beers in his neighborhood in Yokohama, Toru had somehow convinced me that I should just go for it and not worry that the entire audience would be silently judging me and wishing I'd taken a few more years to rehearse. At first I was absolutely against it.

"Don't get me wrong, Toru," I explained. "I loooove playing the viola. Love it. But only in a room by myself with the shades drawn and sirens blaring outside. Or in a fifty-piece orchestra where the sound of my playing can't possibly be heard."

Toru's brow furrowed.

"Or, you know, with a guy going to town on a gigantic grand piano right next to me."

"What means 'going to town'?"

"I absolutely can't be the only viola player in the room. I need a buffer."

"What means 'buffer'?"

"Besides, you don't want me publicly embarrassing you, do you? You're a great player! What if the wrong person should see us playing together? You could be ruined. Ruined, I say!"

"You are so afraid," Toru laughed. "Why is it? You are American. Americans aren't afraid of what other people are thinking."

He's right. After all, we did invent the deep-fried Twinkie.

"All Americans are not the same," I said, enumerating in my head all the differences between myself and the Olsen twins. "Do all Japanese people have black belts?" I asked Toru.

"Yes," he replied. "Anyway, it not important, the concert. We can play fine at performance, and besides, no people will come."

"Do you really think so?" I said hopefully. I do love Toru's streak of negativity whenever it comes to his own musical prospects.

"Yes, we will invite people and no one will come to see. It will be fine."

He'd said the magic words.

"Oh, OK, I'll do it. But nobody better come."

So now here I am, sweating bullets as I prepare to fool the world (or at least a dozen or so people) into thinking I have musical talent. I'm tempted to make some amendments to the flyer Toru designed, in order to lower folks' expectations just a little. A few that come to mind:

Concert for
𝔓iano and 𝔠heap 𝔖econdhand 𝔠hinese 𝔙iola

and

𝔠im 𝔄nderson on 𝔙iola,
In 𝔥is 𝔣irst 𝔓ublic 𝔓erformance
𝔖ince the 𝔄ccident

But Toru won't give his consent to these changes, so instead I'm going to make my grand entrance by walking onto the stage with a limp.

The studio space has a maximum capacity of fifty people. Toru, in spite of his earlier declaration that no one would come, thinks we should plan on having about twenty.

"You think we'll have that many?!" I stammer, panicked.

"Just in case," he says. He has invited his family and some family friends as well as his piano teacher and some of her other students. And me? Well, despite my mortal fear of playing the viola in public, I decided that, screw it, if I'm going to do it, I'm going to do my best to make people that I know sit through it. So I post flyers at work and give a few to friends.

"It's always been a dream of mine to one day wake up and be able to play the viola," my colleague Udo from South Africa says to me as I hand him a flyer.

"Oh God, me too," I say. "Wouldn't that be awesome?"

On the big day, we arrive early and set up all fifty chairs, and it turns out that the good Steinway people weren't lying with the "fifty person maximum" line. We would've had to tear down a wall to get a fifty-first chair in there. We warm up on our instruments and wait for the people to start trickling in. Toru's mother and sister arrive quietly and sit down in the front row. A few minutes later Toru's piano teacher walks in and sits in the last row, increasing our total attendance to three.

Once we're all warmed up and loose, Toru and I hop off the small stage and mingle with our public. Toru talks to his piano teacher, and I engage in some Japanese small talk with his mother.

Me: Hi, how are you? It's been a while since I've seen you.

Her: Fine, thank you. Your viola playing sounds nice.

M: No, it sounds horrible. I need to practice for five more years.

H: No, it's very pretty.

M: No, you're wrong. My viola is a disaster. A musical earthquake.

H: [silent smiling]

M: Do you like my necktie?

Rachel and Tami, her clubbing sidekick, waltz in with water bottles and bug eyes, proving to everyone in the room that I do in fact have friends—sweaty friends hopped up on drugs, but friends nonetheless—and saving me from having to come up with another way to insult myself in Japanese.

"Did you guys get in really late last night?" I ask.

"We just left the after-party about an hour ago," Rachel says, her kaleidoscopic eyes blazing. And now they're at the *after*-after-party.

A few others show up in the next few minutes: my housemate Akiko and her friend, Kenji and Midori from my work, and an employee of the Steinway Salon, who gives us our receipt for the rental before politely declining my kind invitation for her to please please please have a seat and join in the fun.

Since we only have the place reserved for a few hours, Toru and I decide we should go ahead and start playing, even though our audience is only ten strong. I get up on stage, start the show with a few words in Japanese and English—thanking everyone for coming, inviting them to enjoy the show, and requesting that they please not throw anything—and then Toru and I launch into our Brahms sonatas.

People say that when you're nervous on stage, you should simply imagine the audience in their underwear and it will calm you down. Or people always say that people always say that, but anyway, I decide it's inappropriate to imagine Toru's mother, sister, and piano teacher in their underwear. I find I always respond much better to imagining Marky Mark and the lead singer of A-ha lying on a double bed in their underwear. So this is what I do. It relaxes me and strengthens my bow stroke.

Now, I've also found that playing the viola on a bare stage with piano accompaniment and a silent and respectful audience is quite different from playing drums in an experimental rock trio with no discernible song structures and a singer who wouldn't know a melody if it kissed him full on the mouth. For one thing, if you make a mistake in the latter, it may be noticeable, but it's also the nature of rock and roll to take mistakes and run with them. Further, you can blame it on the booze and the drugs. However, if you make a mistake on the viola, there's nothing to cover you. You are left naked and neutered in front of an audience that wants every note to be precise and clear; that counts on the steady harmonic cooperation between viola and piano; that is not likely to readily accept that you fucked up that high C because you were doing Jaeger shots before the show or because you are still reeling from the cocaine you had one of your roadies inject into your anus before you came onstage.

It's the expectation of precision that scares me. One's ear need not be classically trained to hear a stringed instrument falling far short of the intended note. But, thankfully, Rachel, knowing I'll be on the verge of a nervous breakdown, gave me a Xanax yesterday, which I downed about twenty minutes before beginning to play, so instead of fearing that every note I hit is being ruthlessly judged as hopelessly deficient by the audience, I'm floating on a cotton-candy cloud, playing my golden viola flawlessly for an audience of young virgin males in tunics. Drugs make everything so much easier!

Jo and Grant sneak in at the tail end of the first sonata, bringing the audience total to twelve and giving me that extra burst of adrenaline I need to attack the furious climax of the piece before bringing it to a soft and sweet, if slightly squeaky, conclusion.

The rest of the show continues without a hitch, except for a few problems with the high notes that make me sound as if I am strangling my viola rather than playing it. Strangling it real good. And my cell phone rings during the somber and romantic fourth sonata: Shunsuke, calling because he's lost and can't find the studio. Thankfully, though, he arrives in time to see Toru and I take our bows and leave the stage.

"Oh my God, Tim, that was great!" Rachel and Tami say in unison as they each hug me.

"Oh, please. That's the drugs talking."

"No, seriously," Rachel says, petting me on the shoulder and taking a swig of water from her humongous plastic bottle. "I really don't think it is. Tami, is it? It was good, right?"

"Oh, yeah," Tami smiles, trying to stop her legs from moving to the beat inside her head.

Toru introduces me to his piano teacher. We exchange greetings in Japanese, and she lies through her teeth about enjoying the concert.

Her: I enjoyed your playing.

Me: No. It was horrible. I'm very sorry.

H: No, the music was very pretty.

M: My viola sounded like a...a car accident. Like a car accident.

H: No, no.

M: But Toru played very beautifully.

H: [silent judging of Toru]

M: Do you like my necktie?

H: You are so tall.

I'm thrilled that my Tokyo debut wasn't a complete disaster. This concert will be my goodbye kiss to Tokyo, for I have decided that I must soon take my leave of the city and return to my home planet. Or, rather, Jimmy has threatened to divorce me if I don't come home within the next month. So, because gay divorces can get really ugly—especially when there is a cat and a treasure trove of pop-up books, drug paraphernalia, and David Bowie CDs involved—I must return.

I came to Tokyo to wake myself up, to force myself into uncomfortable scenarios, to go record shopping. After two years, I feel the need to return home, to come back to earth and try to relearn its language. I've spent too much time away from the natural flow of my mother tongue. I see Japanglish phrases on

T-shirts or advertisements, and they're making a little too much sense to me these days. I saw a shirt on a young girl the other day that read:

I squint my eyes and pretend I'm snow board
as I bosh the lip off double overhead power pump.
Melon Papa

I know exactly what that means.

Not that I've totally figured things out. Even the seemingly straightforward T-shirt messages are getting lost in translation: look at that ratty rock and roll hipster chick in the T-shirt that reads "Pretty Stupid" or the Harajuku chickadee whose black tee has "Cum Dumpster" painted in blood red on the front. Funny! But wait. Are they being ironic or brutally honest? Am I meant to a) wink, nudge, and laugh, or simply b) laugh? What used to make sense doesn't anymore, and what didn't does.

Sitting at my laptop one recent night trolling the Internet for cheap music, I came upon a listing for the 1988 Siouxsie and the Banshees album *Peepshow* that is shamefully undervalued. On seeing that there are forty-two used *Peepshow*s available—some for as low as forty-five cents!—I remarked with petulant exasperation to myself, "That a great album, why it used so much?!"

My language skills are compromised. I need to go home.

And besides, the culture wars are in full swing back home in the mighty USA, and it would be a real shame to miss out on that festival of Christian love. My country needs me.

A famous traveler once said, "He who is tired of Tokyo is tired of not being able to get a decently sized pan pizza for under thirty bucks." I'm sure someone said that. And I would have to agree, but I must say, my love for a big fat cheesy pizza notwithstanding, I'm far from tired of Tokyo. Like any great city, it sucks the life right out of you on a daily basis. But it also offers a multitude of small treasures to enjoy as it pummels you into submission: the reliable promptness of the reliably color-coded trains carrying reliably daft young creatures of fashion to their favorite two stops on the Yamanote train: Shibuya and Harajuku; the clash of the old and the new, like when you see a ninety-year-old woman literally fight a teenager for a seat on the train; the takoyaki octopus balls; the unintentionally existential English-language signs you see in random places, like the one I saw at Mos Burger that read, "Always close a door behind you." Or the one on the door of a restaurant in Ikebukuro saying, "We are looking for our staff." How sad. Where on earth did their staff go, leaving them like that?

Change is in the air here, and not just for me. I've heard through the grapevine that my old bookish roommate Ewan is engaged to be married to a Japanese woman, with whom he'll return to Australia and no doubt render his family speechless. Donna also has nuptials in her future, as she's taking her love of a guy in uniform to its logical extreme and getting hitched to an American sailor. And those new Edwin jeans I bought the other day, vouched for in advertisements by Brad Pitt himself, were out of style by the time I squeezed myself into them.

So I've started making preparations to leave. I've sent boxes home, started packing up my room, and attempted to sell anything of value I don't need. I went down the road to one of the consignment shops in Koenji the other day to see if I could get rid of my little boom box, hoping to trade it and use the money to take myself out to lunch. The woman didn't seem too interested in buying it, and after a few unsuccessful attempts to pawn it off on her, I gave up and told her she could just have it. I started to set it down on the floor, but, waving her hands like a hummingbird, she explained that she really didn't want me to leave it, that she would really just prefer if I took it the hell out of her damn store. So I left the store with my boom box after a few irritated bows, left it outside the shop on the sidewalk, and took myself out to lunch anyway. When I walked back past the shop on my way home, the boom box was no longer on the sidewalk. It was probably for sale inside for two thousand yen.

Since announcing my imminent departure, I've received many goodbye gifts from fellow teachers, students, and friends. The folks in my business class threw me a going away party and gave me a huge Japanese flag that they'd all signed. I received a wall hanging from a student and a CD of traditional Japanese music from the mothers of the kids I teach. I've gotten enough handkerchiefs to patch myself together a nice set of bay window curtains, and enough bottles of sake to render me legally blind.

So it's a beautiful Sunday afternoon and I'm sitting in a massive field listening to a Japanese hip-hop band performing for me and hundreds of others at a music festival in the east Tokyo district of Odaiba on Tokyo Bay. One of the main sponsors of the festival is Shane British English School, whose advertisements always show a dorky-looking and pasty-faced British guy hanging off of a double-decker bus, inviting you to study English the way it's meant to be spoken: Britishly.

There are many foreigners in attendance, and all the Japanese bands on the bill have been making admirable efforts to use whatever English they know when addressing the audience. The shirtless rapper wearing a sarong on stage just said, "It's a lock and loll liot!!!" to whoops and screams from the crowd.

I'm here with the usual suspects of Jo, Grant, Shunsuke, and Rachel. A few minutes ago, Jo and I joined the mailing list for one of the Tokyo bands that played called Ex-Girl. They're an all-girl trio wearing dresses and wigs that wouldn't be out of place in a Las Vegas revue, and they play a glammy tribal punk pop of sorts. For obvious reasons, I'm desperate to be friends with them. In the flyers for the festival, it says they are from the planet Kero Kero. I wonder if they have Diet Mountain Dew and wheat bread there. Do they need English teachers?

After chatting to the Ex-Girl girls until our Japanese and their English completely give out, we get some more beers and rejoin the others for a boogie. As we all dance and swig and chatter, I find myself thinking about what I've learned on my Japan odyssey. A cloyingly American thing to do, but I am what I am, and I've got to tie this shit up somehow.

I've learned that sometimes assuming does indeed make an ass out of you and me. When I'd first started teaching and asked my students what they eat for breakfast, many of them had replied, "Rice and miso soup." I'd foolishly assumed that this meant they ate them together in the same bowl, like we Americans do with dishes like macaroni and cheese or Corn Flakes and ice cream. This is not so, as I found out when eating lunch with Shunsuke one day. He saw me empty my rice into my bowl of miso soup, looked around uncomfortably, making sure the waitress and surrounding customers were minding their own damn business, and said to me, "That like cat food. But it's OK, you are foreigner."

Or the time when I wanted to send a Japanese card home to the folks and had bought one at the convenience store, assuming it was an all-purpose card. When I brought it home, Akiko told me it was a card intended for a person whose family member has recently died. I sent it to my folks anyway, telling them that the Japanese translated roughly to, "Happy Earth Day."

But I am tired of teaching. My mojo in the classroom never fully returned, and I've taken that as a sign that I'm meant to move on to something else, something that involves a little less of what some gaijinfolk call Japanger:

> juh-pan´-gur, n.: *the overwhelming feeling of frustration and displeasure, usually of Western people living in Japan, resulting from doing daily battle with the sometimes maddening idiosyncrasies and inscrutable behaviors of the Japanese people*

But I will miss those many moments when I could actually feel my students reaching out to me from the dark corners of the language barrier and communicate from their heart. I asked an advanced class one time to write me a short essay about a person they admire. Most of the students conveniently forgot to do the assignment and simply avoided my classes for a few weeks until they were satisfied that I'd forgotten. One student, a university female, wrote one sentence: "I most admire my cat because her life is so easy." Not really what I was looking for, but at least she'd turned something in. Then, one day a few weeks later, I found a neatly typed essay from Masahiro, a retired banker, on the top of my stack of papers to grade.

The Person I Most Admire

> *As well as my father, I admire my mother the most. During the WWII, our family was living in the northeastern part of China, then called Manchuria. I was born in Shenyang in 1943, and my*

younger brother in Pyongyang in 1945. My father was from Hok-kaido and began working for Manchurian Railroad right after his graduation from a college in Shanghai. My mother, born in Tokyo, married him through an arranged meeting in Tokyo held only once a little before the WWII took place, and left for Manchuria.

Despite of their dream of having better days as a railroad officer when the war ends, my father, like all of Japanese and Manchurian Japanese citizens, was aware that Japan would be defeated by the Allies. And the day came. Our family had to stay in Manchuria but live separately, as he was ordered to take care of Japanese pioneers, who mostly came to this continent to develop lands and engage in agriculture, and merchants to return home in Japan safely. My mother and I fled to north part of Korea, where my younger brother was born. It took him more than a year to get together with his wife and sons.

I was two to three years old then, but I can imagine that she took me on her back and fled to Pyongyang. Soon after the birth of my brother we returned to Manchuria, where father was waiting for us. It was already the time when Manchurian Railroad was no longer operative, and we still had attacks from the Chinese army, rob-bery by Siberian soldiers, and so forth, though the war had really ended in Japan. My parents often took me to the railway area to pick up coals spilt from trains. Those gathered coals could sell and helped our living.

Years passed since we came back to my mother's birthplace, Tokyo. She was so strong physically and mentally like many of other Japanese women at that time that we could be safely flee to anywhere. I admire her power and high spirit to return home, as I learned how tough days they spent. More words would be necessary to describe what troubles and accidents they met if space allows. My father died of cancer 26 years ago and 28 years after we got on board an American frigate leaving for Sasebo from China.

A devastating and lovingly told story. I was full of awe and wonder at the brutal odyssey of Masahiro's life, his honesty, and his skill in retelling it in a language that was not his own. Since I felt that correcting his grammar was completely pointless and, in fact, rude, I simply wrote, "Thank you, Masahiro, what an amazing story," made a copy of it for my scrapbook, and placed it in the graded pile.

Feeling quite overwhelmed, I picked up the next piece of homework with a sigh and saw that it was from Tomoyuki, the young J. D. Salinger freak. His assignment was to list one thing he thinks should be banned and explain why:

Getting on the train in a drunken stupor should be banned. Have you ever taken the Yokosuka Line at night? It's quite terrible. There are a lot of fucked up sons of bitches on the train, tarzans spitting, swaying, etc. Most of them have terrible breath. Some guys throw up on the floor, others begin to fight out loud. It's extremely noisy and stinky in the train. To make matters worse, whenever they make trouble with other sober passengers, the police don't punish them strictly. Japan is a paradise for drunks.

In a word: poignant.

Best of all was the dialogue turned in by Yohichi the movie cameraman, an intermediate student. The assignment was to write a short dialogue in which two people are deciding what to do for the evening, and there must be at least one conflict involved. Yohichi's conversation went like this:

A: What do you want to do tonight?
B: I don't know.
A: How about marijuana? It's very fun.

B: But it's not lawfulness. I don't want to go jail. How about mushrooms instead? It's lawfulness.

A: Sounds great!

Was he listening in on the conversation Rachel and I were having the other night in the lobby? Plagiarist.

In so many ways, Japan is America on Opposite Day, which is what has kept my eyes popping open every morning for the past two years, eager to see what absurdities it would bear witness to in the next sixteen hours. It's not just that Japanese verbs come at the end of Japanese sentences. It's in our very essence that we Westerners feel like we're peeping into the otherworld of the looking glass when we stare into the eyes of a Japanese face. Where in America we tend to go to the movies and have conversations with the movie screen, a Japanese cinema, no matter how funny or exciting the film, is as still and reverential as a Shinto shrine. A good-looking draft beer in America will have at most an inch of foam at the top, and if there's more, we will ask for it to be topped off. Here, if your draft beer comes with less than a quarter of the glass full of creamy, bubbly, delicious foam, the customer will think the beer is old and stale and might ask for a new one. If someone compliments your spouse, saying something like, "Oh, your wife is a great cook," it is customary in America to say, "Yeah, isn't she great? How about that bean dip, huh?" and then perhaps slap her on the butt affectionately. But in Japan, it is considered proper to reply with an insult, like, "Oh, that silly bitch couldn't cook her way out of a to-go box. That shit was take-out." Something like that.

When you walk into a low-end American restaurant, you are lucky to be greeted with a smile or any degree of enthusiasm by any employee. They're usually too busy talking to their coworkers about how they're supposed to be on break and how this is such bullshit that they haven't had their break and when the fuck are they gonna get their break? When you enter a food joint here—no matter if it's the grimiest of noodle bars—you are met with the welcoming screams and cries of the entire staff, starting with a few of the floor people and trailing around the place until every person employed by the restaurant has greeted you loudly with an ear-piercing "HELLO! WELCOME! GOOD AFTERNOON! PLEASE SIT DOWN! HELLO! WELCOME! GOOD AFTERNOON! PLEASE SIT DOWN!" Then just when you think you're safe, you get up to leave, trip the wire, and set off the alarm of "THANK YOU! PLEASE COME AGAIN! THANK YOU! PLEASE COME AGAIN! THANK YOU PLEASE COME AGAIN!" Sometimes it's enough to make you long for the days of being completely ignored by the cashier at the drugstore as she prattles on and on to her coworker about how her boyfriend's ex-girlfriend is a total slutmunch.

No matter how well you think you know this place, no matter how much you think you've got your finger on the pulse of the Japanese psyche, you will always be trumped, be it by rice and miso soup, pixilated pornography, Dance Dance Revolution, or thirteen-year-old girls swooning over animated images of young men falling in love with each other and doing it all night.

After the concert, Rachel and I go out for a sayonara dinner in Shibuya, and as a goodbye gift, she gives me a wallet and a framed picture of me sitting in the Vagina Room. Rachel has been telling me for months, ever since she found out I was planning to leave, that I'm not really going to leave, that I will chicken out at the last minute and try to move in with her in the studio apartment she recently rented in Okubo.

"Are you excited about not going home?" she asks as we feast at a table by the window of our favorite Indian curry shop. "The Chemical Brothers are playing a show next week." Then she sings in her best falsetto, "I can get us into the after party…"

"I'm torn," I say, fumbling with my cool new holographic wallet. "I really want to go home to Jimmy, and, you know, find something new and different to do with my life, like, I don't know, study dog grooming or something. You know, I've got to get serious. I'm not going to be young and handsome forever, and eventually I'm going to lose…"

She looks at me with sad, puppy-dog eyes.

"Oh my God, really? Where are the Chemical Brothers playing?"

I look out at the bustling city around me, the city that helped once again unlock my sense of adventure and awe as it smacked me affectionately in the face every morning and said, "Time for breakfast rice and salmon!"

"I'll tell you what, though, I am going to continue studying Japanese," I say.

"Really?"

"Yeah. You know, I've already dedicated so much time to it. I figure, well, why not?"

"Yeah, that's true," Rachel replies, thinking maybe she should start taking some lessons. "Then again, you know, *why?*"

She has a point. Japanese will be about as useful to me back home as a Hello Kitty diaphragm. I guess it's my way of clinging to my Japanese experience and making sure it stays with me even after I'm gone. Whatever, I plan to continue my study of the language at least until I get my first job back home as a temporary substitute data entry clerk.

I hang out at Rachel's place in Okubo until about three a.m., say goodbye, and walk down her tiny side street towards Shinjuku Station. I will wander around for a few hours until the station opens and I can get on the first Yamanote train. Maybe I'll take it around a few times and enjoy the view of the city waking up. Perhaps I'll fall asleep on the shoulder of a drunk, sweaty salaryman and then get beaten awake with an umbrella by a 103-year-old obaasan, who will then kick me out of my seat so her older sister can sit down.

On my way to the station, three different Korean prostitutes offer me "massages," and I politely decline. It's an honor just to be asked. Just a few feet beyond where the third prostitute approached me is a bike stand where two policemen struggle to wrestle what must be a stolen bike free from its chain.

I do have some regrets. I'm still in debt. I still have no great job prospects or get-rich-quick schemes. And the closest I came to meeting a Japanese lesbian was when I saw an older woman on a passing train sporting a classic feathered Alabama mullet.

Most disappointing of all, I was never asked to be on Japanese television. But really, once you're on Japanese television, where is there to go but down? Anyway, you can't have everything, and besides, once I get home and brush up on my English, the world will be mine for the taking.

As I hunch down into the seat of the 5:35 train, I think about the sign I saw posted on that glass door leading to Mos Burger:

Always close a door behind you.

Sound advice, but I think maybe I'll leave this one open.

ACKNOWLEDGMENTS
感謝

I absolutely must get on my knees to grope all of those who offered encouragement along the way as this project morphed from a series of mass e-mails to a series of longer mass e-mails to an excitable and overwrought outline and finally to a manuscript that would need to be hacked and carved into this, its final perfected form that could probably still use some work.

Muchos arigatos, first of all, to Terry Goodman, my editor at AmazonEncore, for discovering Tune in Tokyo and enthusiastically bringing it aboard the Amazon Publishing train. Not only is Terry the reason you are reading this now, he is also the recipient of the 2010 Holly Golightly Award for Most Appropriate Surname. Congratulations, Terry!

Thanks to Jane Hobson Snyder for encouraging me to develop my stories into a book; to Janet Reid and Kristen Elde, whose contributions to and feedback on this manuscript have been heroic to say the least; to Valerie Tomaselli and Hilary Poole for their most excellent support.

Special thanks to my sister Laurie, who has always encouraged me to continue with my writing even though it would likely embarrass our mother.

265

To my boyfriend Jimmy, who never had a doubt that this book would make us rich beyond imagining and allow us to live like the gays we see on the teevee. (Sadly, Jimmy is often wrong.)

An extra special thanks to Kristin Matwiczyk (www.kmatw.com), who created the original version of the mammal head you see on the cover.

Many thanks to Aiko Ogata and Junjiroh Sumikawa for their translation assistance.

Also, to the city of Tokyo, without which the title of this book would only make partial sense: どうもありがとうございました! この本は　どうもすみません。日本語で　タイピングするのが　たのしいいいいいいい。。。。 To Toru, Rachel, Josephine, Shunsuke, Akiko, Sato-kun, Mamta, Suzie, Charlie, Bronwyn, Julia, Ruth, Tony, Tami, Holly, and Grant, as well.

And to you, the reader who heard about *Tune In Tokyo* through a friend of a friend of a friend of an ex-fuckbuddy or weed dealer and took a chance on it. I hope you had fun.

ABOUT THE AUTHOR
著者について

Photograph by Rachell Lee Roth

Tim Anderson has done many amazing things in his short life. Well, two amazing things. OK, one thing that he did twice. But he's got nothing on his older brother, who can play his teeth like a xylophone with his thumb.

Tim has been a waiter, a data entry clerk, a photocopier repairman, a freelance writer, a middle school teacher, and a depressed employee of the State of North Carolina. He hopes to one day be an underwear model/ bookie. He is a graduate of UNC-Chapel Hill, where he was inducted into both Phi Beta Kappa and the Golden Key National Honor Society. These distinctions have yet to pay off.

Tim is an editor in New York and lives in Brooklyn with his boyfriend Jimmy and his cat Stella. He blogs at seetimblog.blogspot. com and plays viola in the band simpleshapes. His favorite Southern state is Hawaii.